# Fix It No

D1358947

## Rediscover the Con
## Get America Out of Its
## Fiscal Death Spiral

### Table of Contents

| | |
|---|---|
| Preface | 3 |
| The Trump Phenomenon | 5 |
| Introduction | 35 |
| American Is Robbing Its Children | 43 |
| Basic Principles | 67 |
| Terms of the Debate | 91 |
| Limited Government | 117 |
| Unlimited Government | 123 |
| Balanced Budget Amendment | 189 |
| Are Republicans Ready to Lead? | 197 |
| Social Security & Medicare: The Problem | 221 |
| Social Security & Medicare: The Solution | 235 |
| Move Faster on Rest of Budget | 241 |
| Fiscal Conservatism Needs Social Conservatism | 249 |
| Conclusion | 255 |
| French Dessert | 279 |
| Merry Capitalist Christmas | 285 |
| Famous Quotations on Debt | 287 |
| Maxwell Bio | 295 |

*Increasing America's debt weakens us domestically and internationally. Leadership means that "the buck stops here." Instead, Washington is shifting the burden of bad choices today onto the backs of our children and grandchildren. America has a debt problem and a failure of leadership. Americans deserve better. I therefore intend to oppose the effort to increase America's debt limit.*

**U.S. Senator Barack Obama (D-IL)**

Senate Floor Speech
March 16, 2006


*Washington depends on the American people not paying attention.*

**U.S. Senator Ted Cruz (R-TX)**

Senate Floor Speech
September 24, 2013

# Preface

*When a nation goes down or a society perishes, one condition may always be found; they forgot where they came from.*

*Carl Sandburg, 1948*

I started writing this book almost a decade ago. I have made hundreds of changes over the years in response to changing factors. I made one last round of changes to freshen it up after the 2020 general election, including adding The Trump Phenomenon after this preface.

The main points of the book have *not* changed, and never will, because the main principles of political society do not change.

This book is designed to remind people, or explain to them for the first time, where we came from as a nation. It's for the general public, not a scholarly work. It's like an extended political column in the newspaper.

In a letter to Henry Lee in 1825, Thomas Jefferson said:

> *This was the object of the Declaration of Independence. Not to find out new principles, or new arguments, never before thought of, not merely to say things which had never been said before; but to place before mankind the common sense of the subject, in terms so plain and firm as to command their assent . . . . Neither aiming at originality of principle or sentiment, nor yet copied from any particular and previous writing, it was intended to be an expression of the American mind, and to give to that expression the proper tone and spirit called for by the occasion.*

My goal is to present the common sense of the subject

3

in terms so plain and firm that anyone who reads this book is ready and willing to defend the Constitution and American founding values. You might call this book secular apologetics. In religion, the tradition of apologetics refers to defending the faith against criticism. Critics say this; here is our response. This book is a practical set of talking points for people who know the nation is going the wrong way, but get bullied and shouted down by those hostile to the Constitution and founding values. There are many good books about politics, but I don't see many that go into the nitty-gritty political and emotional arguments with which people are hit in the face in everyday conversation. This book does.

There may not have been anything new in the political philosophy of the Declaration, but the arguments were presented in an original and convincing way. I hope to do the same: present timeless principles in a fresh and persuasive way, animated by personal anecdotes and observations.

The core question of politics is: How do we provide the best life for the most people? Some say we provide the best for the most by growing government and having it take over more of society. Read on to learn why limited government as outlined in the Constitution is the way to provide the best for the most.

Budget numbers come from government websites available to the public. Fiscal projections are speculative because of variables that depend on whether new policies are adopted. Numbers fluctuate from year to year. Don't let any of that cloud the main point: We need to restore limited government under the Constitution to fix our fiscal crisis, and we need to fix it now.

# The Trump Phenomenon

I voted for Donald Trump in 2016 and 2020, and will vote for him again if he runs in 2024. In some circles, that makes me the equivalent of a Christian in Nero's Rome, someone to be loathed, persecuted, and "canceled."

I don't care. As a conservative, I hit the jackpot with Trump: most pro-life president ever; Supreme Court justices who respect the Constitution; tax cuts benefiting working- and middle-class Americans as well as the wealthy; deregulation benefiting small business; best job and economic numbers in 50 years; Dow Jones Industrial Average hitting 30,000 *in a pandemic year*; improved border security; utilizing domestic resources to achieve energy independence; progress in foreign policy areas stagnant for decades, with foreign leaders nominating President Trump for the Nobel Peace Prize; breakthrough foreign trade deals; cessation of the IRS's harassment of conservative people and organizations; warp speed production of covid vaccines.

Invoking the anti-science delusion of transgenderism, males barge into female bathrooms and sports, threatening personal dignity and safety in the former, and destroying competitive balance in the latter. The Trump administration pushed back against these assaults on decency and fair play.

Most 2020 exit polls showed that Trump won a record share of the minority vote for a Republican. Why? Because he did more for minorities than any president in the last 50 years. The number of food stamp recipients surged to a record 48 million during the Obama administration. The Trump economy drove that number down to 36 million.

People of all races receive food stamps, but the remarkable reduction in poverty reflected in the food stamp numbers is in large part a result of minorities experiencing record low unemployment rates and record high job numbers.

Despite "so much winning," one of our U.S. senators from Nebraska, Republican Ben Sasse, is not pleased. He despises what he calls the "weird worship" of Trump. The Trump phenomenon is weird to Sasse because he is a classic Washington politician. He left his home state to make connections with, and learn the ways of, the political ruling class in D.C. He returned home and, with the help of those D.C. political and financial connections, won a seat in Congress to secure a prime position in that ruling class.

Sasse plays the game well. What's "weird" is that he ran as a hardcore Tea Party candidate in his first Senate race in 2014. Then he rejected Trump, the embodiment of the Tea Party, and became a D.C. darling.

With President Trump leading the way, Republicans began making America great again in all the ways listed on the previous page. Sasse voted for most of it. He brags about his conservative voting record. Yet in September 2018, the angst-ridden Hamlet of the Plains – to be (a Republican), or not to be, that is the question – said he woke up every morning wondering if he should leave the Republican Party because it had become too Trumpish.

Sasse went noticeably silent on Trump in 2019 as his 2020 Senate primary approached. The only noise he made about Trump was to make sure Nebraska voters knew that he and the president spoke regularly and got along fine.

Trump rose above Sasse's prior carping and endorsed

him. Sasse thanked Trump by snubbing him. After getting the Trump seal of approval vital for a Nebraska Republican, Sasse made it clear that he did not ask for it, thus preserving his "purity." (I told you he plays this game well.)

Sasse's general election Democratic opponent offered no serious competition, so once the primary was safely behind him, Sasse resumed unloading on Trump. He would go on to vote for conviction of Trump on the impeachment charge of inciting insurrection.

And now we weird worshippers of Trump have been scolded by a disapproving Senator Sasse. I am grieved.

God is the only being I worship, but I do support Trump.

*How can you support someone impeached for inciting a deadly insurrection at the Capitol?*

Trump did not incite an insurrection. At a White House rally, he expressed the frustration many of us share over the 2020 election. He told the crowd to go to the Capitol and *peacefully* urge Congress to challenge the election result.

The White House rally was wrapping up when the violence began at the Capitol. The rally was a mile-and-a-half from the Capitol, a half-hour walk for a large crowd. By the time the rally crowd arrived at Capitol Hill, the Capitol was under siege. The rally and Trump speech were irrelevant to the rioters who stormed the Capitol. They had planned their assault before Jan. 6 and were going to act regardless of the Trump event. Some showed up with tools and non-firearm weapons, ready to rumble. Some caught on video, such as John Earle Sullivan, were from the political left. ("The left" means Democrats, liberals, progressives, socialists, communists, those on the left side of the political spectrum on page 91, including most of the media.)

For the left, the riot (it was not an insurrection) was a two-fer. It was a chance to bury the investigation of election fraud by declaring it a dangerous lie that got people killed, referring to a protestor fatally shot by a Capitol police officer and a false report about an officer killed by rioters.

It also presented a chance to bury Trump with a second impeachment. Removal by impeachment is a two-step process. If the House votes to impeach (charge with a crime), then the Senate holds a trial and votes on whether to convict on the impeachment charge and remove a president from office. The House impeached Trump based on the Capitol riot. A week later, Trump's term as president ended and he left office. Yet the Senate continued the impeachment process by holding a trial *after* Trump was out of office. It was bizarre. The reason for impeachment no longer existed. Impeachment is for removal from office, not prosecution of private citizens.

Aside from that, as a practical matter, why did Democrats and anti-Trump Republicans (Never Trumpers) go after a president about to leave office, and keep going after him when he was gone? Because of 2024. Democrats fear losing to Trump in a non-fraudulent election. Never Trumpers also want Trump out of the way, especially the presidential wannabes. Conviction on an impeachment charge disqualifies a president from running for the office again.

Trump haters said they tried to convict Trump, even though he was out of office, to protect America by sealing him off from the presidency like toxic waste. They failed to convict, but they knew a conviction was unlikely. They hoped a second impeachment by itself would be enough to place Trump in permanent political quarantine.

The continuing fuss about the riot is about "canceling" other prominent Republicans along with Trump, especially 2024 presidential contenders. The left says those who challenged the 2020 election result have "blood on their hands." Leftists want all of us on the right to be paralyzed with shame and fear, afraid to speak or act because of the riot.

Ignore them. The only people with blood on their hands are those who spilled it. Those trying to use the Capitol riot to bury all forms of opposition are the same people who ignored, or described as "mostly peaceful," the bloodshed, burning, looting, and death produced in recent years by anti-Trump, anti-Republican, anti-conservative mobs. The left's newfound shock and horror at political violence is cynical and deceitful. Do not be fooled or intimidated by it.

Republicans are not barred from speaking and acting on our conservative beliefs because a group from our side went berserk on one occasion. If that were true, Democrats would have to remain silent all the time in the public arena given the repeated mayhem caused by their political allies. If we on the right make a habit of getting violent – if we start acting like the left – then we will lose the moral high ground and have a problem.

*How can you support a racist who said white supremacists at Charlottesville were "fine people"?*

Trump did not call white supremacists at Charlottesville fine people. He strongly condemned them. The audio with his exact words is included as part of my Charlottesville podcast at anchor.fm/checkwithchip on April 30, 2019.

Trump did say there were fine people *on **both** sides* of the dispute over removing a statue of Robert E. Lee. He said there were fine people who were not racist, but believed removing the statue was an unwarranted attack on a hallowed symbol of duty, valor, and honor in Southern culture. On the other side were fine people who believed Lee was too closely connected to slavery and had to go.

Trump also said there were bad people on both sides: white supremacists on the pro-Lee side and leftist militants on the other side who showed up looking for a fight. It was an excellent analysis of a complex situation.

Charlottesville was one of many "fake news" leftist lies about Trump. You've heard leftists shriek that Trump "put children in cages!" Fake news. The Obama administration housed in fenced enclosures children of illegal immigrants detained at the border. The Trump administration *ended* that policy. The left also told you that Trump encouraged people to drink bleach and inhale disinfectants to kill the pandemic virus. He never said either. More fake news.

On a related racial note, the left claims Trump said all Mexicans are rapists and drug dealers. Still more fake news. Trump said when the border is not secure and immigrants are not properly screened, criminals from Mexico come into the USA, which is true. He did not make a blanket statement denouncing all Mexicans as criminals. If you look at Trump's history in business and in community development projects, you will see that minorities have fared well and often have saluted Trump for his support.

*How can you support a traitor who used Russia's help to steal the 2016 election?*

Speaking of fake news, this allegation was investigated by several government bodies and exposed as baseless.

The only presidential candidate trying to use Russian help to swing the 2016 election was Hillary Clinton. Her campaign hired a firm that hired a British ex-spy to reach out to Russian spies for "intelligence" that would damage Trump. The Russians fed the British dupe a dossier that was spectacularly false. The dossier was delivered to the Clinton campaign. The Clinton campaign shared it with the media. The media ran fake news stories about it. Those stories were used by federal investigators to justify warrants to spy on the Trump campaign and presidential administration, and pursue impeachment.

Leftists angry at Trump for challenging the 2020 election result shouted "not my president" as they rejected the 2016 election result and tried to oust Trump from the presidency. Their ongoing "resistance" was based on fake intel in a fake dossier leaked to fake news to justify a fake warrant to fuel a fake investigation of a fake allegation.

The left's fallback position was: The investigation failed to find collusion because of obstruction of justice by President Trump! That pathetic argument went nowhere.

*How can you support a thug who was impeached for bullying Ukraine to produce dirt on Joe Biden?*

That was preposterous. When first asked about the phone call during which the president allegedly pressured Ukraine, the U.S. ambassador on the call said there was no "quid pro quo" (something for something) demanded by the president. The ambassador said he asked the president what he wanted out of the situation. He said the president became agitated and said I don't want anything, just tell them to do the right thing if there was anything corrupt going on.

A few weeks later, that ambassador did a 180 in testimony to a House impeachment committee and basically said: "Now that I've had more time to think about it, the president *did* pressure Ukraine for dirt on Biden." Pardon my skepticism, but Trump was impeached for something that did not happen, and in any event was not a "high crime or misdemeanor" worthy of impeachment.

Quid Pro Joe Biden was the one shaking down Ukraine. As vice president, Biden ordered Ukrainian officials to fire the prosecutor investigating the corrupt Ukrainian energy business that had his son, Hunter, on its board. Otherwise, Biden threatened, Ukraine would not get $1 billion in aid promised by the U.S. Search YouTube for "Biden brags Ukrainian fired" to see video of Biden bragging about getting the prosecutor fired. Or have Big Tech overlords removed that video in their effort to protect Quid Pro Joe?

*How can you support a nonstop liar?*

Have you heard the one about Donald Trump telling 18,000 lies? It popped up during the 2020 campaign in our local newspaper and other places. If you ask for specifics, you are dismissed as blindly loyal to Trump for asking. Dig into these alleged lies and you find that truthful statements are called lies, and every repetition is counted as another lie. When Trump repeatedly tweeted that the allegation of treasonous collusion with Russia was a hoax, each tweet was counted as another Trump lie.

To lie is to say something you know is false. A person may say something false, but believe it to be true. Trump says things that turn out to be false, wrong, mistaken. So do I. So do you. So do all the people criticizing Trump.

In September 2019, Trump was accused of lying to and irresponsibly scaring Alabamians by saying Hurricane Dorian might hit Alabama. It turned out to be mistaken, but Trump was reacting to a projection by the National Oceanic & Atmospheric Administration, a federal agency of weather experts. The experts said Alabama was in play, so the president alerted Alabamians. But critics cited it as an example of how you can't trust anything that comes out of the mouth or Twitter feed of Donald Trump.

The *Washington Post* criticized Trump for claiming at rallies in March and April of 2020 to have generated the best job numbers and economy in 50 years. His presidential term is not completed, the *Post* said, and the 2020 numbers may rival the Great Depression.

The truth-righteous *Post* left out a little detail called a *pandemic*. Aside from that, check out these numbers:

## Wage growth by income level

The lowest-earning quartile of workers is seeing the biggest wage increases in a decade.

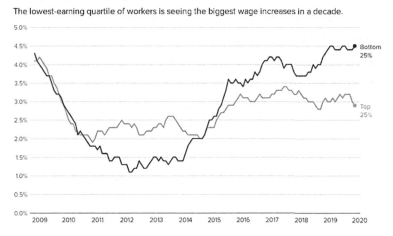

Source: Federal Reserve Bank of Atlanta

Trump's reduction of tax and regulatory burdens ignited a burst of economic growth not seen in decades, benefitting Americans in all economic classes. That is rock-solid fact.

The pandemic virus broke up the game. That does not change the reality that Trump delivered on the promise to make America's economy great again for everyone.

Yet the *Post* said Trump misrepresented the success of his economic policies. It's contemptible. It's insidious. It's unworthy of serious attention. And yet it worries me. People hear relatives, friends, colleagues, and major public figures repeat such things and conclude: there must be some truth to it. So I will keep launching truth mortars and shelling with facts those who lie about lying.

*How can you support a divisive, hateful egomaniac?*

Trump is no more divisive or hateful than the rest of us. The second impeachment trial provided examples of leftists calling for political violence in language much more direct and incendiary than anything Trump has said. Indeed, the left is the main generator of divisive hatred in America.

Leftists produce overwrought narratives about the violent right. Occasionally a rightist militia group does something unhinged, like the one in Michigan that wanted to kidnap the governor – and called President Trump a "tyrant" and an "enemy." Normally, though, right-wing extremists keep to themselves and want to be left alone. They're not the ones occupying and terrorizing American cities.

I had never heard of the Proud Boys until the left began portraying the group as Trump's personal stormtroopers. Critics say the group is racist, but there are people of color in leadership positions. Some Proud Boys are charged with storming the Capitol to support Trump, while others are harshly critical of Trump, calling him a failure. The group became known because members showed up to counter the violent left at public events. They were unofficial security for conservative persons or groups. They fought back when leftist thugs showed up and attacked.

I bring it up because the left acts as if the existence of the Proud Boys balances or justifies violence by the left. The Proud Boys and rightist militias will have to get awfully busy to match the domestic terrorism of the angry left.

The angry left specializes in division and hatred. Leftists crashed 2016 Trump campaign events, provoking fights and heckling Trump until they were removed. MoveOn.org bragged about getting a 2016 Trump event canceled in Chicago because of its menacing protesters. After Trump won, leftist belligerents in helmets and body armor, brandishing weapons and waving Soviet communist hammer-and-sickle flags, attacked peaceful events all over America. Leftist militants converged on Charlottesville to tangle with tiki torch marchers. Riot-loving, police-hating Black Lives Matter zealots rampaged all over the country.

The left generated and exploited the divisive hatred that plagued the nation during the Trump presidency, and then had the nerve to declare: that's Donald Trump's America!

Sometimes the smear campaign was more subtle. A video went viral from the day the Obamas and Trumps went to lunch before the change in presidential administrations. In a clip just a few seconds long, Trump moved ahead of the others toward the door of the restaurant. As he grabbed the handle and opened the door, the video stopped. Look at that boorish jackass, critics thundered, pushing ahead of his wife and the president and first lady to go in first.

The rest of the video, the part the critics deleted, showed that Trump had moved first to open the door and hold it open for the rest of the party to enter ahead of him. No correction or apology by leftist liars.

That cheap shot was small potatoes compared to major hit jobs like Charlottesville, Russia, and Ukraine, but it was part of the left's nonstop siege of defamation to make Trump look like a monster. Any Republican president gets the same treatment. They don't come much nicer than Ronald Reagan and the father-and-son George Bushes, but the left made monsters of them, too.

It's a different story for Democrats. Eventually the left will declare that America is more serene because Biden is a uniter, not a divider like Trump. That's not the reason. The divisive barking stops because leftist attack dogs become fawning lap dogs when a Democrat becomes president.

When U.S. covid deaths exceeded 50,000 in the spring of 2020, a reporter asked President Trump how he could run for re-election with a covid death toll higher than the U.S. death toll in the Vietnam War. It was nonsensical garbage meant to reinforce the narrative that covid deaths were the president's fault.

If a resurgent covid or some new virus wreaks havoc, will that reporter ask Biden how he can show his face given whatever number of deaths occur on his presidential watch? Of course not. Biden won't be blamed. He shouldn't be, but neither should Trump.

Trump has a healthy ego. (Show me a politician who doesn't.) He boasted about successes and sometimes swung wildly at critics. He was combative, but I cut him some slack because he was under siege all the time. In the public arena, Trump was gouged in the eyes, elbowed in the teeth, kneed in the gut, kicked in the groin, and sucker-punched from behind by waves of assailants. Then critics were horrified when Trump did not follow Marquess of Queensberry Rules in defending himself.

It reminds me of professional wrestling. Part of the fun is "selective" refereeing. The referee enforces the rules on the good guy, but somehow does not see the bad guy grab a chair from ringside and bash the good guy over the head with it. If the good guy tries to respond in kind, suddenly the referee rediscovers his righteousness: "Hey! Put down that chair! That's against the rules!"

In a "rassling" spectacle, the outrageous double standard adds to the rollicking good time. In politics, it's a vile betrayal of the public trust.

I'm not in the mood for self-righteous lectures from the left about the alleged excesses of Trump or the right. The left needs to clean up its own act.

In 2017, a nationally known comedian posted pictures of herself holding a fake-but-gory severed Trump head. Later she apologized. Then she put the image back on social media after the 2020 election. I'm not sure what's more disturbing: the severed head, or the 60,000 "likes" it got.

Imagine the reaction from the left – and the right – if someone had walked around with a severed Obama head. The outrage and denunciation would have been universal.

The left raged when a rodeo clown did a routine wearing an Obama mask. It was the same type of mask-wearing skit he had done for two decades poking fun at every president, but he was vilified and fired for lampooning Obama.

Severed Trump head? No problem.

The mock beheading was an example of a political condition called Trump Derangement Syndrome. A lefty commentator on a comedy channel is a poster boy for TDS. In cruder language than I will use, he said President Trump's mouth was a receptacle for Russian President Vladimir Putin's private part. He would have been "canceled" for saying something like that about President Obama. He was celebrated by the left as a hero for saying it about Trump.

There was much heartburn about Trump's use of Twitter. As a morning drive talk radio host, I spent two years going through Trump tweets every weekday. I challenge you to examine a section of 100 consecutive tweets in the Trump Twitter feed from any time during his presidency. In any segment of Trump tweets, a few might be cringe-worthy. Most will be vigorous and cogent corrections of fake news, often directing entertaining zingers at deserving targets. Twitter was the equalizer allowing Trump to counteract the barrage of fake news crashing down on him 24/7.

The media described Trump rallies as hatefests. They were not. I went to a couple and watched several more. The mood was buoyant. There was heckling of media figures, and booing and chanting at the mention of certain people and policies, but it was boisterous political theater – not vicious and dangerous like the leftist street mob that attacked people leaving the White House after the president's speech concluding the 2020 Republican National Convention.

The Capitol riot was not rambunctious fun. I condemn it, as did Trump and every legitimate voice on the right. However, I do understand how people who feel pushed beyond the point of tolerance might snap.

In November 2020, I almost took a swing at a guy while speaking at a local Stop the Steal rally organized by Moms for America. He was not social distancing. He was right next to me, jumping up and down while screaming and ringing a cow bell. The nutjob crowding me was one of a couple dozen leftists roaming amid our gathering of about 100 people. They harassed us with obscene words and gestures, trying (unsuccessfully) to break up the event. One guy shouted into a microphone attached to a large speaker that he pulled around in a wagon. (He later made news leading a protest featuring severed pig heads at a local police union hall, and for his arrest in New York for slamming a woman's face into a wall with concussive force, choking her into unconsciousness, and stealing her car.) It was a slice of hell on Earth – crazed, howling demons spewing bile.

The Moms for America leader politely asked the protestors to tone it down as there were children present with their mothers. The protestors got louder and more abusive.

Police were there. I called 911 when protestors used large barricades and their own bodies to try to block my car and others from entering the park where the rally was held. During the event I asked a cop why the protestors were allowed to plow right into our midst and raise a ruckus. He said as long as they didn't get physical, they could be as obnoxious as they wanted. I disagree, but I suppose the cops have been told to avoid the kind of confrontations craved by protestors and media eager to portray police negatively. I nonetheless reject the idea that any degree of verbal harassment is OK. That violates my First Amendment right to free speech and peaceful assembly. If people can invade my speaking space and make it nearly impossible for others to hear me, amplifying their noise mechanically and electronically, then I have no meaningful right to speech and assembly. Generating a racket of speech-blocking noise may be standard operating procedure for the left, but it should not be legal in a public park when organizers have gone through proper procedures to secure that venue.

*How can you support a destroyer of democracy who falsely claimed the 2020 election was stolen?*

Trump haters were aghast to learn that when a Republican congressional leader asked Trump to stop the Capitol riot (as if he could), Trump replied, "I guess these people are more upset about the election than you are."

Exactly. We *are* upset. We are aghast that our betters in D.C. were enraged at Trump for something beyond his control, but were fine with a stolen election.

The left calls this allegation of a stolen election "the big lie." This is the same left that said Trump put children in cages at the border; Trump told people to drink bleach to cure covid; Trump colluded with Russia to steal the 2016 election; Trump pressured Ukraine for dirt on Biden; Trump called neo-Nazis at Charlottesville "fine people" and all Mexicans criminals; Trump Supreme Court nominee Brett Kavanaugh organized "rape trains" while in high school; a Trump-supporting, white, pro-life high school student provoked a racist confrontation with an American Indian protester in front of the Lincoln Memorial. All false.

I spoke at a Stop the Steal rally because I believe the election *was* stolen – from regular folks as well as Trump. I am not convinced that a failing 77-year-old who spent most of the 2020 presidential campaign in a protective shell inspired record support – 12 million more votes than the previous record of 69 million for Barack Obama in 2008. Our votes are rendered meaningless and we no longer have a functioning democratic system if the other side is allowed to measure the margin by which it trails on election night, then make enough votes materialize over the next 24-48 hours to close the gap and win.

An executive branch investigation by Trump-hating deep-state bureaucrats found no fraud. Imagine that.

Trump haters said state and federal courts rejected all allegations of fraud. Not true. Most courts rejected petitions on technical or procedural grounds, not factual.

Citizens, some of them election officials, swore under oath to the following: dead people voted; postal workers backdated ballots that arrived after election day to make it look like they arrived on election day so they would not be rejected as late; Republican election observers were barred from vote-counting areas; vote-counting systems, human and electronic, attributed votes to the wrong candidate; electronic voting systems were accessed via the Internet and manipulated by people outside the voting systems.

I don't know enough about computer systems to evaluate the cyber-hijacking claims. I do know that on election day some voters showed up at polling places and discovered that others had voted in their name earlier in the day or by mail-in ballot. Yet the left insists there's no voter fraud problem and no need for voter identification.

Mail-in ballots – what a gift for fraudsters. Tens of millions of mail-in ballots went out. No one knows for sure who filled them out under what circumstances. It's virtually impossible to prove fraud, especially when state officials waive deadlines, signature verification, and other requirements designed to prevent fraud. (Fun Fact: Amazon wanted its warehouses to conduct in-person voting on whether to unionize because of the risk of fraud in a mail-in vote. But it's OK to choose a president by mail-in vote.)

The more ballots there are floating around, the greater the opportunity to produce truckloads of counterfeit ballots delivered overnight after election day, as happened in several states – again, according to sworn witness statements.

Even if you reject all the sworn testimony, it is statistically (and laughably) impossible for hundreds of thousands of legitimate votes to materialize after election day, all for Biden, in just the right places and just the right amounts.

C'mon, man! (as Biden likes to say). This is not a democratic process that reflects the will of the people. It's a vote-manufacturing process that rewards fraud.

For Trump haters, the 2020 election spin went through three cycles: 1) there was no fraud; 2) there may have been fraud, but not enough to make a difference; 3) it's OK if the election was stolen because Trump had to be removed.

Critics said Trump attempted a coup by challenging the election result. A coup was attempted *and accomplished* by the election stealers. That's my position until sworn statements of election irregularities have been investigated and proven meritless, and every mail-in ballot has been authenticated as on-time and non-fraudulent.

*How can you support a misogynist who bragged about groping women?*

This is proof, Democrats declare, that Republicans have no morals. They are shameless hypocrites, especially those so-called Christians. They will support any scoundrel they think can win.

This from the same crowd that worships Bill Clinton and other Democrats of low moral character. In the midst of the controversy about the groping comment, Trump noted that Clinton "said far worse to me on the golf course." And of course Clinton has **done** far worse. We could go through a rogue's gallery of former Ku Klux Klan leaders and other reprobate Democrats who have enjoyed rock-star treatment by the same crowd critical of Trump.

However, that would not justify support of Trump. How could so many devout Christians support Trump?

The groping comment was made in 2005. It was repulsive. It happened when Trump was finishing a wild ride in his private life. He married Melania Knauss in 2005 and stopped churning through marriages.

For me, the requirement to forgive people is the hardest thing about being Christian, yet redemption is part of the package. If Trump still bragged about groping women, I would not support him. He does not seem to be the same man he was before he married Knauss. She is reported to be a practicing Catholic. Perhaps that had something to do with

Trump's change in behavior, including his transformation from pro-choice to pro-life on abortion. Critics mocked Trump for clumsy references to Scripture, but as president he was not shy about invoking God and faith. There's always a path to good standing for those who repent and reform. Christians are supposed to celebrate such occasions.

\* \* \*

Are you still having trouble understanding my support for Trump? Let me try an example from history that others also have used to explain their support for Trump.

At the outbreak of the Civil War in April 1861, George McClellan was a Ben Sasse among generals, a rising star of the political ruling class. Nicknamed Young Napoleon, he had fine family, educational, and military pedigrees. He was handsome and intelligent, a consummate officer and gentleman. He was politically sharp; he would be elected governor of New Jersey in 1877. It was no surprise when McClellan was named general-in-chief of the Union army in November 1861.

There was one problem. McClellan was great in strategy sessions in the war room, but not as good in actual battle in the field. The adage in the military is that no plan survives contact with the enemy. A battle often does not follow the script drawn up by strategists. McClellan proved to be a very cautious commander who waited to make a move until conditions were perfect. Since conditions in battle rarely are perfect, McClellan became known for failing to adapt and take the kind of risk required to succeed. He blamed failures to achieve battlefield objectives on the failure of the commander-in-chief, President Abraham Lincoln, to provide enough men, weapons, and equipment.

Senator Sasse shows a similar tendency toward paralysis when he does not feel he controls a situation, and instead might have to take a risk to prevail.

As a member of the Senate Judiciary Committee, Sasse did a fine job shepherding two conservative Nebraska attorneys through leftist minefields in the confirmation process on their way to becoming federal judges. In contrast, Sasse was AWOL during a major judicial battle that was beyond his control and very risky for combatants. Sasse is not shy toward cameras and microphones, but he hunkered down and took cover when the left unleashed a diabolically false and vicious personal attack on Supreme Court nominee Brett Kavanaugh. Sasse later said he was "working behind the scenes" to advance the nomination. OK, but it's possible to walk and chew gum at the same time. He could have joined fellow Judiciary Committee member U.S. Senator Lindsey Graham (R-SC) on the firing line in the public arena, defending Kavanaugh and denouncing the left's demonic attempt to defile him – and still lobbied colleagues privately on the matter.

Sasse also was AWOL on the effort to repeal and replace Obamacare. He ran in 2014 as the man with the plan on health care, but when political bullets were flying and the Obamacare battle reached its peak, Sasse was invisible and inaudible, neither seen nor heard. His absence from the fray was so noticeable that our local newspaper ran a "Where's Ben?" story.

Back to McClellan. A rift developed between Lincoln, the rustic from the frontier, and the Eastern patrician

McClellan. McClellan wrote to his wife that Lincoln was "a well-meaning baboon." He publicly referred to the president as a "gorilla." Soon after being appointed general-in-chief, McClellan came home one evening and was informed that the president was in the front parlor, where he had been waiting an hour to see McClellan. The general-in-chief went straight to bed without acknowledging the presence of the commander-in-chief.

Lincoln overlooked the personal insults. He could not overlook what he considered too much excuse-making and not enough winning. In March 1862, Lincoln removed McClellan from the position of general-in-chief but left him in command of the Army of the Potomac, the main Union force in the Eastern Theater.

McClellan's criticism of Lincoln intensified, as did Lincoln's frustration with McClellan. In November 1862, Lincoln removed McClellan from the Potomac command.

Their beef came to a head in the presidential campaign of 1864. As the Democratic nominee, McClellan challenged Republican incumbent Lincoln. He lost, perhaps due to voters' "weird worship" of homespun populist Lincoln.

Ulysses S. Grant was the general Lincoln eventually put in command of all Union forces. Like McClellan, Grant was a graduate of the U.S. Military Academy at West Point. There the similarities ended. Grant was a hard-drinking commoner from the Midwest (Ohio), rough around the edges. What appealed to Lincoln was that Grant found ways to win with whatever men and matériel were available. He did not whine about logistics. He attacked, even if conditions were not ideal, and did not stop until the enemy was totally defeated. A quip of that era was that Grant's initials "U.S." stood for Unconditional Surrender.

Republican politician Alexander McClure wrote about his meeting with Lincoln in 1862 to complain about Grant's deficiencies. At that time, Grant led an army in the Western Theater. McClure said he urged Lincoln to remove Grant from command. According to McClure, Lincoln denied his request for this reason: "I can't spare this man; he fights."

And there you have the reason for the Trump phenomenon: *he fights*, with a ferocity too seldom seen in Republicans. The nastier the conflict, the more forcefully Trump engages and the harder he goes for unconditional surrender.

Sasse is a McClellan show horse. He has shown admirable guts on pro-life issues, but otherwise avoids conflicts that are anything less than a sure win for him.

Trump is a Grant work horse. It's not always pretty, but he plows into conflicts regardless of the odds because the good of the nation requires it.

I suppose Trump also is part show horse. He has been a pop culture icon. He drew and entertained crowds in the tens of thousands at political rallies. Yet he is not a traditional political show horse. If a conservative work horse also is an elegant show horse, such as Reagan, great. If not, I'll take a grinding work horse over a preening show horse.

\* \* \*

Trump was the first president to attend the annual March for Life. When he left the stage after speaking, it seemed strange that the exit song was *You Can't Always Get What You Want* by the Rolling Stones. It seemed insulting to the president. Then I learned that the song was a staple of 2016 Trump campaign rallies. That tells me that despite the bluster and bravado, Trump must have a humble streak and a sense of humor.

The more I thought about it, the more the song fit. It says that while you may be frustrated at not getting what you want, "you just might find you get what you need." In the 2016 Republican presidential primary, I wanted just about everyone except Trump. When it came down to Trump and Senator Cruz, I wanted Cruz. Maybe Trump was what we needed. I'm not sure anyone else could have withstood the unceasing onslaught of the left.

President Trump's accomplishments were enhanced by the way he convinced me that he *loves* America. He didn't need the job; he donated his salary to charity. Trump's passion is to make the American Dream work for regular people like me. I have not sensed that from any president since Reagan in the 1980s.

After the Capitol riot, a CNN anchor said pro-Trumpers would "go back to the Olive Garden and to the Holiday Inn . . . to have some drinks and talk about the great day they had in Washington." That comment was shared and adored on social media by snooty leftists and Never Trumpers who apparently would not be caught dead at either establishment. They reveled in the notion that people barbaric enough to support Trump also slum it at the Holiday Inn and consider the Olive Garden fine Italian dining.

The Holiday Inn is high-end for me. I have numerous children who love the family dogs, so you are more likely to find me at a bargain motel with iffy air conditioning and a dog-friendly policy.

I have dined at the Olive Garden. (More salad and bread sticks, please.) I don't care whether the salad dressing and the lasagna are considered gourmet Italian cuisine. The food tastes good and is affordable.

I don't care if the elitist left considers Trump as vulgar as it does the Olive Garden. I like what Trump serves, as reflected in the "menu" of accomplishments on page 5.

I realize that Trump probably does not eat at the Olive Garden or stay at the Holiday Inn. I don't care. What matters to me is that he respects those of us who do, and fights for us against the CNN anchor and his fellow elitists.

Trump was resilient. We on the right enjoyed what some called the "Road Runner" aspect of his presidency. In the cartoon featuring the small, fast-running bird, the villain trying to catch and eat the Road Runner is Wile E. Coyote, self-described "super genius." His schemes and devices blow up in his face, often literally.

The same thing happened to critics of Trump. In ways large and small, profound and petty, leftist "super geniuses" kept going after Trump. Seemingly every week the left burst out with a new slam on Trump and declared that *this* would be the death blow to his presidency. Everything they tried, including impeachment, blew up in their faces. So they quit trying to beat Trump in the public arena and went into the shadows where vote fraudsters work their mischief.

Maybe another Road Runner moment will be Trump winning back the presidency in 2024. I want Trump, or someone like him, to be the Republican nominee. I won't accept a typical establishment Republican capitulator. I want Grant, not McClellan.

My support for Trump isn't just about him. I support Trump for *my* sake. The attempt to take down Trump is part of a larger takedown of all things conservative. Look at the left's purge of conservative thought and speech in social media. The left's call for "unity" means extinction for the right. The left is targeting me as well as Trump.

Leftists construct pretentious facades of rhetoric and worship at them as political altars. They produce fussy word salads to justify "disappearing" Trump and anyone or anything connected with him.

As this book is being finalized, angry leftist employees at publisher Simon & Schuster are accusing their employer of betraying "the public's trust in our editorial process" and accommodating race-based "structural oppression."

Gosh, sounds bad. What happened?

Simon & Schuster contracted to publish a book authored by Republican Mike Pence. Pence is a former Indiana congressman and governor who served as vice president in the Trump administration. Regardless of whether you agree with his politics, he deserves basic respect as a dedicated public servant and an exemplary Christian husband and father. It is petty and pathetic to declare that such a man should not be allowed to publish a book in America. You don't see the right trying to block publication of books by former President Obama and other leftists.

The left is like a bratty child holding his ears while screaming and demanding that the competing noise stop because he does not want to hear what challenges him. (See "howling demons" pages 19-20.) The sniveling snowflakes at Simon & Schuster whined that publishing a book by Pence would treat "the Trump administration as a 'normal' chapter in American history." It's not enough for the left to win the 2020 presidential election. History must be revised and sanitized so that the Trump presidency did not happen, or at least is not acknowledged as a valid event.

Some who support Trump are exhausted by this perpetual harassment. They dread another four years of negative drama that would accompany another Trump presidency.

That's how the left rolls. It keeps pounding on you until you lose your will to fight.

Don't give in. Don't let the left pick our candidates.

Sarah "Barracuda" Palin, vice-presidential candidate on the Republican ticket with presidential candidate John McCain in 2008, should have been the presidential candidate in 2012 instead of "Milquetoast" Mitt Romney. Republican leaders said we can't run Palin; the left has beaten her up so badly she would be dead-on-arrival as a candidate.

It is true that the left pummeled Palin. A decade ago, one of my children, in high school or college at the time and actually rightish politically, was laughing about Palin. You know, my child said, the goofy one who said she was an expert on Russia because she could see Russia from her house in Alaska. I said it was an actress playing Palin on a comedy show who said that, not Palin. It was part of an overall campaign to make Palin look like a ditzy airhead. It would have been denounced as sexist hate speech if it had been directed at a woman on the left.

My child insisted there were sources confirming that Palin had said it, but was unable to produce one.

That's because Palin never said it. The derogatory myth was based on an interview about foreign policy and national security during the 2008 campaign. The interviewer, who traveled to Alaska to talk to Palin, noted the proximity of Alaska to Russia. Palin, a former governor of Alaska, pointed out the geographical fact that from an island that is part of Alaska, off the western edge of the mainland, you can look across the Bering Strait and see Russian coastline. She said we must avoid another Cold War and build a good relationship with "our next-door neighbor." She never said anything about seeing Russia from her house.

The point is that we on the right cannot let the left create a mirage of failure around our champions. A friend who generally supported Trump's policies called Trump's presidency a "**** show" (rhymes with "spit"). We can't let the left run over our champions and then declare them roadkill to be abandoned as unfit for further duty. Unfit? Says who? Says the left that splatters them with excrement and then calls them filthy? Says the Republican establishment afraid to challenge the left? Candidates worthy of our support will be bludgeoned by the left; those bloodied-up the most ought to be at the top of our wish list.

I spent a few of the preceding pages taking apart lies about Trump to dispel the false darkness created and perpetuated by the left. After the dismal economic performance and increased racial hostility of the Obama presidency, the Trump presidency should have been sunshine and clear skies, a Reaganesque "Morning in America" 2.0

with jobs and prosperity for all. Instead, even before the pandemic hit, the left drenched the nation with "mourning in America" lies such as: the president is a treasonous Putin puppet; only the rich do well in the Trump economy; a white supremacist president presides over a racist nation.

Christmas came early in 2020 for the left in the form of the pandemic. The death and economic devastation caused by covid were not Trump's fault. Still, it's a tough time to be president when Americans are dying in a global pandemic, and state and local lockdowns suspend or wipe out the jobs and businesses of millions of Americans.

Leftists and Never Trumpers said a national nightmare ended when Trump left the presidency. May Trump 2024 blow up these super-genius coyotes and allow the rest of us to pick up where we left off in making America great again.

\* \* \*

President Trump had many achievements, but there was no fiscal reform. Even before crisis spending on pandemic relief, federal spending during the Trump presidency outpaced revenue, producing deficits and adding to the debt.

In December 2020, there was public outcry over a pandemic relief bill. Pandemic relief spending was rolled in with a mishmash of the kind of spending that drives fiscal conservatives crazy, including: $10 million to Pakistan for gender studies; $1.3 billion to the Egyptian military; $500 million to Central American nations; $134 million to Burma. Foreign governments and lobbyists did well.

So did D.C. insiders. They got goodies such as $1 billion to the Smithsonian Institution, $154 million to the National Gallery of Art, and $40 million to the Kennedy

Center (entertainment venue closed during the pandemic).

The spending bill of more than 5,000 pages was filled with special items inserted by office holders, bureaucrats, and lobbyists. It was approved by Congress the same day it was introduced. That meant it was impossible to determine everything in it before voting on it, but that was the point.

The general criticism was: How dare you use pandemic relief as cover for a feeding frenzy of appalling spending! The anger was justified. The spending was grotesque. However, let's be sure we understand what happened:

> **It was business-as-usual spending that drew unexpected attention because of its connection to pandemic relief.**

Yes, be angry, but for the right reason. This was not a one-time splurge trying to hide under covid cover. These are items routinely funded year after year.

Another pandemic relief bill is moving forward as this updated edition of the book is finalized. This one *is* using covid as cover for special political favors unrelated to pandemic relief. Less than 10% of the nearly $2 trillion total goes to actual pandemic relief. Coming after that is an "infrastructure" bill that in its current form would spend $1 trillion on actual infrastructure and an additional $3 trillion on a leftist wish list of social and environmental programs.

Cramming taxpayer-funded favors into legislative bills often is called pork-barrel spending. Load enough pork into the barrel to please everybody.

Whether the pork is special-order or built into the regular budget process, we need to fix this problem. We need to fix it now.

# Introduction

Our nation's future is threatened by our federal government's debt. It has grown alarmingly, as indicated in this chart from the Federal Reserve Bank of St. Louis:

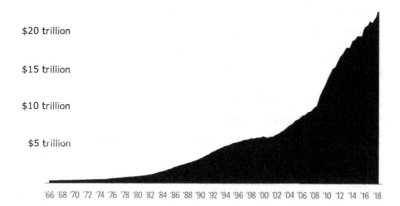

$20 trillion

$15 trillion

$10 trillion

$5 trillion

'66 '68 '70 '72 '74 '76 '78 '80 '82 '84 '86 '88 '90 '92 '94 '96 '98 '00 '02 '04 '06 '08 '10 '12 '14 '16 '18

It has gotten worse with pandemic-related spending in 2020-21. Yet the reaction of some is: Who cares? That doesn't affect my life.

Yes, it does.

When the government doesn't have enough money in the treasury to pay for all the spending it has approved, it sells bonds and other financial instruments called securities. Money raised from these sales is poured into the treasury and spent on government programs, but of course holders of government securities eventually must be paid back with interest. When investors watch the government run up more debt year after year and see the increasingly steep growth curve in the graph above, they get nervous. They wonder if the federal government will ever get in position to pay back all the debt it is accumulating. The government must offer a higher interest rate to get investors to keep buying bonds and supplying money to cover government spending. But that means it will be even more expensive for we taxpaying citizens to pay off all of that debt.

That's not the only way we are hurt. When the government succeeds at attracting buyers of its securities, the increasing flow of investment capital into the federal treasury causes interest rates for other loans to go up because there is less investment capital available in the private sector. Do you need a mortgage or a car loan? Do you need a loan to expand your business or buy a combine or go to school? These loans become more expensive as interest rates rise.

The government sometimes generates more currency to lower interest rates, but that causes inflation that makes the dollars in our pockets worth less.

Retired Admiral Michael Mullen, former chairman of the joint chiefs of staff and chairman of the Coalition for Fiscal and National Security, has said the number one threat to national security is our debt – not terrorism or some other external threat. We can't afford the best military in the world and adequately protect America at home and abroad if the value of our currency collapses and our economy collapses. The failure of the Soviet Union, despite its world-class military, provides a lesson confirming that point.

Let's fix the debt problem now by doing the following:

- **adopt a balanced budget amendment that is phased in over 10 years;**
- **phase out Social Security and Medicare for those under 55 by reimbursing them for their contributions;**

- **dismantle over the next decade the rest of the federal welfare/entitlement system and return federal spending authority to the limits established by the Constitution;**
- **provide social services at the state and local levels;**
- **launch a national effort similar to the 1994 Contract with America to build in Congress a majority of crusaders for limited government.**

The Contract with America was an 8-point program of government reform used nationally to rally voters to the Republican congressional ticket in 1994. It helped produce a Republican majority in both houses of Congress for the first time in 40 years.

In 1994, Republican congressional leaders led the effort to bring a new majority to Washington. Some in today's Republican leadership would join Democrats in resisting a serious push for limited government. It will be difficult to replace the current majority in Washington with a majority serious about limited government.

But that's the mission. It will be a healthy development for our national politics. The only good thing about our fiscal crisis is that it offers an opportunity for people to rally to something on which everyone can agree: We can't keep going the way we have been and bankrupt the nation.

\* \* \*

The remaining pages explain why we must tear down a federal welfare/entitlement system nearly a century in the making. It's sobering stuff.

Yet I write this with a smile. Conservatives need to smile more. We're the bold, freewheeling, joyful adventurers of the American political scene. We are champions of freedom, not political correctness. We call for adherence to a basic code of universal values, then leave people free to live their lives.

As a father of seven children ranging in age from 17 to 31, I understand the concern about conservatives being perceived by the young as nosy busybodies who want to micromanage people's lives, especially regarding sexuality. I stand with 4,000 years of Judeo-Christian teaching on sexuality, but let me assure you that I don't care about your sex life. If you pressure me to endorse or accommodate your sex life in ways I don't want to, then I'll push back. Maybe we agree. Maybe we don't. Reasonable people don't agree on everything.

Now can we focus on the fiscal crisis that will mangle all of us regardless of social beliefs? This is about math and economics and number-crunching – or us being crunched by the numbers – regardless of party affiliations or positions on other issues.

Young Americans should be the first to rally to the call for limited government. It's their future that is most threatened by out-of-control spending and growth of the debt. Yet they present some of the stiffest resistance to the conservative fiscal message. They take as gospel what they get from their favorite sources for news and political direction, and those sources skew left – teachers, entertainers, Facebook, BuzzFeed, Twitter, Instagram, TikTok (although one of my children has shown me pro-Trump conservative offerings on TikTok). When challenged, some millennials refuse to face contrary facts and retreat to a "safe space." Or they go the other direction and get verbally and physically violent.

We on the right can't give up on them or concede them to the left as a voting bloc. We must break through to them.

It won't be easy.

Nebraska's second congressional district, the Omaha metropolitan area, is considered a "swing" district because of the relatively equal voter registration of Democrats and Republicans. In 2018, the incumbent was retired USAF brigadier general Don Bacon, a Republican and reliable vote for the Trump/Republican agenda. Democratic challenger Kara Eastman, a community organizer active in the nonprofit sector, was endorsed by U.S. Senator Bernie Sanders (I-VT). Eastman is a Berniecrat socialist hardcore leftist: Medicare-for-all, raise the minimum wage, raise taxes on the rich, Green New Deal.

In the 2018 primary, Eastman beat Brad Ashford, a moderate Democrat who held the House seat in 2015-16 and was trying to win it back. He was endorsed by the local and national Democratic Party establishment, which provided him a huge funding advantage. Didn't matter. Ashford, who has been a Republican and an Independent and is known as a reach-across-the-aisle centrist, was not far enough to the left for NE2 Democratic primary voters.

Eastman lost to Bacon in the 2018 general election, but by only 2 percentage points. She ran for the seat again in 2020. This time the Democratic Party at the local and national levels united to support her candidacy, something that happened half-heartedly and too late in 2018. She also had in her favor the growing number of voters, especially young ones, enchanted by the siren song of socialism.

On that second point about the appeal of socialism, William Shirer noted in his famous book *Rise and Fall of the Third Reich* that youth indoctrination was a top priority for the most prominent socialist in history:

> **[Adolph Hitler] had stressed in his book [Mein Kampf] the importance of winning over and then training the youth in the service "of a new national state" – a subject he returned to often after he became the German dictator. "When an opponent declares, 'I will not come over to your side,'" he said in a speech on November 6, 1933, "I calmly say, 'Your child belongs to us already. What are you? You will pass on. Your descendants, however, now stand in the new camp. In a short time, they will know nothing else but this new community.'"**

We ignore *der Führer's* point at our peril.

In 2015, I had a disheartening conversation with an intelligent, articulate man who seemed to be in his 20s. I was running for Congress against the aforementioned Don Bacon for the open Republican spot on the 2016 primary election ballot. (In the interest of full disclosure, Don and I became and remain friends.) The young man asked why I was running. I said I was concerned about the increasing debt and would push for a return to limited government under the Constitution to get government growth and spending under control. He smiled with exasperated liberal/progressive smugness and said: "The Constitution? That was written in 1787. Haven't we evolved beyond that? Don't we want more out of government?"

I was impressed that he knew the Constitution was drafted in 1787, but alarmed by his cavalier dismissal of it. I tried to show him that he and his generation are being buried alive by the debt we are running up as we blast way beyond the boundaries of the Constitution. I got nowhere. He was unmoved by the numbers.

A 2018 Gallup poll said 37% of Americans had a positive view of socialism. The poll said among Democrats, 57% were positive on socialism while only 47% were positive on capitalism. Apparently some confused folks were positive on both. But then consider that plenty of capitalism-loving Republicans embrace socialism in the form of Social Security. In recent years, 36 states and the District of Columbia have voted for Medicaid expansion. That's a lot of red states (including mine, Nebraska) voting for bigger government and an expanded federal welfare/entitlement system. Some polls indicate growing numbers of Republicans joining Democrats in the call for Medicare-for-all.

In that Gallup poll, the overall 37% positive view of socialism has been steady since 2010. But something dramatic is happening in the youngest age group. The poll said among Americans 18-29, the positive view of capitalism plummeted from 68% in 2010 to 45% in 2018. We are losing the youth of America to those who demonize capitalism.

If you doubt that young people are being turned ferociously against capitalism and other founding values, have a conversation about politics with your children, grandchildren, nieces and nephews, or any young people in your life.

Be prepared. In fact, check their social media for references to ACAB (All Cops Are Bastards) and other signs that they march to the beat of the leftist drum. They've been told by teachers, social media sites, and pop culture icons that terms such as "Constitution," "capitalism," "rule of law," "property rights," "religion," and other core values of American society are synonymous with "white supremacy," "selfishness," "unfairness," "ignorance," "intolerance," and more-graphic terms not suitable for a family-friendly book. They may gasp in horror at your conservatism and wonder how anyone living in the 21st century could believe in such things.

In our 2020 local congressional race, Democratic challenger Eastman lost to Republican incumbent Bacon. On the national level, Republicans gained seats in the House. However, Republicans still are in the minority in the House.

And of course the Republican Party lost the presidency and its majority in the Senate. Fraud likely was a factor, but the loss of the presidency will become permanent, and other races (state and local as well as federal) will start going to the left permanently, if we keep losing waves of young voters to the mindset that rejects American founding values.

It isn't just the youth. Plenty of adults have been bullied into believing they are moral lepers if they embrace American founding values and reject the move toward bigger government with an expanded welfare/entitlement system.

I'm trying to get everyone on board for limited government – young and old, religious and secular, all races and ethnicities, whatever sexual orientation and gender you believe you are. Limiting the federal government to the spending authority defined in the Constitution is the only way to fix our fiscal crisis.

# America Is Robbing Its Children

By permission of Gary Varvel and Creators Syndicate, Inc.

The cartoon above by Gary Varvel of the *Indianapolis Star* is even more potent in color, with angry orange lava spewing out of the Capitol dome and glowing orange channels running through the black, smoldering, menacing flow. Even in black and white, you get the picture.

Some relatives and friends are shocked to discover that I want to dismantle the federal welfare/entitlement system. It's simple. It bothers me that America is robbing its children by sticking them with trillions of dollars of debt to fund that system. Does it bother you? If so, please read on. If it doesn't, keep reading anyway, especially if you're a young person being enveloped by the molten glacier of debt generated by your elders.

Since 2001, in round numbers the federal government's debt has grown more than 300%, from $6 trillion to $27 trillion. In 2019, the federal government took in $3.4 trillion and spent $4.4 trillion. We taxpayers provided roughly 77 cents of every dollar the federal government spent. We paid for only 77% of the government programs and services we consumed. We borrowed to cover the rest.

Imagine I'm a tenant and I tell my landlord that during the year I will pay only $770 of the $1,000 monthly rent, but the landlord can keep track of the other $230 per month and add it to the rent of the next tenant, my child. So my child will pay full rent plus the unpaid $230 per month racked up by me.

That's what we are doing to our children. The ratio changes as deficits vary from year to year, but the debt keeps growing because we spend more than we take in. It's one generation effectively robbing the next to pay for today's overspending. I went to a high school and a college run by the Society of Jesus, a Catholic order of priests and brothers also known as the Jesuits. My Jesuit education taught me that I am supposed to leave the world a better place than I found it. We are leaving younger generations buried under a mountain of debt. Even if you don't have children, do you have a conscience? No one with a conscience can be comfortable with this intergenerational theft.

My two sons in their 30s are living the American Dream. They are immigrants. They are college graduates. They have good jobs. They are careful with money. They are working hard and playing by fiscally conservative rules.

And they will be crushed financially by their federal government. Their future earnings will be taxed severely to pay off the debt we are running up now. We in effect are pillaging their and other young people's future earnings.

We are reaching into the future and into their pockets to grab dollars to pay for our present overspending. That's what then-Senator Barack Obama meant (page 2) by "shifting the burden of bad choices today onto the backs of our children and grandchildren." He was right.

You might say: "I am not robbing anyone! I pay taxes and put more into the system than I get out of it." I don't mean to insult you. You are a net contributor helping to cover the portion of government spending for which we actually pay. The fact remains, though, that as a society we borrow to cover the rest of our annual spending and leave the tab to those coming after us. What a legacy. We really are robbing our children if we vote for politicians who raise the debt ceiling (thereby increasing that legacy tab), preserve the federal welfare/entitlement system, and reject the call to restore limited government under the Constitution.

President Barack Obama convened the National Commission on Fiscal Responsibility and Reform, also known as the Simpson-Bowles Commission, in 2010. The commission noted that by 2025 *all* federal revenue will be consumed by interest on the debt, Medicare, Medicaid, and Social Security. That leaves nothing for national defense or anything else.

Annual defense spending is roughly $700 billion. The federal Office of Management and Budget says the current annual interest payment on the debt is about $350 billion, and by 2025 will exceed what we spend on defense.

In 1980, our $900 billion debt equaled a third of the Gross Domestic Product, which measures the annual value of goods and services produced by the national economy.

Today our nearly $27 trillion debt is roughly a third larger than our $20 trillion GDP. According to Simpson-Bowles, by 2035 the debt will be roughly twice the size of GDP. Our debt will be twice as big as our economy.

The Congressional Budget Office makes a similar prediction. Greece, which has fallen into financial chaos and panic because of a debt crisis, has a debt-to-GDP ratio that has hovered around 180% in recent years, meaning it owes almost twice as much as it makes annually. That's like saying Greece makes $100,000 a year but owes $180,000. Sounds terrible, right? We're on the same path as Greece. The CBO says that by 2037 our debt-to-GDP ratio will be 200%. We will owe twice as much as we make annually.

From 2001 to 2013, the number of food stamp recipients nearly tripled, going from 17 million to a record high 48 million. That's roughly 14% of the national population.

America has just over 100 million full-time workers. According to the U.S. Census Bureau, over the last decade there have been years in which the number of people receiving means-tested government benefits has surpassed the number of full-time workers. That is ominous. It brings to mind conservative commentator Dinesh D'Souza's wagon analogy. For most of our history, most Americans have been outside the wagon pulling it forward, while those who are incapacitated have ridden in the wagon. We now have an alarming number of people, including able-bodied citizens, riding in the wagon instead of helping to pull it.

The media often report that the unemployment rate floats between 4% and 6%, but that number includes only people actively searching for work. The media do not report the number that includes people who have given up looking for work – not retirees, but people who have become discouraged and are no longer searching for a job. If you count the total number of people not working, the true unemployment rate hovered around 14% during the Obama presidency. That number dropped into the single digits post-Obama, but this and other economic indicators prove that we have been moving dramatically in the wrong direction.

\* \* \*

I have been told that I am much harsher in print than I am in person or on the radio. There's a sharp edge to my message because I am trying to cut through the numbing effect of status quo conformity. I'm challenging notions considered settled for decades.

I have relatives and friends on the left side of the political spectrum – liberals, progressives, a few socialists. I am very critical of "the left" in this book, but I'm talking about people whose life work is politics, people who prepare the marching orders for the left, people who riot. I'm not talking about regular folks who sincerely believe that what the leadership of the left advocates is best for America. I tell what I believe is the unsparing truth about what the left is doing to our country because I believe it's the only way to shatter the false narrative presented by the left and persuade good-hearted people that it's time for them to shift to the right politically. I'm not saying well-intentioned people on the left are stupid or evil; I'm saying they are mistaken.

\* \* \*

Limited government as defined in the Constitution is the right policy for America. Yet in 2008 and 2012, America elected a president who ignored constitutional limits on his office and the federal government. President Obama believed in greater control of society by the federal government. A powerful array of elite activists – media, academia, government, and crony capitalists who benefit from big government – promoted a politically savvy community organizer as a catalyst for expanding the federal government's control over society.

The elites don't have to worry. They're taken care of. The nation's highest concentration of wealth is now the Washington, D.C., metro area. Note the effort on Capitol Hill to cushion government insiders from the full impact of Obamacare. When such policies produce job growth stagnation and higher taxes and inflation, the rest of us caught in that economic grinder must fight harder to win more converts to limited government.

The 2016 presidential election was a step in the right direction, away from big government, but Donald Trump was not a limited-government conservative. As president he cut taxes and business-inhibiting regulations, but did not shrink government and reduce spending.

Now we have Democrats controlling the presidency and both houses of Congress. They want to pick up where President Obama left off and resume the march to socialism.

The Tea Party is pushing to restore limited government, but it won't succeed without some basic education of the general public. People who consider themselves neither conservative nor Republican must be convinced of the need for limited government to get spending under control. The Tea Party message can be jarring to the modern citizen trained to believe that government is the answer to every problem, and anyone who disagrees is cruel and ignorant. Decades of liberal/progressive indoctrination by the education establishment must be undone.

Tea Party activists in their 50s, 60s, 70s, and 80s today were in their 20s, 30s, 40s, and 50s when they rallied to the candidacy and presidency of conservative icon Ronald Reagan in the 1980s. They comprised a market for what Reagan was selling because they were taught basic American founding values.

Does that market still exist? Most people in their 20s, 30s, 40s, and 50s today were educated in a system lukewarm or hostile to American founding values.

It was no accident that radical anti-American agitator and eventual Obama mentor Bill Ayers switched from terrorist bomber of public buildings to professorial shaper of public education. He became a college professor of education – a teacher of teachers – because he decided that the way for the left to win the battle for America was to capture the minds of young people, and thereby capture the future. (See Hitler quotation on page 40.)

Here's an instructive story from a friend:

> *Last Christmas [2011], we were at a gathering of my wife's family in small town Iowa. All of the folks there are solidly upper-middle-class, work hard, and live below their means. Before dinner, some of 's were sitting around the table discussg the economy, investing, farm prices, ·. I had just closed out some stock 'es that were very profitable. A couple e brothers-in-law following my lead lso done well.*

*My 14-year-old nephew joined the conversation and almost immediately came out with, "The stock market is only for the rich, and rich people are evil." He was deadly serious and you could have heard a pin drop at the table.*

*I asked my nephew, "Where did you hear that and why do you think it's true?" It was from his small-town Iowa social studies class, with the teacher reinforcing that conclusion through the use of examples of companies like Enron, WorldCom, etc. As we tried to explain the reality of how the stock market works and who benefits from it, it was obvious we were not making much of a dent.*

*In the end, his father walked over to the Christmas tree and picked up my nephew's envelope from me. It contained $500 in cash for his college fund and was a substantial portion of his Christmas. His father opened it in front of him, handed me the cash, and said, "Give this to the Salvation Army or Goodwill, since your nephew thinks it's evil."*

*And I did so. Now there's a lesson that I guarantee my nephew learned and will never forget.*

My friend made a secret contribution to his nephew's college fund. The saga continued over the next year:

*We had our annual Christmas dinner with family yesterday [Dec. 25, 2012] in western Iowa. What a difference a year makes when it comes to the nephews' knowledge and appreciation for what personal finance is all about.*

*During the past year, we had all made a concerted effort to combat the progressive propaganda and indoctrination that the boys get in the public schools. Their* parents made a point of involving them in the family's everyday financial life – income, paying bills, managing a family budget, saving, retirement planning, giving to charity, etc.

I introduced both boys to investing and trading. They've learned quite a bit about the basics and I guarantee they are both now committed capitalists.

Instead of a set dollar amount for their college fund Christmas gift, we agreed to a "simulated hedge fund" for 2012. I spotted them both enough capital to buy an initial allocation of shares in the stocks that I trade. They were tasked with tracking their holdings and I "consulted" with them when making buy and sell decisions throughout the year. For my "management expertise" I was paid a typical hedge fund management fee.

You should have seen their faces yesterday when they opened their Christmas envelopes, which were 8½ x 11 manila envelopes instead of the typical Christmas cards. The envelopes contained their year-end "account statements" and a check for their "profits" less my management fee, trading fees, and a reserve for "taxes." Since their "hedge fund" had a great year, the checks were impressive.

The really impressive thing was sitting at the table between them going over their statements. They understood how capital markets operate.

I'd like to report that their schools have changed and are providing all students with this kind of knowledge, but I'd be lying. However, at least these two now can recognize what's progressive propaganda and reject it out-of-hand based upon their own very real-world experiences. It's sad to realize that even at such young ages it

**takes a concerted effort to expose them early to the very adult world of financial concerns to combat the powerful and pervasive progressive indoctrination that the public schools are committed to pushing.**

I'm not picking on public schools. The same hostile-to-capitalism attitude can be found in private schools. The challenge is to convince Americans of all ages and backgrounds that the capitalism-bashing, pro-big-government path we are on is self-destructive.

\* \* \*

The "it" in *Fix It Now* is our fiscal crisis, but in a larger sense we have to fix our broken system of government. Federal agencies bully religious institutions and conservative organizations while spying on reporters and the general citizenry via phone records. The U.S. Supreme Court distorts the Constitution and finds Obamacare constitutional. The system we now have makes a mockery of the idea that the federal government is supposed to be subject to the will of the people according to the terms of a written charter of government called the Constitution. Combine all that with our fiscal crisis and reasonable people worry about our country coming apart at the seams.

The Tea Party is not trying to push America out on an extremist limb. America already is out on an extremist limb. The Tea Party is trying to bring America in from the limb before the limb breaks and America crashes.

Tea stands for Taxed Enough Already. Some have joked that it should be Sea Party (Spending Enough Already) or Bea Party (Borrowed Enough Already). All are true. The "extremist" Tea Party message is that we can't keep indulging in unlimited government. It's not foaming-at-the-mouth extremism. It's practical, pragmatic, good old American common sense. Using the federal government to take care of everyone and everything is unconstitutional, it doesn't work, and we can't afford it. The extremists are those who won't face this reality.

Americans have become shockingly selfish. We want a certain amount of government, but we're not willing to pay for it. So we steal from the future by borrowing. For decades, Democrats and Republicans have been raising the debt ceiling, borrowing more money, and pushing the cost off to future taxpayers. The only reason it's an issue now is because the Tea Party is rising up and shouting, "No!"

This book is a call to Republicans to quit supporting the status quo. It's a call to Democrats to reject the dogma that good government automatically means big government. It's a call to citizens of all political stripes to demand the end of the federal welfare/entitlement system and a return to the limited form of government created by America's founders.

Who will answer such a call?

Libertarians want to reduce the role of the federal government in the life of the nation.

There are Republicans who care more about the fate of the nation than insider party politics.

Plenty of Truman/JFK Democrats reject the politics of whining victimhood and the push toward socialism promoted by the leadership of their party.

Many middle-class and working-class people don't care at all about party politics but are tired of funding a federal welfare/entitlement system that creates more problems than it solves. Workers not in government-employee unions might be tired of paying for public sector salaries, benefits, and especially pensions that exceed what similar workers get in the private sector.

Young Americans: the Tea Party is the only force fighting to save you from a fiscally horrendous fate.

Then there are people who have quit on the electoral process. They see no point in going through the motions when the status quo always prevails. They might engage if they believed there were candidates who would be faithful to the voter/taxpayer and rein in the federal government. They don't care about party labels or liberal/conservative debates. They just know the system is failing and they want candidates willing to tell the truth and genuinely try to fix it. They may not consider themselves part of the Tea Party, but they see that we are sliding into fiscal catastrophe because status quo leaders of both parties are unwilling to stop the slide. These are the voters who put Trump in the White House. The Tea Party sees things in the same common-sense way they do.

Americans have been so thoroughly propagandized on the legitimacy of big government that many have no idea what the founders built, and why. It's necessary to briefly review American political history to explain the system of government that made America great, and what has happened to it. There's a better chance of lighting a fire in people if you show them how their political heritage has been hijacked and taken drastically off course.

This hijacking has been accomplished not by terrorists,

but rather by elected officials, bureaucrats, judges, and activists operating through regular channels of government and politics – with the support of enough of the general public to allow it to happen. The process can be reversed if enough citizens engage and flex their political muscles.

Let me guess: the numbers are so big and the problems seem so overwhelming that you don't want to think about them. The last time I checked the mesmerizing display at usdebtclock.org, which shows how fast the debt is growing, the first six columns of numbers were changing so quickly that I couldn't follow them. The debt was growing by just over $2 million per minute, about $37,000 per second. The debt per citizen was $91,000; per taxpayer, $242,000.

And we're not even getting into the ways America's fiscal blunders are threatening to end the U.S. dollar's reign as the basis for world commerce, which would hit the American economy like an earthquake.

You're not comfortable with the way things are going, but you don't know what to do. Political disagreements can be nasty. You are told you are stupid and don't know what you're talking about if you question the existing system. So you steer clear of politics and turn back to family and work and church and social circles and sports and popular culture and other things in life. You avoid political scraps and let politics take care of itself. Maybe you vote, but not with any guiding passion.

Here's the problem: we don't have the luxury anymore of paying little or no attention to politics. Politics is about to break into our bank accounts and other areas of our lives in ways previously unimagined in America.

*The important thing to remember is that your uninterest in politics will not mean that the various tasks will not be done; they will be done, and usually in a way unsatisfactory to you.*

**John Kennedy, 1956**

I included the statement by Senator Cruz (page 2) about people paying attention because we need a whole new wave of citizens to get involved in the effort to restore limited government.

Leaders of media, academia, government, and crony capitalism are trying to turn America into a society dominated by the federal government. Despite evidence of the damage this approach has done to America, they won't stop. They acknowledge that there might be suffering now, but they believe the end justifies the means. They insist their approach will produce a government-managed utopia. They disregard reality.

For instance, on Obamacare we were lied to about its cost and the ability to keep one's insurance plan. The rollout was a snarled cyber mess. It was such a bureaucratic disaster that implementation of key parts was delayed. But its advocates said: trust us, all will be well. President Obama said of those who tried to defund Obamacare, "I'm not going to allow them to inflict economic pain on millions of our own people just so they can make an ideological point."

That's my take on Obamacare. Its advocates inflicted economic pain on the masses by turning the health insurance industry inside-out and upside-down. Why did they do it? Because their political creed says government should manage health care – no matter how dysfunctional it is.

Most of us grew up in relatively stable families and have owned or worked for small businesses. Some of us have owned or worked for large corporations. A typical American has had the experience of working in a capitalist system that is basically fair, rewarding those who work hard and play by the rules. It's not perfect, but no other system can match it in generating prosperity for the masses.

Former President Obama grew up in Hawaii outside mainstream America. His adult mentors promoted a left-wing ideology hostile to American founding principles. He went from an unstable childhood to academia to a career combining academia and community activism.

Obama seems to have had little experience working a regular job in the private sector. He was hostile to traditional American business values (you didn't build that). He was a front man for those who want to turn America into a utopia dominated by the federal government.

Such leftists are misguided. We no longer can ignore them or let them have their way. We don't want to live in their failed utopia. I've been there, done that.

Fresh out of college, I taught high school in the Caribbean island nation of Jamaica for the 1984-85 school year as a member of the Jesuit Volunteer Corps, kind of like the Peace Corps but run by the Jesuits. I saw firsthand the damage socialism can do.

When socialist Michael Manley, an avid fan of Cuban communist dictator Fidel Castro, became prime minister of Jamaica in 1972, he declared that there were "five flights a day to Miami" for critics who didn't want to live under his anti-capitalist policies. Wealth and talent fled the country.

According to the Country Studies research on file at the Library of Congress, in the 1950s and 1960s Jamaica experienced average annual GDP growth of 4.5%. Under Manley, there were seven consecutive years of negative economic growth. The rising price of oil was a factor, but Manley's policies were the main cause.

Manley was voted out in 1980, but four years later I was living in a society still trying to recover from the type of economic mismanagement that utopians inflicted on Jamaica, and are trying to inflict on America. We don't want that. We don't want our children to live most of their lives in a society ruined by a domineering federal government.

\* \* \*

Everybody is exasperated by the fighting between Democrats and Republicans in Washington. Why can't they be reasonable? Why can't they get along? Why can't they agree on common-sense solutions?

Let me ask you this: Why can't you agree on common-sense solutions in your marriage, your family, your church, your school, your work place, your social club, and other areas of your life? Agreement sometimes is impossible to achieve because reasonable people are not going to agree on everything. Despite President George Washington warning against it, the party system developed in the 1790s because reasonable people disagreed and gravitated into like-minded coalitions on how to set up a national financial system, manage relations with England and France, treat civil liberties (including freedom of speech to criticize the government), and other important issues. That's why, in our political life, we vote on things and proceed by majority rule.

Part of the cause for the partisan bickering and gridlock in Washington is the pressure generated by intense 24/7 media coverage. But the main reason is that senators, representatives, and presidents try to do too much. They are trying to solve problems that are supposed to be handled at the state or local level. The nation is bogged down in arguments that aren't supposed to happen on Capitol Hill.

In a 1995 budget showdown, Republicans found themselves under attack by the left because they wanted to reduce the proposed increase in federal spending to subsidize school lunches. The federal government still would have spent more money on school lunches than the year before, but not as much more as some on the left wanted. Instead of arguing dollar amounts, Republicans should have said: We shouldn't even be fighting about this; funding school lunches is a matter for state or local governments, not the federal government.

The best way to reduce the partisan clamor and break out of the cycle of infuriating standoffs is to restore limited government. This is not a partisan argument. Again, it's about math and economics. The lava flow of debt is advancing on us because the federal government exercises far more power than allowed in the Constitution. There is not supposed to be so much power concentrated in the federal government. The temptation is overwhelming. People fight tooth-and-nail for control of that power – even if it means making promises that require looting the federal treasury and running up the debt to please various voting blocs.

Some people want change, but nothing as dramatic as restoring limited government. They want compromisers who seek more moderate solutions.

I cringe when I hear people call for "moderation" and for politicians who can "get along with the other side." Generally in life, getting along is a good thing. In politics, though, getting along is code for protecting the business-as-usual status quo. Defenders of business-as-usual are good at manipulating get-along moderation to neuter any effort at true reform, as they have for most of the last century.

I want politicians whose first priority is telling the truth, not getting along. Even Jesus rejected get-along moderation if it meant sacrificing the truth. What's the point of getting along and finding common ground if the result is an agreement to do nothing meaningful? That doesn't do the nation any good. Cases of much-ballyhooed bipartisan cooperation get special designations – Gang of 4, Gang of 8, Gang of 16, Grand Bargain. These alleged examples of statesmen rising above partisan politics to achieve common-sense solutions too often produce nothing to warrant the hype.

Look at the December 2013 Ryan-Murray budget deal approved by Congress and signed by President Obama. Named for its two main negotiators, U.S. Representative Paul Ryan (R-WI) and U.S. Senator Patty Murray (D-WA), it was celebrated as a triumph of bipartisan accomplishment, proof that Democrats and Republicans can get along. They got along and reached an agreement because they agreed to do *nothing*. They voted to preserve the status quo.

If the Ryan-Murray deal was such a dramatic breakthrough, why did Congress raise the debt ceiling and borrow more money to fund continued deficit spending two months later? I thought the Ryan-Murray deal was "a step in the right direction" leading to "true structural fiscal reform" and no more crisis-driven spasms such as raising the debt ceiling. Or has raising the debt ceiling become part of regular fiscal policy for Washington?

We need people who think differently than the majority now in Washington. We do not need more compromise and getting along. We need a new approach, a new center of gravity, a new majority in Washington committed to restoring limited government. There will be plenty of getting along in Washington when we restore limited government and reduce the power for which federal politicians compete. Good will and cooperation will flourish when a new majority of federal politicians is unified in the quest to restore and preserve limited government.

I am not persuaded by proposals to fix our fiscal crisis with mixtures of spending cuts and tax increases, revised Social Security and Medicare formulas, and other variations on the status quo. They sound like an alcoholic saying he's going to adopt a "balanced" approach. He's not going to abstain from alcohol – that would be "extremist." Instead, he's going to limit his alcohol consumption to a "reasonable" amount.

The analogy isn't perfect. We do need a federal government. That's why the Constitution was written. But the founders were right: if we let the federal government operate outside the parameters established in the Constitution, then forget about it; we won't be able to limit it. How many times must the founders be proven right? We have decades of evidence. Fiscal discipline is overwhelmed by relentless pressure to accommodate legislators and special interests whose support is needed for passage of a bill.

I'm old enough to remember a Democrat, U.S. Senator William Proxmire of Wisconsin, giving spoof Golden Fleece Awards for examples of out-of-control spending by the federal government. They often were small and amusingly bizarre projects.

The "Cornhusker kickback" – a special Medicaid deal for Nebraska that secured the final Senate vote needed to advance Obamacare – was an example of something more serious and more dangerous to our future. It was further proof that Washington politics knows no constitutional boundaries. Add the pressure to grow government coming from those who benefit from it – government employees, recipients of government money and programs, and crony capitalists who profit from big government – and you have the spectacle we now see: government keeps growing with seemingly unstoppable momentum, like an alcoholic who can't help himself and keeps increasing consumption until he suffers a total breakdown.

## Limited Government

federal
authority

The Constitution creates a circle within which federal authority is to be contained. The federal government can do only what is defined in and allowed by the Constitution.

That has not stopped the federal government from pushing beyond its constitutional boundary.

# Unlimited Government

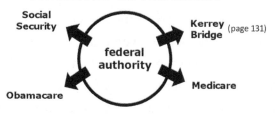

Social Security — federal authority — Kerrey Bridge (page 131)

Obamacare — Medicare

When you break out of the circle of authority established by the Constitution, it's open season. The circle of limitation is destroyed, and with it any hope of fiscal discipline. Growth of government spins out of control, as does the spending to pay for it. In the example above, maybe I should add an arrow for gender studies in Pakistan. We would need more than a thousand arrows to account for all the breaches created by unlimited government.

Once the boundary is breached, there is no logical place to draw a new boundary. Every proposed exception and expansion of government is justified by a compelling reason for it. Once the game is rolling, you don't even need a good reason to justify another breach of constitutional authority. You just point to all the other exceptions as justification.

In December 2009, then-U.S. Senator Ben Nelson (D-NE) was on the radio defending his vote that allowed Obamacare to advance toward enactment. A caller asked where in the Constitution Senator Nelson found authority for such an expansion of government. Senator Nelson did not try to justify Obamacare constitutionally. Instead, he said if you reject Obamacare based on that argument, then you have to shut down Social Security and Medicare because there's nothing in the Constitution authorizing those programs, either.

Well said, Senator Nelson.

There is no logical or moral basis to approve one exception and deny another, so everything gets a green light. I'll say yes to yours, you'll say yes to mine, and we'll be hailed as enlightened compromisers who can find the magical moderate middle ground – and hasten the fiscal self-destruction of America.

Either the federal government is limited as enumerated in the Constitution, or it is unlimited. There is no magical moderate middle ground. That's a mirage. The search for this nonexistent fantasy land is a waste of time and effort. The get-along compromisers just dodge tough cuts and authorize more spending to placate all parties, regardless of the impact on federal taxpayers.

Some ask: "Why should I care about the Constitution? What good is that outdated piece of parchment to me?" That piece of parchment, if we follow and enforce it, is the only thing between us and financial disembowelment by our federal government.

How do we who see what is happening get the attention of family and friends and explain it to them? Does cartoonist Gary Varvel (page 43) need to go a step further and show children being incinerated and consumed by the debt? Maybe we need to send Americans to Greece so they can experience what happens when a persistent debt crisis wipes out the value of a nation's currency and puts its economy in a condition in which people can't get money from the bank, and store shelves empty as desperation sets in.

Maybe people would be moved by images of children engulfed by a deluge of water or earth representing the debt.

Imagine anguished little faces covered by rising flood water or an avalanche. Little hands reach out in desperation before disappearing beneath trillions of cubic feet of water or earth. Maybe millennials should be the victims to get them to focus on the truth. We must show young people that the cool leftists they idolize are *selling them out.*

Who other than the Tea Party is doing anything to stop big-government utopians from inundating the young with an immoral debt burden? We have to make the Tea Party cool. If "cool" is too ambitious, I'll settle for "trusted."

I have emceed local Tea Party rallies. I realize that the Tea Party makes some people uncomfortable, even on the right. Establishment Republicans, maybe even more than Democrats, want the Tea Party to go away. Even some friends of the Tea Party believe it is a spent force.

The Tea Party is not as visible as it was a decade ago, but its spirit remains alive and well. The Trump phenomenon is a manifestation of Tea Party spirit. The Freedom Caucus of roughly 40 robustly conservative members of the House of Representatives is an example of Tea Party spirit.

Former Democratic presidential candidate Hillary Clinton knows the Tea Party spirit lives. In the home stretch of the 2016 campaign, she said half of Republican candidate Donald Trump's supporters were "irredeemable" members of a "basket of deplorables" she defined as "racist, sexist, homophobic, xenophobic, Islamophobic – you name it." (I'll bet they eat at the Olive Garden and stay the Holiday Inn, too.) Her leftist audience laughed and relished the arrogant dismissal of the conservative rabble.

Instead of pouting or rioting, Trump supporters started

wearing shirts proudly identifying themselves as "deplorables." The deplorables were the ones celebrating on election night 2016.

*  *  *

I'd rather not mark the centennial of the Great Depression in the 2030s by reliving it. That means rolling back unlimited government. The only way I can see to do it is to shut down the game of unlimited government and restore the limits defined in the Constitution. That eliminates the pressure to expand the game. There is nothing over which to bargain. There are no temptations to resist.

If someone has a better plan than what I propose, that's great. I'll abandon mine and get behind the better plan. But "better" means actually fixing our fiscal crisis, not tinkering at the edges. "Better" also means *specific*; no more vague blather about finding middle-ground solutions – in other words, preserving the status quo that is ruining our country.

I admire the work of the Simpson-Bowles Commission and other reformers proposing plans to reduce the debt. What stops me from embracing their proposals is that they allow big government to continue. They don't bring us back to limited government. Well-intentioned reformers seem to believe the crisis can be solved by tweaking tax rates and social programs while still allowing the federal government to operate beyond the circle of authority established by the Constitution. Only a return to limited federal government as defined in the Constitution will cure what ails us.

# Basic Principles

I am a populist conservative with a single guiding political principle: the best for the most. I want a system that produces the best life for the most people.

That kind of rhetoric makes some people nervous because those who favor government control of economics say the same thing. They want government to redistribute wealth so that everybody's standard of living is the same.

Remember then-Senator Obama, as a candidate for president in 2008, telling Joe the Plumber that it was all right for government to use tax policy to "spread the wealth around"? That's not what I'm talking about. I'm talking about a system in which government stays out of the way and lets citizens create personal and communal wealth through the dynamo of capitalism.

As an adjunct professor, I have taught an intense American civics course at Bellevue University in Bellevue, Nebraska. Undergraduates are required to take the course. The school is concerned that students are emerging from the American education system without a firm idea of the nation's founding values. The class distinguishes between issues and values. Diversity of experience and opinion has produced healthy political debate on issues throughout American history, but there must be commonly held values for a nation as large and complex as the United States to function. The focus of the course is the erosion of the foundational values on which America has been built.

The groupings on the next page are adapted from Bellevue University's American Vision & Values curriculum.

**Issues:**         Abortion  Death Penalty  War
Education  Taxation  Social Services
Health Care  Foreign Policy  Same-Sex Marriage
Immigration  Affirmative Action  Social Security
Medicare  Medicaid  Environment

---------------------------------------------------

**Values:**  Natural Law  Life  Liberty  Property Rights
Two-Parent Family  Capitalism/Free Markets
Self-Government  Self-Reliance  Personal Responsibility
Democracy/Majority Rule  Work Is Good  Rule of Law
Communal Associations  Religion  Limited Government

The values below the dotted line used to be universally accepted in America. For instance, there used to be no debate over the premise that democracy and capitalism produce the best for the most, the most freedom and prosperity for the most people.

America is a republic, a representative democracy with an elected head of the executive branch. But the operating principle is democracy, with decisions by majority rule. There may be representative and appointive bodies and special procedures involved, but the crucial democratic thread running through our entire system is majority rule.

We make decisions in our republic by majority rule. That's how legislators and the chief executive are chosen. That's how legislators make law. That's how panels of judges decide cases. That's how ballot measures are decided by the people. That's how fundamental rights are identified and protected in federal and state constitutions.

Majority rule maximizes freedom. Reasonable people will not agree on everything. When public policy disputes arise, we go in the direction most people want to go. Sore losers in majority-rule competition call it tyranny of the majority, but it's not tyrannical if decision-makers are free to advocate whatever course of action they want. Make your best argument; the position that gets the most support wins. That's the fairest way. It would be tyrannical to let the minority force society to go down a path most people oppose.

In a republic, majority rule must be exercised according to established procedures. Protest turned to riot as union activists in Wisconsin in 2011 and pro-abortion activists in Texas in 2013 stormed their state capitols and prevented the operation of their state legislatures. That was sour-grapes mob interference with the legitimate exercise of self-government by majority rule. America is a constitutional republic whose charter of government requires a republican form of government in each state – not arbitrary bullying by angry mobs that can't win a fair fight by majority rule in the legitimate lawmaking process.

That doesn't mean the majority is more virtuous than the minority. It could be the other way around. Or both sides might have good arguments. Eventually, though, a course of action must be taken. A policy must be adopted. The proposal that wins a majority prevails. It fits perfectly with our capitalist approach to economics. It's a free and competitive market. The ideas deemed the best by the most people win.

\* \* \*

I love the film *Mr. Smith Goes to Washington,* but I hate the filibuster. It's a procedural tactic in the Senate to block a bill and make exasperated supporters withdraw it so the rest of the legislative agenda can move forward. It takes a three-fifths majority (60 votes) to overcome a filibuster, rather than a simple majority (51). You used to have to "earn" it by talking continuously on the Senate floor. Now you simply announce that you are filibustering a bill.

Supporters call the filibuster "the soul of the Senate." In the famous film, heroic Mr. Smith used it to block corrupt legislation. The truth, though, is that the filibuster is a corruption of our system based on majority rule.

The term "filibuster" comes from 19th century Spanish and Portuguese "filibusteros" – pirates who captured ships and held them for ransom. How fitting. Neither individuals nor minority factions are supposed to be able to hold legislation hostage and thwart majority rule.

To support the filibuster, some cite the maxim attributed to George Washington that the Senate exists to cool what is produced by the hot-tempered House. The cooling effect is not from the filibuster, which did not exist in Washington's time. The cooling effect is from length of service and electoral distance from voters. Senators serve six-year terms. Before election of senators by the people began in 1914, senators were chosen by their state legislatures. Even with direct popular election, the six-year term (in theory) sobers the judgment of senators because they have more time between elections, and thus more electoral distance from voters' immediate passions, than do members of the House, who serve two-year terms.

The Constitution authorizes both houses of Congress to make procedural rules, but they can't make rules that violate the Constitution. Defenders of the filibuster say there is nothing in the Constitution that prohibits the Senate from applying a supermajority requirement to legislation as it sees fit. I disagree. The Constitution identifies special categories for supermajority votes, such as overriding a presidential veto or proposing a constitutional amendment. Otherwise the business of Congress is supposed to be done by simple majority rule. The Senate cannot in effect amend the Constitution by applying a supermajority requirement to legislative business outside the supermajority categories specified in the Constitution.

The pro-filibuster crowd ignores *The Federalist Papers*, a series of pro-Constitution newspaper columns written by founders James Madison, Alexander Hamilton, and John Jay. The filibuster is not in the Constitution because the founders created a system that maximizes freedom. Drafters of the Constitution considered a supermajority requirement for the legislative business of Congress. They rejected it as an assault on liberty.

Federalist Paper 58 said:

> **The fundamental principle of free government would be reversed. It would be no longer the majority that would rule. The power would be transformed to the minority.**

Federalist Paper 22 went into more detail:

> **To give a minority a negative upon the majority (which is always the case where more than a majority is requisite to a decision) is . . . to subject the sense of the greater number to that of the lesser . . . to destroy the energy of the government . . . . The public business must, in some way or other, go forward. If a pertinacious minority can control the opinion of a majority . . . the majority, in order that something may be done, must conform to the views of the minority . . . . [T]he measures of government must be injuriously suspended, or fatally defeated.**

The founders were right. A society based on liberty maximizes freedom by going the direction that most people want to go. Otherwise we're stuck with tyranny of the minority, as we've seen on Capitol Hill in recent years.

Why does the Constitution authorize the vice president, serving as president of the Senate, to break 50-50 ties? Because the business of the Senate is supposed to be done by simple majority rule, and the vice president provides that majority-making vote when it's needed to reach a decision. The vice president is in effect amended out of the picture if the number for making decisions is 60 votes or some other supermajority because there are no ties. There is no constitutional authorization for the vice president to provide the supermajority-making vote needed to end a filibuster.

Senator Ben Sasse said abolishing the filibuster would be a "suicide bombing blowing up the deliberative structure of the United States Senate," "turn[ing] the Senate into just another House of Representatives" operating by majority rule. U.S. Senator Mitch McConnell (R-KY), quoting U.S. Senator Chuck Schumer (D-NY), called the filibuster "the most important distinction" between the House and Senate.

They are wrong. The Senate is distinguished from the House by the six-year term, and by the powers assigned solely to the Senate by the Constitution.

As for the "deliberative structure" of the Senate, it already has been destroyed – by the filibuster. Sasse often complains about the dysfunctionality of the Senate, yet defends the most dysfunctional thing about the Senate, the filibuster. When a majority believes it's time to decide an issue and move on, that's what should happen.

According to the Brennan Center for Justice, in the late 1950s roughly 25% of bills introduced in the Senate became law. By 2010 that number had fallen to just under 3%. We on the right like to joke about government impotence being good for the nation – a government too weak to do anything can't do any mischief. But it's not healthy for our republic when it becomes nearly impossible for the legislative branch to enact anything but noncontroversial measures.

This enervation of the legislative branch has the added negative effect of driving more policy-making action to the executive and judicial branches, further undermining the principle of representative government by majority rule. As Congress recedes into policy-making paralysis, presidents are more assertive in issuing executive orders, and judges are emboldened to fill policy voids with court rulings.

It kills me to hear conservatives argue that some items are so important they should be subject to supermajority approval. That's what the left says when it can't win in majority-rule competition. Or some on the right say, "That filibuster sure comes in handy when we're in the minority and want to stop something." That's a loser mentality, and it's faithless to the Constitution. It's OK to ignore the Constitution and the fundamental principle of majority rule to stop an idea you don't like? When we deviate from the Constitution and operate outside of proper procedures, we move farther away from being a constitutional republic.

If Sasse and McConnell believe so fervently in the filibuster, then why have they collaborated in the suicide bombing of the deliberative structure of the Senate when it comes to approval of Supreme Court nominees? Surely that process should be subject to a filibuster and a supermajority vote if the filibuster is so vital to proper Senate decision-making. If the filibuster is so important, then you can't discard it when making the momentous decision of whether to put someone on the highest court in the land. Yet Republicans have used procedural maneuvers (previously used by Democrats) to neutralize the filibuster and get judicial nominees confirmed by simple majority vote.

Please understand: I'm glad Senate Republicans have done so. Majority rule is the way the Senate is supposed to operate. I want them to do it for everything not designated by the Constitution for supermajority approval.

If you want supermajority approval for more categories of legislative business in the Senate, or for all legislative business in the Senate, then amend the Constitution to make it so. Otherwise stop whining, follow the Constitution, win elections, and govern boldy by majority rule.

But isn't it good for our political system to require the broader consensus needed to reach 60 votes?

No. It's too hard to get anything done. That's why the founders rejected it (page 71).

If 60 is such a good idea, wouldn't 67 be better? A two-thirds supermajority used to be the requirement to end a filibuster. Wouldn't three-fourths (75) be even better? How about 100%? If we're serious about protecting minority rights, then allow a single senator to grind the Senate to a halt indefinitely until his sense of righteousness is satisfied.

A pro-filibuster voice might say: "C'mon, that would be extreme; we just want to strike a reasonable balance." That

74

sounds nice, a reasonable balance. What you really are saying is you want to abandon the Constitution and make it totally subjective based on what feels like the right balance to you or the current crop of senators.

The Constitution clearly provides a system in which the default setting for Senate business is simple majority rule, with the vice president breaking ties. Don't tell me you love the Constitution if you believe it's OK to ignore it to accommodate an arbitrary "reasonable" supermajority.

The filibuster became possible in 1806 when the Senate eliminated the motion to end debate by simple majority vote. The rule was considered unnecessary. Nobody would be so obnoxious as to ramble on endlessly to prevent the constitutional operation of majority rule, right? *Right?*

Wrong. The filibuster emerged in the mid-1800s when pro-slavery Democrats used it against proposals hostile to slavery. It resurfaced in the post-Civil War Reconstruction era when Democrats fought to preserve Jim Crow racial segregation, and in the 1950s and 1960s when pro-segregation Democrats unsuccessfully filibustered civil rights legislation. That's the glorious history of the filibuster.

A Senate rule put into law in 1974 says everything is subject to a filibuster except a narrowly defined category of budget items. Again, if the filibuster is crucial to Senate decision-making, then why exempt decisions on taxes and spending, some of the most important that senators make?

Both parties threaten to filibuster everything. Research by the Brookings Institution shows that annual filibusters grew from a half-dozen or so in the 1970s to more than 150 in recent years. It's making our nation ungovernable.

In 2016, conservative voters delivered the House, the Senate, and the presidency to the Republican Party, but some of the main reforms promised in that election were at the mercy of a handful of senators from the party that lost the national election in which those promises were made. That is disenfranchisement of the voter. An American's vote means nothing if a tiny faction can block what was approved by a majority of electors in the last election.

The filibuster helped defeat the effort to repeal and replace Obamacare. Conservatives complained that the solution proposed did not accomplish the goal. Republican leadership replied that anything stronger would trigger a filibuster in the Senate and doom the effort. (A more modest "skinny repeal" proposal failed in a simple majority vote 51-49 because several establishment Republican senators could not stomach even that weak sauce.)

The federal government was partially shut down in late 2018 and early 2019 because Democrats didn't want to fund a border wall. The House passed a budget bill including border wall funding. The president was ready to sign it, but the threat of a Senate filibuster produced a stalemate. Senate Republicans had 51 votes, but not the 60 needed to beat a filibuster. Injuriously suspended and fatally defeated.

The filibuster tips the scale too far in favor of the minority. It gives too much power to the losers in our electoral system. Nine people from the party that lost the most recent election should not control the Senate's agenda. This is the tyranny of the minority described on page 71.

Friendly voices have warned: criticizing the filibuster scares some on the right. Too bad. It's the truth. The filibuster is a procedural deviation disrupting the operation of majority rule established by the Constitution.

"Gridlock is good" Republicans are timid defeatists. Gridlock means we keep drifting leftward, racking up deficits and debt. It means we never restore, or even move in the direction of, limited government. I'm fired up about this because I see no chance of restoring limited government while the filibuster exists. Exercising majority rule is how we restore limited government and reclaim our political system from the elites who have hijacked it. However, it will be hard to build a *simple* majority for this project, never mind a *super*majority.

The filibuster is part of the effort to make public policy via the executive and judicial branches instead of by majority rule via the legislative branch. It was developed by those who could not win majority support for their flawed positions; they had to find ways around the constitutional procedure of majority rule in our democratic republic.

If we believe in the self-evident truth of conservative principles, then we should not fear majority rule. As the left becomes increasingly totalitarian woke, we on the right have in our political quiver the greatest arrows of all time: the Declaration of Independence, the Constitution, natural law, and 4,000 years of Judeo-Christian teaching. With that monumental advantage, if we fail to successfully educate the electorate and win elections and hold majorities, then we deserve to suffer under leftist misrule.

Restore the motion to end debate by simple majority vote. Govern by majority rule as the founders intended. Republicans, don't buckle when you are accused by

Democrats (and some Republicans) of using the "nuclear option" by eliminating the filibuster. It's not the nuclear option. It's the constitutional option.

Actually, Democrats changed their tune on the filibuster heading into 2021. They talked of abolishing the filibuster upon taking control of the Senate and the presidency. In a sad spectacle, Republicans now read old speeches of their Democratic colleagues defending the filibuster.

Senator McConnell threatened that if Democrats abolish the filibuster, someday a future Republican majority will respond with:

> **Nationwide right-to-work for working Americans. Defunding Planned Parenthood and sanctuary cities on day one. A whole new era of domestic energy production. Sweeping new protections for conscience and the right to life of the unborn. Concealed-carry reciprocity in all 50 states and the District of Columbia. Massive hardening of security on our southern border.**

Incredible! Does he understand how that enrages the conservative base that in the 2016 election empowered him to do exactly that? He presents that agenda as if it's an outlandish, beyond-the-pale, end-of-days, Armageddon scenario. It's basic conservative policy that McConnell and other Republicans promote in their campaign flyers and speeches. Why isn't it already done? It should have been done during the Trump presidency. Trump said let's get rid of the filibuster and, for a change, deliver to voters everything we promise in campaigns.

I don't want Democrats to expand the Supreme Court and pack it with leftists, add states to the Union to pack the

Senate with leftists, nationalize elections (though that likely would be overturned by the Supreme Court), and work other leftist mischief, but majority rule is the Constitution's default setting. Maybe restoration of majority rule in the Senate will motivate Republicans to crush voter fraud, and then win elections and maintain majorities by actually practicing the conservatism they preach.

* * *

Presidents Obama and Trump were accused of dictatorial behavior by their critics, and there is justifiable concern about presidents increasingly using executive orders for major public policies, not just for routine bureaucratic matters. Nonetheless, the greatest threat to American democracy has not come from the executive branch. It has come from the judicial branch as judges claim authority to decide which political ideas are best and make public policy from the bench. This violates the constitutional principles of separation of powers, checks and balances, and representative government.

The judicial branch is not where public policy is supposed to be made. There's a misconception that judges are supposed to be champions of minority rights even if it means defying the will of the majority by identifying and protecting new rights. That view is mistaken. Judges are like referees in a football game. They apply rules made elsewhere by a policy-making body. They are not supposed to pick sides. They are not supposed to favor an underdog. They are not supposed to be for the little guy, the big guy, or any other guy. They are not authorized to bend or change the rules because they feel that one side might have a competitive advantage. They are supposed to apply the rule of law to protect rights identified by legitimate policy makers. They exceed their authority when they identify and protect rights not specified by authorized policy-making bodies.

Judges are supposed to make sure statutes and ballot measures comply with state and federal constitutions. If constitutions are silent on an issue, a court has no business getting involved. The people and their elected lawmakers are free to make public policy in that area.

Much of the misunderstanding of judicial authority can be traced to the landmark 1803 *Marbury v. Madison* Supreme Court decision. *Marbury* established the principle of judicial review, the idea that the Supreme Court determines whether a law is constitutional.

Right before leaving office, President John Adams appointed William Marbury to be a federal justice of the peace. The commission of office had not yet been delivered when Thomas Jefferson succeeded Adams as president. Jefferson told his Secretary of State, James Madison, not to deliver the commission to Marbury. Marbury sued. The Supreme Court said Marbury is right, he is entitled to the position, but the Constitution does not give the Supreme Court authority over this type of case, so we can't issue the order Marbury seeks mandating that the executive branch deliver his commission. The court can do only what it is authorized to do by the Constitution. Congress passed a law that seems to authorize the court to issue the order, but issuing such an order is beyond the grant of authority given to the court by the Constitution, so we can't do it.

The Supreme Court did its job as defined in Federalist Paper 78. The court reviewed whether a law complied with the Constitution. It took the occasion to *limit* its authority to only what is allowed by the Constitution.

The problem is this sentence from the opinion:

**It is emphatically the province and duty of the Judicial Department to say what the law is.**

That is wrong. It is the province and duty of *Congress* to say what the law is. The court's job is to make sure the law defined by Congress does not violate the Constitution. That's it. The court is not authorized to "interpret" the law, examine the motivation or justification for the law, or read into the Constitution phantom provisions to justify a ruling.

That changed in the 20th century as the left used that sentence from *Marbury* to turn judicial *review* into judicial *supremacy*. The founders did not see this coming. Federalist 78 noted that the judicial branch does not control the money or the military, so it is (in theory) the weakest of the three federal branches and poses the least threat to the republic. The modern left has used that sentence from *Marbury* to claim authority broader than what is proposed in the Constitution. That sentence has been carved into the wall of the Supreme Court building and worshipped as a basis for courts to "say what the law is" and strike down validly enacted laws and constitutional provisions, or impose policy mandates on legislative and executive bodies.

This perversion of judicial authority has spread throughout federal and state courts.

In 1993, the Hawaii Supreme Court ruled that it was unconstitutional for Hawaii to deny marriage licenses for same-sex couples. The court said the state failed to show a "compelling interest" to justify the policy.

That's judicial activism – judges going off the rails of proper judicial authority and making public policy decisions based on political beliefs. The U.S. Supreme Court has used similar arguments to justify judicial meddling in similar cases. Courts conjure up requirements, standards, and tests not specified in the Constitution. It does not matter whether a judge thinks the reason for a law is compelling or wise or fair or moral. That's a political evaluation. Judges are not supposed to make political evaluations of laws. They are supposed to *apply* the law, not *make* it. Judges who want to make law and set public policy should turn in their robes and run for legislative offices.

In the two decades following that Hawaii court ruling, citizens in 41 states amended their constitutions to ban same-sex marriage. That should have been the end of it in those states. But starting in 2012, courts all over the country began striking down such amendments. This judicial attack on valid state constitutional amendments was promoted as evidence of society's embrace of same-sex marriage in the march toward "marriage equality." No, it's evidence of how a minority gets around the legitimate lawmaking process: get judges to act as arbitrary policy tyrants and wipe out laws produced by majority rule.

Nebraska was one of the states whose citizens by majority vote put in their state constitution a ban on same-sex marriage. A federal judge in Nebraska struck down that provision. He called it "repugnant" because he believed it was damaging to children raised by same-sex parents.

The word "repugnant" means offensive, disgusting, revolting, unacceptable. The Supreme Court said in *Marbury* that a law repugnant *to the Constitution* is void, but the Nebraska judge said the state constitutional provision was repugnant in a moral or political sense.

What's repugnant is a judge violating his constitutional duty by injecting his personal opinion into a court ruling. Every judicial bench in America should have ejector buttons to expel from the courtroom judges who defy the will of the people validly expressed by majority rule. A judge is free to harbor his personal opinion of a policy. In his ruling he can criticize the people for adopting the policy. He can resign from the court and try to change the policy by running for the state legislature or starting a petition drive to change the state constitution. He is *not* free to strike down a constitutional provision properly enacted by voters. The amendment to the Nebraska constitution defining marriage as a union of one man and one woman was not repugnant to the Constitution. It was irrelevant to the Constitution, which is silent on marriage.

The point is not whether one is for or against same-sex marriage. Swap in whatever subject matter you want. I am against the death penalty, but I do not want judges to strike down death-penalty laws that were validly enacted by the people or their elected lawmakers. The burden is on me and like-minded people to swing the majority to our position.

When Nebraska's ban on same-sex marriage was challenged in court, some conservative voices said, "Why fight something that's probably inevitable and isn't a big deal?"

You fight because once society breaks away from 4,000 years of Judeo-Christian teaching on human sexuality, it's open season, anything goes. Look how quickly we went from same-sex marriage to anybody can claim to be any of dozens of genders, with men ruining women's sports.

You also fight because there is more at stake than a position on one issue. Who calls the shots? Who makes public policy? It's supposed to be the majority, through ballot measures or elected lawmakers. If the minority can win by judicial tyranny and force society to go in directions most people don't want to go, then we are no longer a democratic constitutional republic that maximizes freedom. We are no longer a democratic constitutional republic if a judge can strike down a validly enacted law or constitutional provision because he happens to find it repugnant.

Advocates of same-sex marriage celebrated a Supreme Court ruling declaring same-sex marriage a constitutional right. I did not want the court to rule for or against same-sex marriage. I wanted the court to say it's not our call. The Constitution is silent on this. If citizens amend their state constitutions to legalize same-sex marriage, so be it. If Americans amend the federal Constitution to identify and protect a right to same-sex marriage, so be it. That settles it for the entire nation. But it's a public policy decision that must be made by majority rule.

Minority rights are protected to the extent approved by the majority. The Bill of Rights, properly cited as protection of minority rights from majority pressure, was a product of majority rule. Those beloved first 10 amendments became part of the Constitution because a majority of deciders in a three-fourths majority of states decided that certain rights deserved protection no matter what. We the people are free to add to or subtract from that list of absolute rights by amending the Constitution, but it must be done by majority vote in a supermajority of 38 states. No one, including a judge, is authorized to unilaterally define something as a right and declare it absolute.

Any uncertainty about the primacy of majority rule was settled by the Civil War. The Constitution prohibits states from entering into any treaty, alliance, or confederation with other nations. What if a state says it's not entering into anything, it just wants to unilaterally disengage from the USA? History's answer – provided by the result of the Civil War and an 1869 U.S. Supreme Court ruling – is that if you join the USA, that's a one-way journey unless the majority amends the Constitution to allow states to secede. The peace and stability of our democratic republic cannot be maintained if states can leave the Union because they don't want to abide by majority rule.

The founders knew the dangers of democracy and majority rule. They believed the republic was so large and diverse, with majority coalitions changing from issue to issue, that no person or faction could dominate.

A system based on majority rule can deteriorate. A self-governing democratic republic is free to ruin itself with bad decisions. The never-ending challenge is to elevate civic virtue to the level required to maintain good government:

> *I know no safe depository of the ultimate powers of the society, but the people themselves; and if we think them not enlightened enough to exercise their control with a wholesome discretion, the remedy is not to take it from them, but to inform their discretion by education.*
>
> *Thomas Jefferson, 1820*

We cannot continue to let judges, or presidents with a pen and a phone, usurp the policy-making authority of the people and their elected lawmakers. (In a tantrum over the failure of Congress to pass the type of legislation he wanted, President Obama said he would use his pen and phone to issue executive orders generating the policies he wanted.) Elites who influence or work the controls of big government and benefit from it will use the judicial and executive branches to block the effort to restore limited government via the legislative branch. Restoration of limited government will happen when a critical mass of citizens rediscovers majority rule and exercises it through the legislative branch or direct votes of the people. A good start would be electing senators committed to eliminating the filibuster.

\*   \*   \*

In America, policy-making power is supposed to flow from the bottom up by majority rule. The founders advocated "power to the people" nearly two centuries before it became a popular slogan of the left. It fits with capitalism. Democratize political and economic power. Leave political and economic decisions to the free flow of thought and speech and action. The most-compelling offerings flourish.

That has been the American formula for success, though it is under attack today. It generally has been rejected in Europe, except in Britain when the late Baroness Margaret Thatcher was prime minister from 1979-90. She extolled one of capitalism's greatest virtues: economic mobility.

Search YouTube for "Thatcher on socialism" to find a short and entertaining defense of capitalism by then-Prime Minister Thatcher. In a 1990 debate in Parliament, socialist

# Thatcher on Rich/Poor Gap

## Socialism          Capitalism

adversaries complained that the gap between rich and poor had widened under Thatcher's capitalist policies in the 1980s. Thatcher replied that the gap may have widened, but the entire spectrum had shifted upward. The bottom rung of the ladder was higher. The poor were better off than they had been under socialist policies and were free to go higher.

The same is true in America. The rich get richer but the rest also are better off. Middle-class families lost ground economically over the decade or so preceding the Trump administration, but numerous studies show how the typical standard of living for a family considered poor by today's standard compares favorably to the standard of living for a typical middle-class family in previous generations.

It was 1970 or '71 – I was 8 or 9 years old – when my parents called the neighbor's house where I was playing and said to send me home. I wondered who had died. My parents summoned me home in the middle of the afternoon to reveal a wondrous addition to our living room – a *color* TV. The sound and picture quality were primitive by today's standard, but 50 years ago it was a big deal for a basic American middle-class family.

Amassing wealth is not my main motivation in life, but I do not begrudge the wealthy their success. Prosperous people hire other people. They spend money, which fuels the economy. They pay taxes that fund government. They donate to the kind of do-gooder organizations for which I have worked.

It does not bother me that our capitalist system allows some people to make more in one year than I will make in my lifetime. The same system offers the best chance for me and others of any means, or no means, to make a good life for ourselves and our families. Your effort to raise your standard of living produces benefits not only for you, but for me and the rest of society. That's what Scottish philosopher Adam Smith wrote about in his famous book about capitalism, *An Inquiry into the Nature and Causes of the Wealth of Nations*. He said giving free rein to the "invisible hand" of mutually beneficial self-interest was the best way to raise everyone's standard of living.

There is a negative perception that capitalism is based on exploitation. It's true that capitalism can be twisted to serve exploitative agendas. Such cases usually involve fraud, intimidation, or some other ethical perversion that distorts the mutually beneficial nature of capitalism.

President Obama called conservative critics of his fiscal policy advocates of a "you're on your own" economy in which "everyone is left to fend for themselves and play by their own rules." He misrepresented free-market capitalism. It's not based on rogue actors destroying each other. It's based on mutually beneficial transactions. Properly functioning capitalism motivates all parties to accommodate each other. People succeed to the degree that they satisfy the needs of fellow citizens. Sellers produce what buyers want; buyers reward sellers who produce what buyers want at the best prices. This fosters cooperation and agreement on a common set of rules, not fending for yourself and playing by your own rules.

It is competitive in that those who provide the best goods and services at the best prices will enjoy the most success, but that's healthy competition that produces the best for the most, raising the communal standard of living.

Commentator Bill Bennett says one measure of a successful country is the "gates test." If you open the gates to your country, do people rush in or rush out? We know the answer for America. People try to rush in even if the gates are closed. They do so because America provides the best for the most, the best chance on the planet to make the most out of life for yourself and your family.

Is that changing? Do we now have people coming to the United States not for opportunity, but for social services?

Has Americans' perception of America changed? The revised American Dream seems to be: live on government welfare; if you have to work, get a government job with better pay, benefits, and retirement than private sector workers get; if you can't swing that, hang in there working in the private sector until 65; after that, the federal government will provide you a pension (Social Security) and subsidized health care (Medicare); if you finish life in a care facility and run out of money, the government will cover it with subsidized health care for the poor (Medicaid); if you're clever about it, you can hide your assets and have Medicaid cover your costs all along the way.

President Obama denounced as "social Darwinism" the

effort to scale back the federal welfare/entitlement system. It is becoming extremist hate speech to say that Americans ought to be responsible for themselves.

\* \* \*

Often in politics, people say incremental change is the smart play. Confronted with a federal government that has become the overreaching behemoth the founders feared, some preach gradualism. Take small bites. Slice off a few billion dollars from the federal budget here and there, and declare victory. Don't be a fool and go after the main items in the budget such as Social Security and Medicare.

Advocates of big government do not practiced gradualism. The liberal/progressive agenda that has dominated the last century began in the 1930s with the New Deal as the federal government burst out of the cage of limited government built for it by the founders. The Great Society welfare program of the 1960s was another dramatic expansion of the federal government. The Obama administration continued the movement toward a larger federal government by taking over an auto company, recasting the health care industry (Obamacare), and giving billions of dollars to political allies in the guise of "economic stimulus." Will the Biden administration resume that agenda and make America look more like socialist Europe? Some European nations are experiencing a tug-of-war between fiscal austerity and the fiscal abyss of the modern welfare/entitlement state. Will we switch places with some of them as we move left on the political spectrum while they move right?

We are abandoning our constitutional founding principles. That's the problem. We need to fix it now.

# Terms of the Debate

| Statist | Radical Socialist | | Liberal | Conservative | | Libertarian |
|---------|-------------------|--|---------|--------------|--|-------------|
| Fascist | | | | | | |
| Communist | | Progressive | Moderate | | Reactionary | Anarchist |

| Total Government | Natural Law/Rights | No Government |
|------------------|--------------------|--------------|

That's a political spectrum I developed for the civics course I mentioned. I revised models used by political scientist Leon Baradat. It's based on two questions:

1. **How much control should government have over society?**
2. **What degree of political change is acceptable?**

Above the horizontal line are points on the political spectrum. Below the line is a simpler summary of the spectrum. Those who favor individualism and want no government are on the right wing. Those who would sacrifice individualism for total control of society by government are on the left wing.

The founders believed the best combination of liberty and security was a point on the spectrum between the extremes, a balance based on natural law and natural rights. The individual surrenders some autonomy for the common good, but freedom remains the top priority.

The key to the founders' approach is the doctrine of natural law. Many great minds have explained it. My favorite explainer is C. S. Lewis, whose views are reflected here.

Natural law refers to rules governing human behavior that, if followed, maximize happiness and fulfillment. These rules are inherent in human nature and can be discovered by reason. They do not originate from religious or governmental bodies. They existed before, and transcend, human institutions. They are universal principles written in the minds and hearts of human beings that apply to all people and societies regardless of time or location.

Natural rights – such as life, liberty, and the pursuit of happiness – flow from natural law.

Natural law sometimes is misperceived as a nicer way of saying "survival of the fittest," with the additional misperception that the challenge of human society is to overcome natural law with civility. That's understandable, but mistaken. Nature can be brutal, with the strong preying on the vulnerable – among humans as well as animals. Natural inclinations in humans to act on urges toward sexuality, material gain, and other things can produce individual and societal damage. The philosophical doctrine of natural law does not deny that these appetites are part of human nature. Natural law says individuals and societies will do best if they follow certain principles and manage those appetites properly. Natural law is a formula for acting on those appetites in ways that benefit the individual and society.

The foundation of Western civilization is 4,000 years of Judeo-Christian teaching. It began with Abraham and the dawn of Judaism in 2000 BC, then continued with Jesus Christ to the present. It helped produce the greatest society in history – the United States of America.

Judeo-Christian teaching has stood the test of time because it is rooted in natural law.

I believe God is the author of natural law. Nonetheless, an atheist can believe in natural law. Even absent the Ten

Commandments, humans have an innate sense that it's wrong to lie, harm others without justification, steal others' possessions, or mess with others' spouses. That's natural law. The sense that adults ought to provide special care for children is another manifestation of natural law.

The younger you are, the more likely you are to bristle at the concept of natural law. Most young people like to think they can do whatever they want. For nearly half a century, our education system and popular culture have saturated people in relativism. Everything is relative to the individual's preference, meaning truth is *sub*jective rather than *ob*jective. There are no objective, absolute values. "Truth" depends on the individual's perspective. People are encouraged to be gods unto themselves. "Right" is whatever the individual believes it is. Don't dare question another's view of right and wrong.

It's a recipe for chaos. I heard a priest describe it well in a sermon. Imagine a football game in which one side declares that it only has to cross the 50-yardline for a touchdown instead of going all the way down the field. Then the other team declares it is not bound by the sidelines because it believes the field is too narrow. In sports and in all of life, we need rules and common reference points. Otherwise there is no order, no stability, no progress, no enjoyment of civil rights, no American Dream that rewards people who work hard and play by the rules.

There always has been a relativist camp in Western thought that says to hell with absolute values. Some high school and college students are delighted to learn that from Protagoras in ancient Greece (man is the measure of all

93

things) to Nietzsche in modern times (God is dead), famous people throughout history have validated the youthful rebellion against any kind of absolute code of values imposed by God or society.

Relativism helped launch judicial activism (pages 81-82). In the first three decades of the 20th century, progressive U.S. Supreme Court Justice Oliver Wendell Holmes Jr. greatly influenced American jurisprudence. His relativist judicial philosophy denied any "eternal order" and declared that the law is "what is understood to be convenient."

Because relativists reject natural law, they don't accept limitations on what government can do. They do not recognize a higher, objective standard that people and governments must obey. People and governments can do whatever they want. This is why the millennial I mentioned earlier (page 40) declared that we have "evolved beyond" the Constitution and the limits it places on government.

Those who accept natural law believe in objective, timeless truths to which people and governments must adhere if they want to prosper. We are not gods unto ourselves. For this reason, believers in natural law are more likely than relativists to accept limitations on government.

The importance the founders placed on property rights came from natural law. They drew heavily from 17th century English political philosopher John Locke, who said if you apply labor and resources to a parcel of land, then you have earned an ownership right in that land and in whatever it produces. The classic Locke formula identified property, along with life and liberty, as natural rights derived from natural law. The Declaration of Independence adopted the broader term "pursuit of happiness" instead of "property," but security of property rights was at the heart of the founders' idea of happiness. The Fourteenth Amendment says no one shall be "deprived of life, liberty, or *property* without due process of law."

Closely related was the idea that work is good. It might be hard today to understand how revolutionary that concept was. In 17th and 18th century Europe, work was considered dirty, embarrassing, a necessary evil to be avoided if possible. America flipped that view. Birth and family connections did not determine your destiny in America. You could rise to whatever level your work ethic took you, and there was nothing embarrassing about it. Success resulting from hard work was a badge of honor – even a sign of divine favor in some faith traditions.

The founders wanted the best for the most – well, the most among white male property owners, preferably Protestant. In drafting the Constitution, the founders did not go as far in guaranteeing "unalienable rights" for "all men" as the Declaration of Independence required, but they were on the right track, and farther down that track than any other society had gone. Their guiding principle was that a society would prosper to the degree that it aligned itself with fundamental values based on natural law and natural rights. They believed that the more rigorously a society incorporated natural law and natural rights into its system of government, the more successful it would be.

In our time, there's a misconception that advocates of limited government are simply engaging in blind reverence to the founders. Not so. Passion for limited government comes from the fact that it maximizes freedom while protecting the safety of citizens. It does so because it respects natural law and natural rights.

Part of the founders' genius was realizing that natural law is as binding in the political world as the law of gravity is in the physical world. The farther we stray from it, the more we invite disaster. You can jump off the roof of your house, flap your arms, and declare that you are flying, but your flight won't last long and probably won't end well.

The same is true with natural law. We can pretend that marriage, family, property rights, economic self-interest, personal responsibility, and other founding values rooted in natural law are not binding on human society. Eventually we will run our society into the ditch.

Natural law is the key to American exceptionalism. American exceptionalism is derided by the left as code for white supremacy, but it has nothing to do with race, ethnicity, or nationality. America is exceptional to the degree that it follows natural law, promotes natural rights, and protects those rights by the rule of law. It's that simple. Any nation can be "exceptional." America has produced more freedom and prosperity than other nations because it has been the most successful at following the formula for exceptionalism based on natural law, natural rights, and the rule of law. That's why people all over the world want to make a life in America. They want to live in a society where people who work hard and play by the rules are rewarded with prosperity and the freedom to enjoy their natural rights.

The communist Soviet Union rejected natural law, and the political and economic rights that flow from it. In the

Soviet system, government was the supreme, unquestioned authority imposing political and economic decisions from the top down. There was no say for regular folks. This defiance of natural law was as misguided and doomed as the "flight" of the fool jumping off the roof of his house. A "planned" economy is a stagnant economy. In the Soviet economy, the government controlled what sellers could sell and buyers could buy. Production was determined by government edict – not by an individual's desire to make more money by better serving a market. The Soviet Union eliminated the chance for personal gain, which also eliminated personal initiative and the incentive to produce. The result was a 70-year failure that finally collapsed when too many people decided they wanted more food, clothing, and other goods than the government-managed economy could deliver. Additional factors contributed to the fall of the Soviet Union, but its citizens' demand for economic improvement was a major one.

In the early 1620s, the Pilgrims of Plymouth Colony made a course correction that saved them from a similar fate. Their society was failing because of its collectivist economic system. All produce from colonists' labor was held in common. Productive people got tired of supporting slackers and thieves. Productivity declined. Colonists were dying. The colony seemed doomed.

A switch in 1623 to a more capitalist economy gave settlers private property and ownership of the produce of their labor. This generated prosperity for those who worked hard and played by the rules, and surplus to provide for the truly needy. It saved the colony and provided the model for producing the best for the most.

The left hates that story. Every Thanksgiving, the late conservative commentator Rush Limbaugh recounted the tale. Lefties accused him of lying about what happened or trying to retrofit something irrelevant from four centuries ago to serve today's conservative agenda.

The problem for the left is that the truth is right there in the journal of William Bradford, governor of Plymouth Colony. The Pilgrims were good Christians trying to look out for each other while providing a return for the project's investors back in England. They tried to live like the original Christians according to an ideology that two centuries later would be the basis of socialism and communism: from each according to his ability, to each according to his need. It sounds wonderful. But as Bradford noted in his journal, the Pilgrims discovered that even devout Christians will take something for nothing if they can.

Private property rights and reward for effort are bedrock principles of natural law that must be honored if you want to produce the best for the most. Not even Christians trying to do what they believe is God's will can ignore, veto, override, deny, or defy natural law.

Those misrepresenting history are leftists who refuse to acknowledge a direct connection between historical facts. There is the fact that Plymouth Colony saved itself by rejecting socialism and promoting capitalism. There is the fact that the modern left, through the federal welfare/entitlement system and Obamacare and other big-government programs, is trying to drag America back to the socialist ideology that Plymouth Colony rejected. It does not matter if the events are 400, 40, or 4,000 years apart. They are related because they involve timeless principles of natural law that apply to human society universally. When you deviate from such principles, you invite disaster.

A more recent example of what happens when you thumb your nose at natural law as it applies to economics is the home foreclosure crisis that rocked our national economy in 2008. What began in the 1970s as a well-meaning effort to combat racial discrimination in housing markets developed into a politically correct mandate that everyone be given a home loan, even people not in a financial position to handle it. Advocacy groups pressured lenders to cooperate. Lenders were threatened with negative business consequences if they denied high-risk loans. These ticking-time-bomb loans were repackaged and sold into the larger financial system, where they exploded and blew holes in the system when high-risk clients defaulted on their mortgages.

Before the explosions, when Republicans raised questions about the dangers of these high-risk mortgages, Democrats dismissed it. Former Clinton administration official and Obama campaign advisor Franklin Raines ran one of the government-sponsored home loan mortgage agencies at the heart of the mess. He told a congressional hearing that concerns were unfounded because the loans at issue were "riskless." The $52.6 million Raines received in bonuses was based on how many such loans were approved.

When disaster struck, the federal government rescued the financial institutions that caused it by bailing them out with hundreds of billions of dollars. Those dollars came from taxpayers, many of whose retirement funds were jeopardized or wiped out by the crisis. This brazen display of elite cronyism helped start the Tea Party movement. It took nearly a decade for our national economy to overcome the negative effect of this defiance of the laws of economics.

The ultimate American example of how disastrous it can be to deviate from natural law came right at the start. The founders built a national government based on natural law and the fundamental natural rights of humanity, but they also preserved slavery. That violation of natural law and natural rights created stresses that ultimately caused a national rupture called the Civil War.

The mistake of deviating from natural law was repeated with Jim Crow racial segregation. This nation based on the fundamental natural rights of humanity abolished slavery, but accommodated American-style apartheid. That mistake guaranteed major future social and political conflict. We're still dealing with the consequences. More on that to come.

*   *   *

Back to the spectrum:

| Statist | Radical | | Liberal | | Conservative | | Libertarian |
|---|---|---|---|---|---|---|---|
| Fascist Communist | Socialist | Progressive | | Moderate | | Reactionary | Anarchist |

Total Government       Natural Law/Rights       No Government

The anarchist wants no government at all. The sovereignty of the individual is supreme.

The libertarian is willing to allow a minimal degree of government, but only enough to keep basic social order.

The reactionary is more accepting of government, but still wants it limited and thinks change has gone too far, too fast. He wants to restore a previous standard under which government had less control over individuals and society.

The conservative shares the reactionary's concern about change and keeping government limited, but is not necessarily calling for a return to a previous standard. His goal is to establish a properly ordered status quo and conserve it.

The moderate is more willing to accept change, including growth in government.

The liberal wants significant change and wants to use expanded government to accomplish it.

The progressive wants significant change and believes government, led by an elite bureaucracy not subject to majority rule, is the main engine of progress for society.

Example: Obamacare has at its heart a bureaucratic panel with the power to ration health care by changing Medicare. Before Obamacare, federal law allowed bureaucrats to recommend changes in health care policy, but no changes could occur without an act of Congress. Obamacare allows bureaucrats to change Medicare and they can't be stopped unless Congress intervenes with a supermajority vote. It is tyranny achieved by the bureaucracy in steps that are small and hard to detect, but it's nonetheless menacing.

Sometimes Congress willingly surrenders its authority to the bureaucracy. When pressed for details on Obamacare, Democrat Nancy Pelosi, as Speaker of the House and congressional leader of the effort to pass the legislation, famously said, "We have to pass it to find out what's in it." Usually progressives are not so obvious and clumsy about transferring governing authority from elected lawmakers to unelected bureaucrats.

Here's another example of progressive bureaucratic overreach: Obamacare threw millions of people off health insurance plans that they liked and could afford and wanted to keep. When citizens complained about it, the federal government told them that their plans weren't good enough. Nanny government knew what was best for them.

"Radical" comes from the Latin word for "roots." The radical wants to rip out the existing order by the roots and completely remake society with government controlling the economy. An anarchist could be considered an advocate of radical change to society, but anarchists have high regard for individuals and their personal rights. As you move left on the spectrum, there is more willingness to override individual rights, especially property rights, to accomplish whatever government thinks is best for society. For a concrete example, take a spin through the Green New Deal, the left's current plan for reorganizing society.

The statist sees the state as all-powerful. The ultimate purpose of the national government is complete control of the people. This also is called totalitarianism, total control of individuals and society by government. The individual exists to serve the state – not himself, his family, or his God.

Communists say they envision a utopia in which, according to Karl Marx, the state "withers away" and individuals enjoy true freedom. But the historical record shows that inhabitants of communist states have been some of the most oppressed and terrorized people on the planet – with the oppression and terror coming from their own governments.

Fascism, authoritarianism, dictatorship, monarchy, and other forms of small-group or individual rule often are wrongly defined as right-wing. It comes from the French Revolution. Supporters of monarchy and the existing order sat on the right side of the legislative chamber, while revolutionaries sat on the left.

You may get pushback on this from people you consider very smart about politics, or from people who consider themselves very smart about politics. That's OK. Calmly explain that where French politicians happened to sit in the 1780s does not truly determine left and right in politics. What truly defines left and right is individual liberty versus control by a national or imperial government. Some monarchies have shared ruling power with other people and groups. However, monarchies and other systems that put all sovereignty into a single person or small group belong on the left wing because they eliminate individual rights and the democratic process, and demand obedience to the ruling person or group.

The left often calls conservatives and Republicans "right-wing Nazis." That's an oxymoron. The terms "right-wing" and "Nazi" are contradictory and mutually exclusive.

The truth is, the left can't handle the truth: the Nazis were fellow leftists. Like today's left, the Nazis wanted a big national government that dominated the life of the nation. The Nazis called themselves the *National Socialist* German Workers Party. The term "Nazi" came from the party name in German: **Na**tionalso**zi**alistische Deutsche Arbeiterpartei. The Nazis were proud leftist totalitarians.

"But we are nice," today's lefties whine, "not like those nasty Nazis." Tell that to people punched in the face and told they are going to hell by Democrats, liberals, progressives, socialists, and communists for wearing a Make America Great Again hat or displaying a Trump sign.

"But the Nazis fought communists in Germany and abroad," the left argues, "so they were right-wingers." No, Nazis and communists were rival leftists. There were rival factions even within Nazism. There were rival leftist factions fighting each other in revolutionary Russia. Leftists fight each other just as viciously as they fight the rest of the political spectrum.

The left also says the Nazis were right-wing because they allowed private businesses to operate. It is true that the Nazis deviated from socialism to some degree in managing the economy. They took a fascist (FASH-ist) approach. To build economic strength, big government *partnered* with big business rather than take it over, but it was a one-sided partnership. Businesses were allowed to prosper if they did what they were told and helped the Nazis build their war machine and totalitarian police state.

The term "fascism" was promoted by Italian dictator Benito Mussolini, an ally of Hitler. It comes from the Latin word for a bundle of wooden rods. A single rod can be broken easily, but many rods bundled tightly together are difficult to break. A bundle of rods, often with an axe head affixed to the top, was used in ancient Rome as a symbol of ruling authority. Mussolini tried to invoke that legacy by resurrecting that symbol and proudly calling his regime fascist. He would bundle individuals into one monolithic mass subservient to the national government. "All within the state, nothing outside the state, nothing against the state." That was the motto of *Il Duce* (ill DU-chay, the leader).

Didn't Mussolini want to go back to the "good old days" of Roman dictatorship as a modern Caesar? Isn't that a right-wing reactionary approach?

Not if it grabs all political power for the ruler and extinguishes the democratic rights of the people and their civic institutions, as the dictatorship of Julius Caesar did to the senate and people of Rome.

It's also not a right-wing operation if you club people over the head to make it happen. Mussolini was a typical left-wing totalitarian thug. Change, including going back to a previous standard, must be voluntary to be of the right. The right respects individual thought and freedom, and believes someone must be *persuaded* to make a change.

There are people or groups who consider themselves rightist, or are perceived by the world as rightist, that use violence. Occasionally a segregationist who wants to undo civil rights laws, a pro-lifer who wants to stop abortion, or a Trump supporter who wants to undo an election result, resorts to violence – and is roundly condemned *by the right*. Meanwhile in 2016 a torrent of leftist verbal and physical abuse was unleashed on all things Trump, Republican, and conservative, reaching a riotous crescendo in 2020 – with virtually no condemnation by the left. Voices on the left were more likely to downplay or even justify the violence.

That's because confrontation and violence are permitted and even expected in leftist politics. Why did businesses in Washington, D.C., close early and board up windows on the eve of the 2020 general election? Were they afraid of marauding Republicans, conservatives, Tea Partiers, Libertarians, Proud Boys, and others on the right? Of course not.

They were afraid of the left. They were afraid of the same people who ambushed U.S. Senator Rand Paul (R-KY) and other Republicans leaving the White House after the president's speech concluding the 2020 Republican National Convention; the same people smashing up and burning down cities across America; the same people overrunning parts of cities, declaring martial law, and hurting or killing people who challenge them. That's how the left operates.

Watch the Project Veritas undercover video of a Bernie Sanders supporter describing how, under a Sanders presidency, anybody who resisted "reeducation" and conversion to full-blown socialism would be imprisoned or executed. The Bernie Bro eagerly explained that they would use the playbook of their hero, Fidel Castro of communist Cuba.

A Sanders supporter opened fire with a rifle on Republican members of Congress at a baseball field while they practiced for a charity event in 2017. The shooter, who nearly killed U.S. Representative Steve Scalise (R-LA), had said on social media, "It's time to destroy Trump and company." That was after marinating in social media sites such as "Terminate the Republican Party" and "The Road to Hell Is Paved with Republicans." Maybe he was a fan of the comedian parading around with the fake severed Trump head.

The left cultivates lethal levels of hatred and violence. That is the unifying thread connecting leftists of yesteryear to the baseball practice shooter and rioters of today. If you don't see things my way, then you are so ignorant and mean-spirited that you deserve to be hated; it's good and necessary for me to hate you, attack you, and, if I deem it necessary, kill you – literally, or by shutting down your social media platform, putting you out of business, getting you fired from your job, or destroying your Trump sign.

If change is coerced, it is of the left – be it socialist, communist, Marxist, Stalinist, Maoist, fascist, autocratic, authoritarian, monarchical, or whatever name it is called. People who use brute force to bully others into submission are on the left side of the political spectrum.

Violent agitators in America today calling themselves "anti-fascists" are the very definition of fascism. They are just like Mussolini's Blackshirts and Hitler's Brownshirts, political street gangs that attacked opponents and terrorized the entire population.

Right there with them as leftist speech-crushers and thought-crushers are Big Tech elites trying to eliminate conservative speech in cyberspace.

The American work place increasingly is dominated by left-wing corporate totalitarian rainbow social justice jack-booted thuggery. Leftist culture commissars are on a mission to politically reprogram employees and eliminate conservative thought and speech in the work place. Does this sound like your human relations department or employee consciousness-raising program, or maybe your union? Beatings will continue until morale improves – meaning you conform to leftist doctrine.

Dictatorship is a left-wing thing. Sometimes the left-wing collective is personified in a supreme leader such as Mussolini in fascist Italy, Hitler in Nazi Germany, Joseph Stalin in the communist Soviet Union, or Mao Zedong in communist China, but the key point is that totalitarian systems negate individual liberty and the democratic process, and instead channel all power to a person or group over which the people have no control. Leaders and policies are dictated to the people.

Granting messianic status and unchallenged governing authority to one person or group, or assertion of such status, also is a left-wing thing. When the people exist to serve and worship Dear Leader, whether *führer* or king or president, you have arrived at the extreme left edge of the political spectrum. That's why some of us were troubled by videos of American school teachers training children to sing songs of worship to President Obama.

An observant reader might note that the names Reagan and Trump pop up a lot in this book. Isn't that the same kind of sycophantic worship of Dear Leader?

A true conservative is motivated by ideology, not by a person or personality. Some conservatives whine about when the next Reagan will come along. The ideology is there for all of us to pick up and carry forward. A conservative pledges allegiance to principles, not Dear Leader.

I took a chance on Trump in 2016 because he was the only hope for conservatism. I became a supporter because Trump did more for conservatism than any president in my lifetime, including Reagan.

I want ideology and rationality to drive politics, but emotion of course is a major force. Presidents Reagan and Obama were revered by their supporters.

A key difference between them, besides their general positions to the right (Reagan) and left (Obama), was that Reagan was defined by decades of clearly identified ideology. Like Obama, he had a winning way with people, but so do most politicians. The Reagan phenomenon was fueled by an ideology based on limited government and American exceptionalism. That ideology was repeatedly explained by Reagan over many years of conservative advocacy and service in public office. Critics teased Reagan about advocating the same positions in 1984 that he did in 1964. He would smile and thank them for noticing that core conservative principles based on natural law and 4,000 years of Judeo-Christian teaching are eternal. They don't change, and only a fool would deviate from them.

Obama was ideological, but he was more vague about it. All that most people knew in 2008 was that Obama was endorsed by Oprah Winfrey as The One offering hope and promising change, whatever that might mean. There certainly was change. As president, Obama defied the Constitution to expand the power of the federal government and take federal policy as far left as he could.

Another difference was that Reagan *gained* votes in winning re-election, while Obama *lost* votes. Obama got 3 million fewer votes in 2012 than he did in 2008, a 4% decrease from 69 million to 66 million. Reagan: 44 million in 1980, 54 million in 1984, a 23% increase. The more of Reagan voters experienced, the more popular he became. The opposite occurred with Obama. Perhaps some who voted for Obama in 2008 were surprised by his performance as president because his ardent left-wing ideology was concealed when he first ran for the office.

President Obama operated in the liberal-progressive-radical range, same as he did as a U.S. senator, and before that as a state legislator in Illinois. President George W. Bush operated in the conservative-moderate-liberal range, though he dabbled in progressivism with No Child Left Behind, the major federal intrusion into K-12 education.

These are generalities. Your position on the spectrum may change depending on the issue. Some people say they are fiscally conservative and socially liberal.

Circumstances can change and leave people in new places. Reagan began his political life as a Democrat. "I didn't leave the Democratic Party," Reagan was famous for saying, "the Democratic Party left me." My Irish Catholic Democrat father felt the same way, though he remained a Democrat because he grew up in an era when, as he put it, if you wanted to go to Heaven, you registered Democrat.

Even as a Republican, Reagan had to run against his own party as well as the Democratic Party. He won because his ideology matched that of most of the electorate, which was moderate-to-conservative. Candidates tend to run to where the media and party establishments are, which is left-of-center. That's not where the people were in the 1980s. At his 1984 political peak when he was re-elected president in a 49-state landslide, Reagan was supported by millions of Democrats and Independents who shared his ideology.

That word "ideology" bothers some people. I realize that conservative forebears such as Russell Kirk and William F. Buckley Jr. rejected the notion of conservatism as an ideology. They were right about many things, but on this point they were wrong. The word "ideology" comes from the Greek terms for "idea" and "word." An ideology is a coherent expression of ideas united by a guiding ethic. The guiding ethic of conservatism is natural law; from it springs a coherent array of ideas – among them the primacy of life, liberty, property rights, the American Dream, and other values discussed in this book.

America was born of ideology. The Declaration of Independence is an explanation of the ideological principles, and violations of them, that led to revolution.

Some voices on the right complain about people being too hung up on ideology, letting ideological convictions block the path to compromises and solutions. This disdain for ideology as unreasonable extremism is a sign of how politically wimpy we have become. We do not suffer from too much political ideology in America. We suffer from a lack of ideological nerve – on the right. The left is ferociously ideological, then cries "Extremism!" when a competing ideology pushes back. Too often, the right crumples and concedes.

The Tea Party is an ideological movement challenging the left-of-center ideology typical in local, state, and federal governments in America. Not surprisingly, people invested in the status quo call the Tea Party divisive and extremist. They call anything that challenges the status quo divisive and extremist. Yet the Tea Party message is unifying. It appeals to the Reagan majority – Democrats, Independents, Libertarians, and members of other parties, not just Republicans. The call to action is to pick up where Reagan left off and demand a return to limited government. The goal is to build a limited-government majority of voters throughout the nation that will elect crusaders for limited government to the presidency and congressional offices.

The American political market place has responded with candidates who challenge the left-of-center status quo in government at all levels. The chapter starting on page 5 called The Trump Phenomenon could have been called The Tea Party Phenomenon since it was Tea Party populist conservatism that fueled the Trump ascendency.

\* \* \*

Medicare is going broke. In 2011, then-Congressman Ryan from Wisconsin (not yet speaker of the House) proposed a modest reform of Medicare that would *not* apply to people 55-or-older. For that display of leadership, he was rewarded with an attack ad showing a Ryan look-alike dumping a senior citizen out of her wheelchair and over the edge of a cliff.

Former Speaker of the House Newt Gingrich tried to shove Ryan off the political cliff by slamming the proposal, but in that tussle it was Gingrich who went over the edge. Gingrich made a comeback as a 2012 presidential candidate by strongly advocating Reagan conservatism. I still see him as part of the Washington insider crowd. He deserves credit for being the main driver of the 1994 Contract with America, but the new Republican majority did not capitalize on the opportunity presented by that historic victory.

Speaking of the 1990s, Democrats love to cite President Bill Clinton as a champion of fiscal responsibility because annual budget surpluses materialized in the final three years of his presidency. It was not due to spending cuts. Spending went up 30% during Clinton's presidency. It was $1.38 trillion in 1992, the year before Clinton took office, and hit $1.79 trillion in 2000, Clinton's final year.

What surprised the left (and some on the right) was that annual revenue rose during that period from $1.09 trillion to $2.03 trillion, an 86% increase. The Reagan tax cuts of the 1980s laid the foundation for the longest sustained period of economic growth in American history. A 1990s technology boom was a factor, but Reagan's tax cuts generated robust prosperity and an unexpected flood of tax revenue during the Clinton administration.

The left says the massive Clinton tax hike of 1993 produced the budget surpluses of the late 1990s. I'm with those who say the economy grew like never before and produced budget-balancing revenue *despite* the growth-inhibiting effect of the Clinton tax hike. I credit Clinton for joining congressional Republicans to enact a 1997 tax cut that made a strong economy stronger, and thus boosted revenue. It was right after that tax cut that the annual federal budget finally broke through and finished in the black for a few years.

Left and right agree that the middle class did well in the 1990s. Figures from the Bureau of Labor Statistics, the Census Bureau, and the Department of Commerce show that during the Clinton administration, people in all economic categories benefitted from the 23 million new jobs created and the healthy 35% growth in GDP. Hourly wages went up 7%. Median household income went up 14%. The corresponding boost in income tax revenue put the annual federal budget into the black with a few years of surplus.

The left admits that in the 1990s our capitalist system increased wealth for regular folks because it happened on President Clinton's watch. Even if you credit Clinton's 1993 tax increase for balanced budgets from 1998 through

2001, remember that it was not accomplished by the fiscal discipline of spending cuts. Clinton's political mantra was a classic liberal/progressive promise that the Democratic Party would use the federal government to safeguard "Medicare, Medicaid, education, and the environment."

During his first term, the only support Clinton offered for a fiscally conservative measure was on welfare reform. Clinton twice had vetoed legislation to reform welfare. He signed it the third time it came to his desk because political consultant Dick Morris warned Clinton that he would not be re-elected in 1996 if he rejected it a third time.

Republicans in Congress at that time were no better. There was no genuine fiscal reform.

I've heard former Speaker Gingrich say the fiscal discipline of Congress produced the budget surpluses of the late 1990s, but Republicans did not significantly reduce federal spending. The Republican Party won majority control of both houses of Congress in 1994. Spending increased 23% over the next six years. That was basically the same average annual rate (nearly 4%) as the previous two years. It was the aforementioned unexpected flood of revenue that balanced the budget for a few years in the late 1990s.

I worked for then-U.S. Senator Chuck Hagel (R-NE) for a brief time spanning 1999 and 2000. He later would become known for aggravating fellow Republicans by criticizing the Iraq war and serving as Secretary of Defense in the Obama administration. In 1999, he was aggravating fellow Republicans by calling them out on budget proposals. What's the point of presenting ourselves as fiscal conservatives, Senator Hagel asked, if we spend more and grow government just like the left when we are in the majority?

Republican George W. Bush was president from 2001 through 2008. There was a Republican majority in the House from 2001 through 2006. There was a Republican majority in the Senate from 2003 through 2006. Despite that alignment of Republican power, there was no Republican-led fiscal discipline. Instead, there was dramatic *expansion* of the federal government such as No Child Left Behind in education (2001), a new federally subsidized prescription drug entitlement (2003), a "stimulus" package of cash handouts to the citizenry (winter 2008), and the Troubled Asset Relief Program bailing out mismanaged financial institutions (fall 2008). From 2001 through 2008, spending shot up *66%*, with annual spending reaching nearly $3 trillion in 2008.

I suppose President Clinton could be considered a fiscal conservative compared to Bush. Spending increased "only" 30% on Clinton's watch, less than half of the Bush increase percentage-wise. The average annual spending increase was 3.75% under Clinton. It was 8.25% under Bush.

Under Bush, the debt grew from $6 trillion to $10 trillion. Some of that debt growth was war-related, but even if 21st century military engagements in the Middle East had never happened, we still would have moved dramatically in the wrong direction fiscally. We are in a fiscal death spiral because we have embraced unlimited government.

For most of the last two decades, Mitch McConnell has been leader of the Senate Republicans, whether they have been in majority or minority status. He has been vocal in the media about how he wants the Tea Party to shut up and get out of the way so the grownups can govern. He says cynical Tea Party leaders profit from financial contributions as they exploit gullible grassroots people. According to McConnell, the Tea Party fires people up with a rousing song-and-dance about conservativism and limited government, but doesn't deliver anything meaningful.

That's what McConnell and establishment Republicans have been doing for decades.

What did Republicans do in the 1990s with their first combined House and Senate majorities in 40 years? They increased spending at basically the same rate established by the Clinton administration in its first two years.

What did they do when they had the House, the Senate, and the presidency in the early 2000s? They increased spending and grew government at *more than double* the rate they did in the 1990s!

What did establishment Republicans do when the Tea Party provided a Republican majority in the House in 2010? They complained about the Tea Party's fiscal conservatism and continued raising the debt ceiling.

Republicans rightly denounce Democrats for failing to produce realistic annual budgets, but Republicans also lack fiscal courage. They are scared to death to propose budgets with meaningful spending reductions.

President Trump dragged establishment Republicans in Congress in the direction of tax and regulatory reduction, but it was a struggle. And even no-more-business-as-usual Trump did not reduce spending and shrink government.

How did we arrive at this situation?

# Limited Government

The government we have had since 1789 was not universally embraced by Americans when it was created. Americans had recently liberated themselves from a dominating central government, but the new confederation of 13 states was more like an alliance of 13 small countries, and it was very shaky. Yet even those who supported a centralized national government were concerned about creating a monster that would grow beyond the control of the people and end up tyrannizing them.

The founders took what they thought were the best elements of governments down through the ages and put together a new model that would provide ordered liberty. They wanted it strong enough to be effective, but limited in its power. In the Constitution, the founders struck a balance between individual freedom and government control, and also between the sovereignty of the states and the authority of the new national government.

Amid spirited public debate, the Constitution was ratified by the states. It was approved because the powers of the proposed federal government were clearly enumerated (defined). The federal government could do only what it was authorized to do in writing by the Constitution.

That didn't prevent disagreement over what it really means to practice limited government.

In 1794, Congress appropriated $15,000 for French refugees who had fled the dangerous chaos of the French Revolution. The aid of France, especially its navy, had been crucial to America in the Revolutionary War.

Despite these factors, then-Congressman James Madison – "father" (main drafter) of the Constitution, co-author of *The Federalist Papers*, future president of the United States – disapproved of the appropriation in floor debate:

> **I cannot undertake to lay my finger on that article of the Constitution which granted a right to Congress of expending, on objects of benevolence, the money of their constituents.**

Here's how the Supreme Court addressed the issue in *Marbury v. Madison*:

> **The powers of the legislature are defined and limited; and that those limits may not be mistaken, or forgotten, the Constitution is written. To what purpose are powers limited, and to what purpose is that limitation committed to writing, if these limits may, at any time, be passed by those intended to be restrained? The distinction between a government with limited and unlimited powers is abolished if those limits do not confine the persons on whom they are imposed.**

The Court went into more detail in 1819 in *McCulloch v. Maryland*:

> **This government is acknowledged by all to be one of enumerated powers. The principle that it can exercise only the powers granted to it would seem too apparent to have required to be enforced by all those arguments [referring to The Federalist Papers], which its enlightened friends, while it was depending before the people, found it necessary to urge; that principle is now universally admitted.**

The founders created a limited government that can do

only what is allowed by the terms of the Constitution.

Nonetheless, advocates of expanded government cite this language from *McCulloch*:

> **We admit, as all must admit, that the powers of the Government are limited, and that its limits are not to be transcended. But we think the sound construction of the Constitution must allow to the national legislature that discretion with respect to the means by which the powers it confers are to be carried into execution, which will enable that body to perform the high duties assigned to it in the manner most beneficial to the people. Let the end be legitimate, let it be within the scope of the Constitution, and all means which are appropriate, which are plainly adapted to that end, which are not prohibited, but consistent with the letter and spirit of the Constitution, are constitutional.**

Expanders use "let the end be legitimate" and "all means which are appropriate" to justify open-ended federal power. They conveniently ignore the modifiers "let it be within the scope of the Constitution," "not prohibited," and "consistent with the letter and spirit of the Constitution."

The case arose because the State of Maryland tried to impede the operation within its borders of the Second Bank of the United States by applying a state tax to the national bank's facilities in Maryland. The Court ruled that states can't interfere with federal government actions that are authorized by the Constitution.

The Constitution does not say anything about the federal government setting up banks, but it does give the federal government power to tax, spend, borrow, and regulate commerce and currency. It is acceptable to recognize *implied* powers, the Court said, consistent with the grant of authority in the Constitution allowing Congress to "make all laws which shall be necessary and proper for carrying into execution the foregoing powers."

The principle of limited government remained unchanged. The point was that in those limited areas where the federal government is authorized to act, it is allowed to do what is "necessary and proper" to carry out its responsibilities.

In 1827, Congress debated a $10,000 appropriation to the widow of a naval officer. Congressman Davy Crockett of Tennessee – king of the wild frontier, future hero of the Alamo – stopped the bill with this argument:

> **We must not permit our respect for the dead or our sympathy for the living to lead us into an act of injustice to the balance of the living. I will not attempt to prove that Congress has no power to appropriate this money as an act of charity. Every member upon this floor knows it. We have the right as individuals to give away as much of our money as we please in charity; but as members of Congress we have no right to appropriate a dollar of the public money [for such a purpose].**

In 1887, President Grover Cleveland vetoed a drought-relief bill for Texas. In his veto statement, he acknowledged that "there seems to be no doubt that there has existed a condition calling for relief," but said he could "find no warrant for such an appropriation in the Constitution." Cleveland also said, "Though the people support the government, the government should not support the people." If he said the same thing today, it might send his fellow Democrats scurrying for safe spaces, or trigger riots.

Cleveland did not advocate leaving to their own devices Texans and other Americans in crisis: "The friendliness and charity of our countrymen can always be relied upon to relieve their fellow-citizens in misfortune."

It is the moral and civic duty of Americans to help fellow citizens in need, but not by having the federal government use federal funds for purposes not authorized by the Constitution.

Modern politicians say the heck with that. They love to give out federal money for disaster relief. It is one example of the devastating transformation from limited government to unlimited government.

# Unlimited Government

*There never was a democracy that did not commit suicide.*

**John Adams, 1814**

No outside force on this planet will take down America. If we fall, it will be because we rotted from within.

A risk of self-government is that voters will gravitate to candidates who promise the most benefits from the public treasury. It's a self-destructive way of providing the best for the most. It descends into political and economic cannibalism of the productive by the non-productive.

\*   \*   \*

The main action in our political system is supposed to occur at the state level. The states are supposed to be the main arena for public policy decisions. Your governor and your state legislators should be the most important politicians in your life, not your president and your federal legislators. The federal government is not supposed to be the driving force of the political life of the nation.

That changed in the 20th century. As champions of the emerging progressive movement, Presidents Theodore Roosevelt (Republican) and Woodrow Wilson (Democrat) brazenly expanded the power of the presidency and the federal government from 1901-20. Responding to the Great Depression in the 1930s, President Franklin D. Roosevelt ignited decades of Democratic Party dominance in national politics by launching the New Deal. It pushed the federal government headlong into territory forbidden by the Constitution. It was a triumph of the leftist belief that government should control the economy. One of the most hallowed legacies in American politics is that FDR's New Deal rescued America from the Great Depression. President Obama cited the New Deal as precedent for his agenda.

While successfully defending **British** troops tried for murder in the Boston Massacre, founder John Adams said, "Facts are stubborn things." Here are the facts: The national unemployment rate was nearly 25% (10% is crisis level) when FDR took office in 1933. Over the next seven years, annual federal spending more than doubled, from $4.5 billion to $9.5 billion. The unemployment rate initially dropped, then fluctuated between 15% and 20% until World War II created virtually full employment in the 1940s.

Stifling micromanagement of industries by new federal bureaucracies, inflation-generating policies, and massive tax increases hindered economic recovery and prolonged the crisis. Nonetheless, advocates of big government repeat the mantra that FDR's New Deal saved the country.

In modern terms, the New Deal was an economic stimulus package. Obama versions featured giveaways of tax dollars to special interest groups. The New Deal included actual job creation for the general public. I've heard people say of the New Deal, "I don't care about the politics or economic theory of it, my father (or grandfather) sure was glad to have a job." Some New Deal projects provided not only jobs for individuals, but also tangible benefits to society in the form of roads and bridges. Of course, those trying to run businesses in construction and other areas where the federal government muscled into the field were undermined or ruined by the unfair competition.

The problem for FDR was that the Supreme Court kept

swatting down New Deal initiatives as attempts to do things not authorized by the Constitution. The heart of the debate was (and still is) Article I, Section 8, which identifies the powers of Congress. That provision has 18 grants of authority such as maintaining military forces, setting up a court system, and, as already noted, exercising various financial responsibilities. It also includes the authorization to do what is "necessary and proper" to carry out those tasks.

The key provision is Article I, Section 8, Clause 1:

**The Congress shall have power to lay and collect taxes, duties, imposts and excises, to pay the debts and provide for the common defense and general welfare of the United States.**

Progressives cited the words "general welfare" to justify government action beyond what is allowed in the Constitution. The argument was that Congress can use its taxing authority to do anything it thinks will provide for the general welfare of the nation.

That's ridiculous. Why would people whose top priority was reining in the power of the federal government draft a provision giving the federal government unconditional and unlimited power? The drafters of that language meant that federal legislation could not benefit targeted individuals or groups – no special favors with the federal treasury. Any benefits produced by federal taxing and spending had to benefit the general public for purposes found in Article I, Section 8 or some other provision of the Constitution.

If the opening sentence of Article I, Section 8 is an unconditional grant of unlimited power, what is the purpose of the remaining 17 grants of power? Why bother? If you've already said Congress can do whatever it wants with its taxing and spending authority, there's nothing more to say.

Article I, Section 8 continues with specific grants of power because the purpose was to limit the federal government to those powers. Here's Madison on this point in a 1792 letter to Edmund Pendleton:

> *If Congress can do whatever in their discretion can be done by money, and will promote the general welfare, the government is no longer a limited one possessing enumerated powers, but an indefinite one subject to particular exceptions. It is to be remarked that the phrase out of which this doctrine is elaborated, is copied from the old Articles of Confederation, where it was always understood as nothing more than a general caption to the specified powers, and it is a fact that it was preferred in the new instrument for that very reason as less liable than any other to misconstruction.*

Here is Congressman Madison, also in 1792, in House floor debate:

> *If Congress can apply money indefinitely to the general welfare, and are the sole and supreme judges of the general welfare, they may take the care of religion into their own hands; they may establish teachers in every state, county, and parish, and pay them out of the public treasury; they may take into their own hands the education of children, establishing in like manner schools throughout the Union; they may undertake the regulation of all roads other than post roads. In short, every thing, from the highest object of state legislation down to the most minute object of police, would be thrown under*

*the power of Congress; for every object I have mentioned would admit the application of money, and might be called, if Congress pleased, provisions for the general welfare.*

Madison's crystal ball was accurate. Without realizing it and certainly without intending that it happen, he charted the course of 20th century liberal/progressive expansion of government at all levels.

Here's one more offering from Madison, in an 1831 letter to James Robertson:

*With respect to the words "general welfare," I have always regarded them as qualified by the detail of powers connected with them. To take them in a literal and unlimited sense would be a metamorphosis of the Constitution into a character which there is a host of proofs was not contemplated by its creators.*

But logic often does not prevail in politics. Besides, the purpose of the expanders is to override the Constitution, not comply with it. Progressives believe society should be planned and managed by those who know what is best for us. Limiting government's authority messes up the progressive plan.

Progressives were incensed that the 1930s Supreme Court was in effect saying of FDR's New Deal: sorry, but however well-conceived and well-intentioned these programs are, they are not allowed by the Constitution; the Constitution is the will of the people in print, and you are governed by it; until the people express a change of their will by changing the words in the Constitution, you can't do what you are trying to do.

FDR declared political war on the Supreme Court for blocking his agenda. He pushed a "court-packing" proposal to allow him to appoint more justices and create a majority favoring the New Deal. He lost the court-packing battle but won the war. His effort to pack the court failed, but the Supreme Court caved in under relentless political pressure and ruled that "general welfare" means Congress can do whatever it wants with its taxing authority. The genie of big government, with the power to make all kinds of wishes come true, was let out of the bottle.

Part of the cave-in was the Supreme Court giving Congress virtually unconditional authority under the Commerce Clause.

Article I, Section 8, Clause 3 of the Constitution gives Congress the power to regulate interstate commerce. The main reason for this provision was to preserve free-flowing economic activity throughout the nation.

As part of its collapse under New Deal progressive pressure, the Court abandoned precedent limiting congressional authority under the Commerce Clause. Instead, the Court said Congress was free to legislate on whatever it thought might affect interstate commerce. The field was open for creative definition and interpretation of activity related to interstate commerce. The federal government took full advantage of it, as an Ohio farmer would find out in a 1942 case of big government versus little citizen.

Roscoe Filburn raised chickens and grew wheat. The New Deal established limits for wheat production to boost the price of wheat. Filburn grew more than his government-approved allotment of wheat, but he did not sell the excess.

He fed it to his chickens. It never entered interstate commerce.

Didn't matter. The federal government sued Filburn for violating the federal wheat quota and won. The Supreme Court ruled that Filburn might have purchased wheat to feed his chickens had he not grown excess wheat, and such a course of action by him and other farmers could affect interstate commerce in the wheat market.

A similar argument surfaced in the debate over the mandate in Obamacare forcing individuals to buy health insurance. I realize that the official name of the law is the Patient Protection and Affordable Care Act. That's galling given the revelation that it will cost $1.76 trillion over 10 years instead of $940 billion, the figure given when the legislation was passed. It's outrageous to call it "affordable" given the budget-busting annual health insurance premiums tormenting middle-class families trapped in Obamacare.

A challenge to Obamacare was heard by the Supreme Court. The Obama administration made the Commerce Clause argument: the federal government can force a citizen to either buy health insurance or pay a fine because the decision by the citizen to not purchase health insurance affects commerce in the national health insurance industry.

The Court rejected that argument. However, Obamacare was found constitutional on the flawed basis that Article I, Section 8, Clause 1 is a grant of unlimited taxing authority. (See discussion on page 125.) The Court said the mandate to buy health insurance is constitutional under the taxing power of the federal government because the ultimatum to buy insurance or pay a fine is a form of taxation, and the federal government can use its taxing authority to do whatever it wants for the "general welfare."

Under current federal policy and Supreme Court jurisprudence, it's hard to imagine any activity or behavior, no matter how private, that could not be tied to either commerce or the taxing power and thus be deemed subject to congressional mandate. As Madison warned about such a broad interpretation of federal taxing power, "every thing would be thrown under the power of Congress."

\* \* \*

Before the rise of the cancel culture, Thomas Jefferson was hailed by Democrats as their party's founder. Yet in 1791, then-Secretary of State Jefferson issued this warning:

> *I consider the foundation of the Constitution as laid on this ground: That "all powers not delegated to the United States by the Constitution, nor prohibited by it to the States, are reserved to the States or to the people." [Tenth Amendment] To take a single step beyond the boundaries thus specifically drawn around the powers of Congress is to take possession of a boundless field of power, no longer susceptible of any definition.*

That's what happened in the New Deal. The Supreme Court said the federal government could go beyond the boundaries drawn in Article I, Section 8 eliminating limits on federal authority. The circle of limitation was broken wide open (page 63). Federal power became boundless and no longer susceptible of any definition.

The Supreme Court gave Congress the green light to let the genie of big government out of the bottle. Congress created dozens of bureaucratic agencies with the power to issue rules and regulations, and to exercise police and judicial powers. It was the progressive dream come true: management of the economy, and society in general, by unelected elitists not accountable to the people.

One of the charges against the king in the Declaration of Independence was: "He has erected a multitude of new offices, and sent hither swarms of officers to harass our people, and eat out their substance." New Deal administrators and bureaucratic "czars" of the Obama administration were the heirs of colonial bureaucratic bullies. Then came thousands of new Internal Revenue Service agents hired to enforce Obamacare under the leadership of Lois Lerner, the bureaucrat who engineered IRS persecution of conservative groups during the 2012 campaign. How appropriate.

The American people share the blame for the transition to unlimited government. Back when the New Deal was taking root, there were members of Congress who resisted the new role as dealers in the political narcotic of federal money and programs. But the holdout senators and representatives discovered what their colleagues were discovering: the people like this new drug, and they like sugar daddy legislators who can deliver the goods.

A $22 million pedestrian bridge spans the Missouri River between Omaha, Nebraska, and Council Bluffs, Iowa. It's named after Democrat Bob Kerrey, a former Nebraska governor and U.S. senator. It's beautiful. It's popular. It's a signature feature of my hometown (Omaha).

I have not set foot on that bridge. One of my goals in life is to never set foot on it. My hostility to the bridge is not a reflection on Senator Kerrey. He lost part of a leg serving our country in Vietnam as a Navy SEAL and was awarded the Congressional Medal of Honor.

I despise the bridge because it's an example of how advocates of big government get the rest of us addicted to it. About 90% of the cost of the bridge was funded by an earmark in federal spending legislation secured by Senator Kerrey. Classic congressional pork. What's $20 million among friends? A little something for you in your district or state, a little something for me in my district or state, and we prove how well we are serving our constituents by providing them with goodies from the pork barrel subsidized by the rest of the nation.

Anyone who complains about it is dismissed as stupid. Nebraskans are funding projects in other states. Get the rest of the nation to subsidize something for you. That's how the game is played.

The left used that argument to get Medicaid expansion passed by Nebraska voters on the 2018 state ballot. In round numbers, we send $500 million per year to other states to subsidize their expanded Medicaid programs; let's get $500 million per year back from the federal government to expand Medicaid here and at least break even on the deal.

There's an Internet rant about 535 people (representatives and senators in Congress) supposedly being out of touch and defying the will of the nation on fiscal policy. It's the one that asks: If both Democrats and Republicans are against deficits, then why do we have deficits?

We have deficits because of the way Americans vote. In our capitalist economic system, you get what you pay for. In our representative democracy, you get what you vote for.

Voters have signaled to politicians that they like the benefits produced by deficit spending to fund big government. We reward looters of the federal treasury by re-electing them. The message is: get us a piece of the action; we'll keep you in office and put your name on a building or a bridge if you can secure federal funding to pay for it.

In a Jan. 26, 2011, column entitled *Can Our Nation Be Saved?*, economist Walter E. Williams put it this way:

> **Everyone who receives government largesse and special favors deems his needs as vital, deserving, proper, and in the national interest. It is entirely unreasonable to expect a politician to honor and obey our Constitution and in the process commit political suicide. What's even worse for our nation is that voters ousting a politician who'd refuse to bring, say, aid to higher education back to his constituents is perfectly rational. If, for example, he's a Virginia politician and doesn't bring higher education grants back to his constituents, it doesn't mean Virginian taxpayers will pay a lower income tax. All that it means is that Marylanders will get the money instead. Once legalized theft begins, it pays for everyone to participate. Those who don't will be losers.**

My existence is Kerrey Bridge-free so far, but I am not free of involvement in federal government programs. For college and law school, I participated in a loan program sponsored by the federal government. I did not return to the federal treasury the "stimulus" check I received in 2008. I'm not claiming to be holier-than-thou on this issue. I'm saying we need to dismantle the federal feeding trough and break out of the get-my-piece-of-the-action frame of mind.

\* \* \*

The New Deal steamrolled over Jefferson, Madison, Crockett, and all the statesmen who warned against letting the federal government do things not authorized in Article I, Section 8 of the Constitution. The left prevailed. The American welfare/entitlement system was born.

The legal and philosophical violation of the Constitution was not the only damage done by the New Deal. It also had a lasting and profoundly negative effect on the American spirit because of the misguided notion that two important lessons were learned from the New Deal:

1. **Pressing the federal Expand Government button is the right solution to economic problems.**
2. **The president is the national savior and protector.**

The Great Depression happened in large part because the Federal Reserve choked. When citizens grew nervous about the stability of the financial system after the stock market crash of October 1929, they began to withdraw their money from banks. The Fed failed to provide the banking system with the extra cash reserves it was designed to provide in such circumstances. A "run" on banks became a nationwide stampede as an increasing number of panicked citizens withdrew money from banks.

The Fed intervened in some cases with infusions of cash for desperate banks, but not on the scale necessary to calm citizens and stop the cycle of doom. The purpose for which the Fed had been created arose, and the Fed blew it. In a few years' time, the national economy would lose a third of its capital, causing catastrophic reduction in the flow of money in the economy, destroying businesses and jobs. The crucial mistake we made was growing the federal government to address the crisis. When a lag in job-generating spending by the private sector left a void, New Deal progressives filled it with federal deficit spending to create jobs and prime the pump of national economic activity. Politicians loved it because it allowed them to "do something" and appear to be champions of the suffering masses. Again, the numbers show that the New Deal did not work, but that has not stopped politicians from tapping into the FDR legacy and pushing the Expand Government button in response to economic crises, even if it means deficit spending.

Which leads to the second point, that the job of the politician, especially the president, is to save and protect us. We've come to expect our presidents to behave as if they have extra-constitutional powers to address all needs of society. We demand that presidential candidates present plans to solve every problem.

While he still was competing for the 2012 Republican presidential nomination, former U.S. Senator Rick Santorum (R-PA) had an unfortunate exchange with a woman who said she needed $1 million per year to pay for her son's medication for schizophrenia. Santorum rightly said we have to allow the market to set prices for drugs so drug companies have incentive to spend the time, effort, and money needed to produce the drugs. He got off track, though, when he said some people spend $900 on an iPad. I'm not sure what the connection was supposed to be. Prioritizing expenses?

Comparing an iPad to medication for a child facing a

debilitating condition was a clunker. Internet comments were savage about the cruel and inhuman beast, Santorum.

Full disclosure: I voted for Santorum in the May 2012 Nebraska primary even though he had withdrawn from the campaign. I emceed a presidential campaign event for him in Iowa in 2015. He has a young daughter with a disability so severe most children who have it don't survive long, if they even survive to birth. He is aware of what parents face in raising children with rare and life-threatening challenges.

Meanwhile, I wonder whether the question about schizophrenia medicine was a set-up. I can find no basis for the $1 million annual cost for Abilify, the drug the questioner said her son needed. I raised the issue while hosting a local talk radio show. A social worker and someone on psychotropic medication were among callers who said the $1 million scenario sounded absurd because there are low-cost options through state and local government programs, and in private sector arrangements with doctors and pharmaceutical companies.

Aside from those concerns, notice that the mother viewed the president and the federal government as responsible for solving her problem. It was reminiscent of the woman at a public event in May 2011 asking President Obama for help in finding a place to live. This is a disturbing development. Imagine American citizens 200 years ago thinking it was appropriate to make their personal problems the public business of the nation and expect the president to solve them. The New Deal sowed the seeds of the modern expectation that the president and the federal government should fix everything.

*   *   *

**_Ask not what your country can do for you._**
**_Ask what you can do for your country._**
**_John F. Kennedy, 1961_**

That famous pronouncement by President John F. Kennedy in his inaugural address would be eclipsed just a few years later by a massive expansion of the federal welfare/entitlement system. In the 1960s, the left used the Great Society and liberation theology to put the growth of the liberal/progressive nanny state on political steroids.

The Great Society was what President Lyndon Johnson, Kennedy's successor, called his package of social programs that included Medicare (federally subsidized health care for the elderly), Medicaid (federally subsidized health care for the poor), and welfare payments to low-income families. The rallying cry was to win the "war on poverty."

The war on poverty is, at best, a stalemate. The number of food stamp recipients rose 50% during the Obama administration, from 32 million to 48 million. The Trump economy drove that number down, but according to the Census Bureau, the proportion of Americans living in poverty has been basically the same for five decades, fluctuating from 11% to 15%, despite federal spending of more than $20 trillion to eradicate poverty.

The Congressional Research Service says that from the American Revolution to the 21st century war on terror, adjusting for inflation, we have spent about $7 trillion on all our military wars **combined**. We have spent nearly **three times** as much on the war on poverty. Why are we not winning? Because we have strayed too far from the founding

137

values of self-reliance, personal responsibility, and reverence for the two-parent family.

The Great Society had at the heart of its anti-poverty plan a program that paid women for having children out of wedlock. The more children you had, the more money you got. But the only way mothers could collect the per-child subsidies was if there was no husband/father in the home. The federal government created a booming growth industry in out-of-wedlock birth and single-parent families.

The arrogance of liberal/progressive ideology was on full display. Builders of the Great Society were too smart and too sophisticated to respect natural law. These modern and enlightened social engineers used the power and tax dollars of the federal government to assault two founding values rooted in natural law – marriage and the two-parent family, institutions on which our society has been built. The liberal/progressive assertion that fathers in the home are not necessary for good family life has blasted the African-American community and is causing severe socio-economic damage across racial and ethnic lines.

In a 2012 study using data from federal government agencies, the Heritage Foundation noted that a child in a two-parent family is 82% less likely to be living in poverty than a child in a single-mother family. At the dawn of the Great Society in 1964, 6% of American children were born out of wedlock. Now it's 42%, including 73% for black children. Heritage produced additional findings cementing the inescapable conclusion that out-of-wedlock birth has become the main cause of poverty in America.

A component of the 1996 welfare reform law signed

grudgingly by President Clinton was a rule change allowing two-parent families to receive benefits. That does not appear to have stopped the momentum of out-of-wedlock birth, fueled by decades of cash incentives to have children as a single parent, and by the liberal/progressive push to deemphasize marriage and fatherhood.

Another provision of the 1996 welfare reform law was that after two years of receiving benefits, a recipient had to be working to continue receiving benefits. It was left to the states to define "working."

In 2005, the Government Accounting Office reported that among activities defined by some states as "work" were bed rest, personal care activities, massage (receiving, not giving), exercise, journaling, motivational reading (to get a job?!), smoking cessation, weight loss promotion, participating in parent-teacher meetings, and helping a friend or relative with household tasks and errands.

Apparently even those "requirements" were too demanding for President Obama. He announced that states could obtain waivers from the work requirement in federal welfare law.

\* \* \*

At the same time the Great Society was being launched, liberation theology, with its "preferential option for the poor," was emerging in Christianity. My layman's take on liberation theology is that society ought to take special care to look out for the underdog. That's exactly what a Christian church should teach. It goes all the way back to Jesus Himself: "Whatever you did for one of these least brothers of mine, you did for me." (Mt 25:40)

The mistake was letting the left work its way into the minds and hearts of Christian leaders and convince them that it is moral to use the coercive power of the federal government to reach into people's pockets for tax dollars to pay for social programs. Never mind that some taxpayers may consider programs ill-conceived or even immoral, such as subsidizing, and thus encouraging, out-of-wedlock birth.

The left succeeded in making support of big government the 11th Commandment. One of the most damaging things Christian churches did to the political conversation in America was add a religious burnish to the assertion that Democrats are more virtuous than Republicans because Democrats favor more government spending for the poor.

When I was a county commissioner, a long-time county worker referred to social services provided by the county as "the Lord's work." This person was sincere, but it also struck me as a way of shielding such programs from fiscal scrutiny – you can't touch them without getting on the fightin' side of the Lord.

The same argument often is used by defenders of the federal welfare/entitlement system: you are unchristian if you challenge it. Some leading Catholic voices have cited the social teaching of the Catholic Church to criticize Catholics such as former Congressman Ryan, his Catholic colleagues in Congress, and Catholic Republicans in general for trying to rein in the federal welfare/entitlement system. They equate spending tax dollars with practicing the faith.

It's a major factor in modern American politics. Catholics provide a significant bloc of support for the left. Some Catholics see a linkage between the social teaching of the

Catholic Church and the FDR/LBJ/Obama legacy that has produced the modern federal welfare/entitlement system. Some secularists have no use for religion, but cite Catholic social teaching to try to neutralize those of us who are Catholic, yet question our church's support for social services provided by big government.

It wasn't always this way. Saint Paul told fellow Christians: If you don't work, you don't eat. (2 Thes 3:10) The Christian position on charity has softened a bit since then, but there is healthy debate about what government's role should be in doing the Lord's work.

The modern social teaching of the Catholic Church began with the 1891 papal encyclical *Rerum Novarum* (*On New Things*) by Leo XIII. It established the principle that later would be identified as "subsidiarity." It means that decision-making, including functions of government, should happen at the local level as much as possible. The higher or central authority is subsidiary to the local – "sit behind" from the Latin *subsidium*. The higher authority is limited to providing supplemental help for the local authority.

Closely related is the doctrine of "distributism," which warns that stifling centralization of political and economic power, with domination of the many by the elite few, can happen under capitalism as well as communism.

Today in America that's called "crony capitalism." Big business and big government make wink-and-nod deals to benefit each other. Such collusion used to bother the left and the right. In the early 20th century, the progressive movement took aim at monopolies and other business practices it considered perversions of healthy capitalist competition. During their combined dozen years in office, Presidents Theodore Roosevelt and William Howard Taft, both Republicans, broke up more than 100 such corporate arrangements. Today, other than the Tea Party and the fleeting Occupy Wall Street circus, it's hard to find opposition to elite cronyism anywhere in the political arena.

I like the way the Catholic Church evaluates systems of government by how they treat the individual. That's the heart of subsidiarity. The church says individuals are likely to be treated best by systems that operate, and are held accountable, at the local level.

It's similar to the modern conservative principle of federalism – pushing power down to state and local levels. Federalism's ideological lineage goes all the way back to Jefferson. In the vocabulary and political context of his time, Jefferson was an anti-federalist, someone opposed to a strong federal or national government. Today he would be a federalist, someone who wants to see governing authority shift back to the states of our federal republic. Jefferson would be entitled to say, "I told you so." He would be appalled at the concentration of power at the national level, with the national government dominating American political life, and citizens increasingly treated as parts of a giant bureaucratic machine.

Section 16 of *Rerum Novarum* says:

> **It is clear that the main tenet of socialism, community of goods, must be utterly rejected, since it only injures those whom it would seem meant to benefit, is directly contrary to the natural rights of mankind, and would introduce confusion and disorder into the commonwealth. The first and**

**most fundamental principle, therefore, if one would undertake to alleviate the condition of the masses, must be the inviolability of private property.**

This was a reaction to socialism and communism gaining ground in Europe in the late-1800s. An absolute *laissez-faire* (leave-it-alone, hands-off) capitalism that ignored the struggling masses was not acceptable, but the church was nervous about a swing to the opposite extreme of dehumanizing control of society by a central government. Open a current edition of the Catholic Catechism to paragraph 1885 and you will see that "the principle of subsidiarity is opposed to all forms of collectivism" and "sets limits for state intervention." The goal is a balance that "aims at harmonizing the relationships between individuals and societies."

In 1931, 40 years after *Rerum Novarum*, leftist totalitarian forces were growing more powerful in Europe and Asia. Leftist pressure was building in the United States for a more assertive federal government. That was the context in which Pius XI affirmed the principle of subsidiarity in section 79 of papal encyclical *Quadragesimo Anno* (*In the 40th Year*):

**That most weighty principle, which cannot be set aside or changed, remains fixed and unshaken in social philosophy: Just as it is gravely wrong to take from individuals what they can accomplish by their own initiative and industry and give it to the community, so also it is an injustice and at the same time a grave evil and disturbance of right order to assign to a greater and higher association what lesser and subordinate organizations can do.**

Got it? It is an "injustice," a "grave evil," and a "disturbance of right order" to resort to big government when "lesser and subordinate organizations" can do the job.

When is national government involvement in economic and social matters justified? In *Rerum Novarum*, *Quadragesimo Anno*, and subsequent papal writings on this topic, there is healthy tension between letting capitalism operate and using government to make sure basic human rights are protected, including the right to earn a living in a fair economic system that respects human dignity. Popes generally have striven to chart a course that adheres to natural law and protects natural rights.

Our American version of capitalism is not a chew-'em-up-and-spit-'em-out system. Labor has rights. There are safeguards protecting consumers from fraud, physical danger, and unfair exploitation.

America's Catholic bishops, though, seem to have focused on language in papal encyclicals justifying government responses to socio-economic problems. They moved left on the political spectrum, endorsing the shred-the-Constitution unlimited power of the federal government characterized by the New Deal and the Great Society.

It happened in part because too many American Catholic leaders let Saul Alinsky set up shop within Catholic institutions in the middle of the 20th century. Alinsky wrote *Rules for Radicals*, the bible of left-wing community organizers. He dedicated the book to the entity he called the first rebel: Lucifer. Alinsky was channeling Satan from John Milton's *Paradise Lost*: "Better to reign in Hell than serve in Heaven." If there is an afterlife, Alinsky said, I want to go to Hell; those are my kind of people.

Why would Catholic clergy welcome this? Because the

Alinsky model is presented as a way to help the underdog get a fair shake in a society dominated by elites. That sounds great to people striving to do the Lord's work in the rough places of society. A similar "don't tread on me" populist spirit animates the Tea Party movement.

The problem is that Alinsky's doctrine is poison. It's all about acquisition of power. It's all about negative pressure generating fear, chaos, and collapse. It's all about class warfare in which Have-Nots vanquish Haves. It's all about using your adversary's goodness against him, making him adhere to his moral code, while you are as obnoxious and ruthless as you need to be. (See "selective" refereeing, page 17.)

I don't know if the left got it from Alinsky or Alinsky got it from the left, but a prime weapon of the Alinskyite left is: accuse your opponent of doing what you do to him.

The left could not compete with Rush Limbaugh, so it accused him of lying and spreading hatred and conspiracy theories to rile into a frenzy his base of dimwitted followers. That describes the playbook of the left, not Limbaugh. Limbaugh was like Trump in that a small percentage of what he said might have been out of line, but 90% was on target. And he magnified the potency of his points by delivering them hilariously. Alinsky's favorite rebel was the devil; what the devil hates most is to be mocked. Leftists go bonkers when the Limbaughs or Trumps of the right catch them lying and use humor to expose it. The left tries to dismiss it as false hate speech, but anyone willing to look at the facts can see where the truth lies.

Let's go back and look at what I'll call the "big three" leftist lies about Trump: Charlottesville, Russia collusion, and Ukraine shakedown (pages 9-12).

Joe Biden launched his presidential campaign with an add saying he was running because President Trump called white supremacists at Charlottesville "fine people." Complete lie. For a detailed breakdown, go to my April 30, 2019, podcast at anchor.fm/checkwithchip about Charlottesville. Yet the left to this day continues to cite Charlottesville as "proof" that Trump is a racist.

The other two cases are more on-point because of the brazen reversal of identity. Collusion with Russia to swing the 2016 election was attempted by Hillary Clinton, not Donald Trump. Shakedown of Ukraine for a personal political favor was attempted *and accomplished* by Vice President Biden, not President Trump.

The facts don't matter to the Alinskyite left. Just keep blasting forward with the false narrative as if it's true and never look back.

Limbaugh coined the term "drive-by media" to describe this practice. Like a gang rolling up on a location and opening fire in a drive-by shooting, the left rolls up on a target and unleashes a hail of false accusations, then drives on to the next target. Let others clean up the mess and sort out the truth, if they can; we did the damage we intended to do. In fact, let's keep moving and overwhelm the opposition with one drive-by after another so the truth detectors can't keep up with us. Plus we'll keep our leftist followers focused on the latest incident so their attention does not wander back to previous incidents where our lies have been discovered. And by flooding the zone with drive-by attacks, we delay such discoveries until it's too late to make a difference.

When Republican Mitt Romney ran for president in 2012, U.S. Senator Harry Reid (D-NV) said a source told him that millionaire Romney had not paid taxes for 10 years. The media ran with it. Romney denied it. He released recent tax returns showing millions paid in taxes. The media still hounded him over it. After Romney was defeated, the media pressured Reid to reveal his source. There was no source. Reid had lied. When pressed on it, Reid said: "They can call it whatever they want. Romney didn't win, did he?"

Somewhere the late Al Davis was smiling. He owned the Oakland Raiders of the National Football League. The Raiders were really good in the 1970s and 1980s, but had a reputation for dirty play. Davis relished the outlaw image. He said his motto was "just win, baby."

In a more recent example, the *Washington Post* ran a fake news story about President Trump allegedly pressuring a Georgia election official to find enough voter fraud in that state to flip it to Trump. This was after the presidential election and before the January 2021 election for the two U.S. Senate seats in Georgia. Trump campaigned for the two Republican Senate candidates, but the smear by the *Post* had people asking whether Trump was helping or hurting. The left was escalating the Georgia phone call into another basis for impeachment. It created a cloud of confusion and negativity on the Republican side. Republicans narrowly lost both seats, which cost them their majority in the Senate.

It was a leftist drive-by lie, but the lie was not discovered until two months after the January election. Schemers in Georgia had secretly recorded the conversation between Trump and the election official. Then they got rid of it – or so they thought. A search prompted by a public information request discovered the recording in a digital "trash" folder. It proved that Trump had said nothing wrong. He said he suspected "dishonesty" in Fulton County and would be grateful if the election official examined it.

It was a classic drive-by scenario: roll up on the target, riddle it with an irresponsible and unsubstantiated lie, and accomplish the damaging result intended.

Back to Alinsky. He did not consider himself a friend of big government, but his method has been adopted by leftist big-government activists. The way the left operates today makes sense if you read Alinsky's rules. Just win, baby.

Alinsky didn't care for liberals or progressives. He considered them members of impotent debating societies. He preferred socialists and communists, the hardcore leftists, because they were violent. They would break bones and shed blood, their own and other people's. They would attack the existing power structure head-on in the streets and refuse to moderate or compromise.

The Alinsky model thrives on dissent – until power is attained. Then dissent is crushed. A constant state of revolutionary hostility is maintained toward any threat to power.

It's the same with leftists everywhere. Six decades after seizing power in Cuba, communists still blame the U.S. and other bogeymen for Cuba's substandard living conditions and political repression. North Korea. Venezuela. The former Soviet Union. Leaders keep their people in a constant state of hysterical fear and hatred toward domestic and foreign "enemies" and "threats" to justify political repression and distract them from economic failure. China has fared better because it allows a modified form of capitalism in its economic system. Yet even China is finding it harder to stop its people from protesting against the repression of political rights by China's communist government.

The record of failure is similar in American cities and states controlled for decades by the Democratic Alinskyite left. People that community organizers were supposed to help are worse off. There is more poverty, desperation, and violence, not less. Chicago, Alinsky's base of operation, has become a killing field. People and businesses who can, flee.

Leftists are great at tearing down existing systems, but never succeed in building the new utopia.

Alinskyites make no apologies. It's not their fault. It's racism's fault. It's capitalism's fault. It's the system's fault – unless they control the system, in which case it's the fault of someone or something else.

They remain fierce and in your face, but they also know how to conduct stealth warfare. Their infiltration of Catholic institutions continues.

I see sports teams at Catholic colleges with the Black Lives Matter "BLM" logo added to their uniforms. BLM is a self-described Marxist organization. It stokes race hatred to tear down not only America as we know it and love it, but also 4,000 years of Judeo-Christian teaching as the basis of our society.

Whether it's Catholic leaders embracing the Alinsky model or Catholic sports teams promoting BLM, it's a form of institutional suicide. It's like a body welcoming the cancer that will overwhelm and destroy the host.

A prime target of the left is Christianity, especially the Catholic Church. Leftists want to rewrite or abolish history and define truth relative to whatever keeps the left in power. Leftists can't allow the existence of a voice that says: truth is absolute and eternal, not relative to your immediate agenda; long-term happiness requires love, forgiveness, and peace, not perpetual revolution; we respect government, but there is a higher loyalty to something above and beyond the state; your ideology is not God; God is God.

The left can't allow that kind of competition. That's why Catholic schools are infected with Alinskyites. The virus attacks from within. Some of the most virulent strains are in theology departments.

*   *   *

The U.S. Conference of Catholic Bishops' 1986 statement *Economic Justice for All* was cheered by the left as criticism of the Reagan administration's effort to reform the federal welfare/entitlement system. The bishops paid lip service to subsidiarity, but embraced the idea that the answer to socio-economic problems is to push the federal Expand Government button.

Subsidiarity did not disappear. The 1991 papal encyclical *Centesimus Annus* (*The 100th Year*) was written by Saint John Paul II to commemorate the centennial of *Rerum Novarum*. It said in section 11:

> **If Pope Leo XIII [in Rerum Novarum] calls upon the State to remedy the condition of the poor in accordance with justice, he does so because of his timely awareness that the State has the duty of watching over the common good and of ensuring that every sector of social life,**

*not excluding the economic one, contributes to achieving that good, while respecting the rightful autonomy of each sector. This should not, however, lead us to think that Pope Leo expected the State to solve every social problem. On the contrary, he frequently insists on necessary limits to the State's intervention and on its instrumental character, inasmuch as the individual, the family and society are prior to the State, and inasmuch as the State exists in order to protect their rights and not stifle them.*

It was more blunt in section 48:

*By intervening directly and depriving society of its responsibility, the Social Assistance State leads to a loss of human energies and an inordinate increase of public agencies, which are dominated more by bureaucratic ways of thinking than by concern for serving their clients, and which are accompanied by an enormous increase in spending.*

That's a future saint calling out big government for draining the lifeblood of a nation with "enormous" spending on a soulless bureaucratic system.

In Section 28 of *Deus Caritas Est* (*God Is Love*) in 2005, Benedict XVI reaffirmed subsidiarity:

*The State which would provide everything, absorbing everything into itself, would ultimately become a mere bureaucracy incapable of guaranteeing the very thing which the suffering person – every person – needs: namely, loving personal concern. We do not need a State which regulates and controls everything, but a State which, in accordance with the principle of subsidiarity, generously acknowledges and*

*supports initiatives arising from the differ-
ent social forces and combines spontaneity
with closeness to those in need. . . . In the
end, the claim that just social structures
would make works of charity superfluous
masks a materialist conception of man: the
mistaken notion that man can live "by
bread alone" – a conviction that demeans
man and ultimately disregards all that is
specifically human.*

There is debate about whether American Catholic clergy endorsed Obamacare. From my layman's perspective, my church seemed to be for it. Then came revelations of bureaucratic panels to manage Medicare (critics call them death panels), indirect subsidizing of abortion, and a mandate forcing religious employers to help provide birth control for employees. By the time the Catholic Church voiced meaningful opposition, the Obamacare juggernaut was rolling and could not be stopped.

I want the American Catholic Church to acknowledge the barrage of evidence from the last 80 years showing that more federal government involvement in social services increases poverty and misery, as evidenced by the record number of people on food stamps during the Obama administration. Big government produces more people in need of help to obtain food, health care, and other necessities. Yet some in Catholic circles still argue for bigger government.

It brings us back to my fundamental question: What produces the best for the most? For more than a century, popes (including some with direct experience of socialism and communism) have warned of the spiritual, psychological, and fiscal dangers of big government. I pray that Catholic leaders heed papal teachings and rediscover the principle of subsidiarity. May they stop hammering politicians who want to restore a health care system, and overall system of government, that produces the best *for the most*, a system that reduces the number of people in need and maximizes the number doing well enough to help the Catholic Church care for those not doing well.

The Catholic Church is not shy about tapping wealth produced by capitalism to fund its many worthy missions. Lots of educators in Catholic high schools and colleges enjoy a good standard of living because of capitalism, which makes it possible for their students' families to pay tuition, and for wealthy donors to subsidize Catholic schools. All the institutions and good works of the church depend on capitalist wealth. That wealth will dry up if national fiscal policy keeps sliding to the left. I look forward to the American Catholic Church speaking up to help stop that from happening.

Please understand that I love my church. A Protestant friend once said, "I've never met people more critical of their church than Catholics, but I've also never met people more loyal to their church." As comedian Norm Crosby would say, "I resemble that remark." People are critical of things they care about because they want the people and institutions they love to be their best. Sports fans know what I'm talking about. So do parents.

*Evangelii Gaudium* (*The Joy of the Gospel*), released by Pope Francis in November 2013, drew attention for its rough treatment of capitalism. I share the pope's hostility to unbridled materialism, and to perversions and distortions of capitalism that result in one-sided exploitation of human beings. However, I'm glad *Evangelii Gaudium* was an "apostolic exhortation," a statement that does not rise to the level of a papal encyclical.

Bishop James Conley of Lincoln, Nebraska, complained in a Dec. 2, 2013, column in *National Review* that Rush Limbaugh tried to turn Francis into "a cartoonish socialist to quiet consciences rankled" by a challenging moral message. I liked Bishop Conley's balanced discussion of how capitalism must operate within moral guidelines.

*Evangelii Gaudium* lacked that balance. Its discussion of capitalism was a litany of feverish assertions about man's inhumanity to man and idolatrous worship of the "golden calf" of profit. There was no acknowledgment of the regulated capitalism practiced in typical capitalist economies. There was no acknowledgement of how **good** capitalism has been for the common man and for the Catholic Church, especially in America.

Here's an excerpt from paragraph 54:

> **[S]ome people continue to defend trickle-down theories which assume that economic growth, encouraged by a free market, will inevitably succeed in bringing about greater justice and inclusiveness in the world. This opinion, which has never been confirmed by the facts, expresses a crude and naïve trust in the goodness of those wielding economic power and in the sacralized workings of the prevailing economic system.**

Never confirmed by the facts? People all over the planet try to get to America because its economic system based on free-market capitalism produces the best for the most. Catholics in America have gone from struggling underdog to leadership because they have used hard work and passion for education to succeed in an economic system that produces more prosperity for more people than any other, certainly more than systems hostile to capitalism.

"Trickle down" is a cynical left-wing description of capitalism in general, and tax breaks in particular. The left denounces as nonsense the idea that wealth retained in the form of tax breaks for successful capitalists will "trickle down" to the masses.

The left does not understand how capitalism works. There's nothing "trickle down" about reducing tax burdens and leaving more money in the economy. It creates a robust flow of capital investment at the grassroots level where most Americans live and work. Investors able to retain more of their wealth have more capital to fund middle-class small business dreams. When more money is left in the private sector, new and established businesses hire people and expand, which generates jobs and economic growth. This produces tax revenue for government plus more people prosperous enough to make donations that fuel the many missions of the Catholic Church, which benefits everyone.

The tax cut promoted by 2016 presidential candidate Trump and enacted by congressional Republicans in December 2017 prompted beneficiaries to give more than a million Christmas bonuses, raise pay, improve benefits, hire more people, and bring billions in investment capital back into the United States. Then-Speaker Ryan said that after the plan became law, a United Auto Workers union member teased him: "I thought your tax cut was for the rich. I'll be $4,000 better off next year because of it. I guess I'm the rich!" The Republican tax cut benefited the wealthy, but it also benefited millions of working- and middle-class folks.

The left is triggered by such capitalist good news. My boss – David Brooks, founder and president of independent financial planning firm Retire SMART – posted on social media that the Trump tax cut allowed him to expand his business and hire more people. A professor at the University of Nebraska-Lincoln attacked the post as false right-wing propaganda. Brooks refuted that claim with more information. The professor said they probably were miserable minimum-wage jobs. Brooks also nuked that assertion. I figured the professor was from the UNL English department, notorious for extreme left-wing polemics and activism. I was wrong. It was someone from the chemistry department. How disappointing. I expect more rationality and less knee-jerk pettiness from someone in the hard sciences.

Back to the pope. *Evangelii Gaudium* implied that a homeless person dying of exposure is considered an acceptable loss by capitalism and its defenders because the demise of the homeless person doesn't make the evening news, while fluctuation of the stock market does. I took that to mean that capitalism's defenders do not care that some people struggle and suffer in a capitalist system.

The dignity-robbing death of a homeless person is a tragedy, but it's not capitalism's fault. I worked in a homeless shelter and developed friendships with some of the guests. That fact remains that most of the guests were substance abusers, ex-convicts having trouble reintegrating into society, or people with mental problems or other anti-social behaviors.

The point is not to be mean. The point is that most of them had made decisions and taken actions that had messed up their lives. They were not victims of "the system." No system can save people from the consequences of crawling into a bottle, breaking the law, behaving in ways that alienate people, or deciding to quit taking prescribed medications because they are feeling better and don't think they need the meds anymore.

A homeless person's death may not make the news, but the mission of homeless shelters is in the news and plastered on billboards all the time. Our American capitalist culture does not ignore the plight of the poor. What a blessing it is that our capitalist system produces enough tax revenue and private philanthropy to fund the efforts of homeless shelters and other public and private programs that help people struggling to survive.

I worry that *Evangelii Gaudium*, coming from such a respected and admired source, will be used by the left to promote the New Deal/Great Society/Obamacare dogma that it's OK, perhaps necessary, for the federal government to grow bigger and more belligerent toward capitalism to save the people. That seems to be the unspoken solution demanded by the statement's attack on capitalism.

There is video of one of my sons at the rope line in St. Peter's Square, waving an American flag and cheering, when the white smoke signaled that Cardinal Bergoglio had become Pope Francis. I still get goose bumps watching that fusion of faith, family, and country all in one overwhelming burst of joy.

How can I not root for the first pope named Francis?

The middle name of my son who was at St. Peter's Square is Francisco, in honor of Francis of Assisi, the saint the new pope invoked as inspiration for his papacy. My middle name is Francis, for Francis Xavier, one of the founders of the Jesuits, the religious order to which the pope belongs.

It is vital for a pope to participate in the conversation happening in the public arena. Yet words must be chosen carefully. Follow-up spin by others saying "this is what he really meant" is ineffective and undermines the Holy Father's credibility.

Some commentators claim that the English translation of *Evangelii Gaudium* is flawed and makes the statement seem more anti-capitalist than it is. But then Francis made waves in May 2014 by saying economic equality includes "the legitimate redistribution of economic benefits by the State." He did not define "legitimate" or "economic benefits." He also emphasized voluntary charity.

I try to see the glass half-full. Francis is not a Marxist; he just sounds like one when he tries to synthesize left and right economically. Let's give this pope a pass on these statements and stick with more than a century of papal encyclicals warning that big government is not the answer to social and economic problems.

\* \* \*

A Catholic priest with a heart of gold, a dear friend of our family who spent much of his life working to improve education for inner-city youth, sent me a commentary – *From the Mouths of Babes*, May 30, 2013 – by *New York Times* columnist Paul Krugman. Krugman, a Pulitzer Prize winner and favorite of the left, extolled what he considers the virtues of the federal food stamp program and ripped into Republicans for wanting to reduce or eliminate it. The priest wanted to know where I disagreed with Krugman.

Krugman said an "overwhelming majority of food stamp recipients really need the help." What does that mean? 85%? Then 15%, 7 million people, are cheating the system for roughly $11 billion per year. That alone is cause to shut down the program.

Krugman said the program must be expanded because in recent years "millions of workers lost their jobs through no fault of their own." That's true, Mr. Krugman; it was *your* fault, not theirs. Policies *advocated by Krugman* such as Obamacare and other government interventions in the market place cost people their jobs, yet he had the nerve to cite lost jobs as support for his argument.

The Obama administration granted exemptions from Obamacare to unions and other favored supporters. Then it had to close down that option because of the stampede of applications for exemptions. Employers who missed the chance for exemption fired people or reduced them to part-time status to avoid the cost of having to provide Obamacare, or pay fines for not doing so. Even absent that phenomenon, employers laid people off, or did not hire new workers and expand their businesses, because they saw the out-of-control spending and borrowing, and worried that the government would raise taxes to pay for it.

Krugman basically admitted it in the column:

> *Why is our economy depressed? Because many players in the economy slashed spending at the same time, while relatively few players were willing to spend*

*more. And because the economy is not like an individual household — your spending is my income, my spending is your income — the result was a general fall in incomes and plunge in employment.*

What he did not admit is that policies he advocates cause such economic stagnation.

Krugman suggested that expanding the food stamp program would increase GDP. Well, then, let's put everyone on food stamps and really grow the economy. Then we all can enjoy the success of Detroit and other places that practice Krugman's brand of liberal/progressive economic policy. I wish Krugman and other lefties could be forced out of their elite cocoons to live in the kind of environment produced by their ideology. That may happen if the left succeeds in turning the whole country into Detroit.

Krugman said food stamps ultimately reduce the deficit because they help children perform better in school, which helps them become productive citizens.

Reality check: The food stamp community (which includes all races and ethnicities) has been in educational, economic, and social free fall for decades – failing in school or dropping out, unable or unwilling to engage in the legitimate work force, producing children out of wedlock with the resulting social chaos.

Krugman referred to children several times. Look again at the headline of the column: *From the Mouths of Babes.* The implication is that the only way for vulnerable children to eat is if federal nanny government feeds them. Anyone who disagrees wants to take food from the mouths of hungry children and let them starve. It hearkens back to the

1995 attack on Republicans over federal funding of school lunches (page 59).

If I seem a little feisty, it's because I resent self-righteous elitists such as Krugman denouncing grassroots people such as me for allegedly starving children to keep a few more dollars in our pockets. We have seen what Krugman's policies do to people and communities – angry single parents trapped in dependency and demanding more accommodations from society; angry children trapped in dysfunctional chaos and grinding poverty, lashing out at each other and the world. I want to help struggling parents and feed hungry children, but not by ruining people as citizens, culturally demolishing entire communities, and bankrupting the country. The Krugman liberal/progressive legacy to America's children would be a suffocating debt burden and no escape because they would be living in a bankrupt nation with a wrecked economy.

Help the underdog the way popes have advocated since *Rerum Novarum* – locally, or as close to the grassroots level as possible.

Krugman might say only the federal government can do the job. Baloney. If you show people a targeted, trustworthy, effective, and locally run food stamp program, they will support it the same way they do other worthy causes. Deliver the help through private citizens or through Catholic Charities, Jewish Family Service, Lutheran Family Services, secular nongovernment social service providers such as Heartland Family Services or the Child Saving Institute, city/county/state agencies, or other entities that are not the federal government.

Within days of the Krugman column, there was in my local newspaper a column by Nebraska religious leaders echoing Krugman's argument: there are more hungry children than ever; private resources can't meet the need; we must increase federal spending on food stamps or desperate children and families will suffer. In calling for expansion of a program that has intensified the crisis at issue, the column cited the same verse from the Gospel of Matthew about helping the needy among us that I cited (page 139).

Given the fact that America's underclass *grows* as we throw more federal government money and programs at it, why are some voices still clamoring for more of the same? In the case of religious leaders, I'm willing to believe they are not experts in politics and are getting bad advice. In the case of politicians, they advocate failed policies because it's safe. Who cares if it works? Who cares if it violates the Constitution, *worsens* the problem, and bankrupts the nation? I can say I did whatever I could to help the struggling. I'm covered, politically and morally.

Some defenders of Obamacare call it Obama Cares. For some politicians, that's all that matters – the perception that you care. It's cowardly, not courageous or noble.

\* \* \*

In a similar vein, politicians calling for a higher minimum wage is one of the most cynical things in politics. Instead of appealing to American exceptionalism, it recycles the socialist class-warfare whining that has ruined Europe and is eroding the American spirit. As with calling for more spending on expanded federal social programs, politicians know that a higher minimum wage won't solve people's economic problems. It's likely to hurt those it's supposed to help. Then why do politicians endorse it? Because they believe they are covered politically and morally if they support increasing the minimum wage.

It's also a way to raise tax revenue. All taxpayers pay the payroll tax for Social Security and Medicare regardless of how rich or poor they are. When the government mandates an increase in wages, a slice of that increase goes to the government via the payroll tax. The purpose is not to pull people out of poverty or whatever justification the left may offer. The purpose is to raise tax revenue for government by clipping taxpayers in the least painful way possible. People getting a raise don't mind giving a piece of the action to the raise-mandator that made it happen.

Democrats succeed with the pitch for a minimum wage increase by convincing voters that it's all about stingy millionaires not wanting to share their profits with employees. It's the same old leftist demand for arbitrary redistribution of wealth; the law should take money out of one person's pocket and put it in someone else's, similar to then-Senator Obama telling Joe the Plumber in 2008 that the power of government should be used to "spread the wealth around."

Minimum wage advocates don't understand how business works, especially small business, the main engine of American prosperity. Small businesses typically operate in competitive markets with small profit margins. The biggest expense is labor. Increasing that cost by even a small amount can be devastating.

If we're serious about the minimum wage pulling families out of poverty, then we should make it at least $15 an hour. Yet even $10 an hour forces an employer to reduce staff. Who gets the axe, a low-skilled adult who really needs the job, or a higher-skilled teenager just looking for spending money? If you put the squeeze on the employer and raise his labor cost, he will keep the employee who provides more bang for the buck. It's a business, not a charity.

On the 2014 ballot, Nebraska voters approved a 24% increase in the state-mandated minimum wage. What about those who lose their jobs because of it? To avoid that scenario, employers must be forced to retain all employees. Government must make it illegal for employers to reduce pay or staff. That's crazy, but that's what you must endorse and enforce if you are serious about the minimum wage.

The left's reaction: "That's how an economic system *should* work. Force employers to retain all employees *and* pay them more. Let the employer dip into his profit to cover the added expense."

The laws of economics do not allow most businesses to comply with such a mandate. And where is the logical end to it? If employers have limitless profits and government should be the Great Leveler, taking from the rich and giving to the poor, then don't be miserly about it. An hourly wage of $10 generates $20,000 of annual income. It's hard for some individuals to live on that, never mind families. Why not $20 an hour? The answer is that the employer's labor cost would be so high that the business would not make a profit, and would fail. Or the price of the product or service would be raised so high to cover the labor cost that no one would buy, again resulting in the failure of the business.

Government should not mess with wage rates. It cannot

identify the profit point for all businesses; it should not impose a one-size-fits-all minimum wage.

The way for people to raise their pay and standard of living is to develop the skills and habits for a better job. If people have developmental disabilities or for other reasons beyond their control can't qualify for better-paying jobs, then of course there should be charitable systems to accommodate them. But don't try to take care of people by having government arbitrarily distort the employer's labor cost. It hurts employers and people looking for entry-level jobs.

\* \* \*

Tea Party opposition to unlimited government is called racist by some critics. There may be fringe voices saying fringe things, but the legitimate Tea Party wants every American to participate in American exceptionalism.

As for "soft" racism, you must look to the left to find the white-man's-burden paternalistic contempt that says: A federal welfare/entitlement system is necessary because, outside of sports and entertainment, we can't expect minorities to compete successfully and live the American Dream; they need help just to survive at a subsistence level; stop complaining, keep reaching deeper into your taxpaying pocket, and be glad you aren't one of the inferior people.

I had a spirited exchange on the radio with a black caller who had no use for the Tea Party. He said African-Americans align overwhelmingly on the left with the Democratic Party because the Republican, conservative, Tea Party, right side of the political spectrum is racist.

I said blacks have been "played" by the Democratic Party for decades. That really set him off. He laughed and said that comment is why blacks gravitate to the Democratic Party; racists on the right think blacks are too dumb to understand what is in their best interest. I said it wasn't about stupidity or intelligence. Very smart people can make very wrong choices. Many blacks have analyzed the political situation and determined that their best interest lies with the Democratic Party. I say they are mistaken, not ignorant.

A new campaign to foment race-based hatred of America and its founding values has been launched by the *New York Times*. It's called *The 1619 Project*, as in the year slaves from Africa arrived in what became the USA. According to the *Times*: "Though America did not even exist yet, their arrival marked its foundation, the beginning of the system of slavery on which the country was built." The goal is to get Americans of all races to hate our heritage and reject our Declaration/Constitution legacy as a fraud.

*1619* is based on the false assertion that slavery was the foundation of America, that America was built on racism and slave labor. Slave labor was a major part of the Southern economy before the Civil War. The part of America **not** dependent on slavery grew bigger, stronger, more prosperous, and more diverse economically. That economic system based on paid labor and economic mobility was the foundation of America. Over the last century-and-a-half, that formula for prosperity has spread throughout the former Confederacy from Atlanta to Dallas.

The *Times* seems to see slavery as uniquely American. Humans of all races and nationalities all over the planet had been enslaving each other for thousands of years before slavery came to America. Africa already was buying and selling slaves (including white Europeans) when Europeans showed up to get slaves for America.

That does not excuse what happened in America. It is tragic that the worldwide scourge of slavery wormed its way into our society that prizes liberty. It took nearly a century from the writing of the Declaration of Independence for America to live up to that document and abolish slavery, but it did happen. You can join the *New York Times* in hating America for bringing slavery here, or you can love America for reforming itself and opening a path to the American Dream for everyone.

What's really happening is that the left is petrified at what President Trump accomplished for blacks who got a taste of the American Dream and want more. The left can't let this continue unchallenged. What if blacks declare that they are done being angry victims manipulated by the left for votes without anything ever changing for them? Yikes. African-Americans might discover that not only do they not need the left; the left is holding them back.

*1619* gets a boost from its anti-white cousins Critical Race Theory and Black Lives Matter, movements generated by Marxists who realized that class-warfare hatred and jealousy can't compete with the American Dream. They sought another way to make people angry enough to overthrow our democratic capitalist system. Hence this effort to make racism the number one issue, the defining characteristic of America. That way the left can say: however good things might seem, it's all contaminated by racism.

It may be working. One of my kids showed me a social media post for Independence Day 2020 by a recent graduate of a local high school. I will call the graduate Riley, which could be male or female. Riley is not the graduate's name. Riley's identity is irrelevant. The point is that this is what the toxic *1619*/CRT/BLM cocktail is doing to students.

Riley, who is black, was a star at a majority-white high school. Good grades. Popular. Athlete. Leader in student government. Performed in musicals. Worked at a fast-food restaurant. Classic all-American kid with a bright future.

The left did a *1619*/CRT/BLM wokeness job on Riley. Riley's social media tirade made it sound like Riley was in agony in the hold of a Middle Passage slave ship. Riley claimed to be in pain, feeling the trauma of ancestors.

Celebrate America's birthday? *NEVER!*

Riley needs to absorb the *I Have a Dream* speech by Martin Luther King Jr. King said the civil rights movement did not want to tear down America. It called on America to be its best, to be true to the principles of the Declaration of Independence and the Constitution, to provide access *for all* to "the great vaults of opportunity of this nation."

King's message would generate standing ovations from today's Tea Party. It was all the more remarkable because, unlike the race protestors of today, King truly did live in a society plagued by systemic racism – attack dogs, water cannons, and "narrow jail cells" for those who peacefully challenged institutional barriers based on racial prejudice. Instead of appealing to justifiable anger and calling for vengeance, King insisted that such evil could be overcome only by "soul force" and American founding values.

Riley's ancestors don't want Riley to be consumed with

rage. They want Riley to shine like the joyful star Riley was, and still can be. That's how to settle the score with slave traders and whip crackers, and vindicate the anguish of ancestors. Win. *Be* the American Dream. Honor MLK by living the dream he had for you.

People all over the world come to America because it's a place where those who work hard and play by the rules are rewarded with freedom, prosperity, and a full array of civil rights – regardless of race, ethnicity, or nationality. African-American Colin Kaepernick can make a fortune playing a game (football), then make an even bigger fortune slamming the patriots who built the system he now enjoys, and falsely demonizing as predatory race-haters the law enforcers who protect the system for him. What a country!

African-Americans have violent confrontations with police more often than might be expected because, though only 13% of the population, they commit roughly half of violent crimes. There are cases of white officers unnecessarily killing black suspects, but they are a tiny percentage of total cases. One is too many, but consider that every year white officers have tens of millions of interactions with African-Americans, including millions of arrests. If racism was "systemic" – built into the system, standard operating procedure – there would be thousands of bigoted brutality cases exploding in the news every year. They would be impossible to hide in this age of police dashboard and body cameras, and citizens with cell phones.

Cell phone video showed a white officer kneeling on or near the back of the neck of African-American George Floyd as he repeatedly said "I can't breathe" just before he died. Floyd died of heart failure rather than failure to breathe, but it was alarming and tragic – and a one-of-a-kind occurrence. If there was systemic racism in America, there would be a daily George Floyd case in the news.

The death in 2014 of African-American Michael Brown in Ferguson, Missouri, is considered the national breakout event for the Black Lives Matter movement. "Hands up, don't shoot!" was the rallying cry.

The whole thing was a lie. Brown was not surrendering with his hands up pleading "don't shoot" when he was killed. Brown was 18, 6'4", and 292 lbs. He robbed a convenience store, assaulting a clerk in the process. A white police officer saw someone (Brown) matching the description of the robbery suspect and tried to stop him. Brown leaned into the police cruiser, attacked the officer, and tried to get his gun. Brown was shot in the hand and fled. The officer pursued and caught up with Brown. Brown was moving toward the officer aggressively, not surrendering, when he was fatally shot.

It became the lead national story. The left was in full cry. Protests became violent. St. Louis Rams pro football players ran onto the field for a game holding their hands up in protest. (Ferguson is near St. Louis.)

The local prosecutor reviewed the case and concluded there was no basis to charge the officer with wrongdoing.

The left was furious. It wanted the officer destroyed. A grand jury was convened. President Obama sent in an army of FBI agents and federal attorneys to nail the officer.

The result: the officer was exonerated.

Yet in 2020, Floyd-fueled BLM rioters in Omaha wrote "Michael Brown" in the street in huge letters, as if Brown was an innocent martyr to deadly police racism.

Some of those rioters attacked downtown Omaha businesses. They smashed the giant glass windows of white bar owner Jake Gardner's establishment. Gardner went out to confront them. Video from surveillance cameras captured the confrontation on the street. Gardner asked the crowd to move along. Some remained combative. He lifted his shirt to display a gun. There was a struggle in which Gardner ended up on the ground. He fired two warning shots and the assailants backed off. But as Gardner was getting up, a young black man named James Scurlock jumped him and applied a chokehold. Gardner shouted at Scurlock to get off. Scurlock refused. Gardner fired his gun over his shoulder at Scurlock, hitting him in the neck killing him.

Scurlock became Omaha's Michael Brown or George Floyd, a martyr to systemic racism. There were press conferences, protests, and T-shirts. Justice for James!

As happened in Ferguson, the local prosecutor examined the evidence and concluded that the accused had acted in self-defense. Also as happened in Ferguson, the left erupted. Social media exploded with wild and unfounded claims about Gardner being a white supremacist who was shouting racial slurs when he proudly murdered Scurlock.

A grand jury was convened. It indicted Gardner for manslaughter, terroristic threats, and other offenses.

Gardner killed himself. Perhaps Gardner had other demons tormenting him. Or he concluded: They have ruined my business and my life; I'm a white Trump supporter; they are going to twist or trample the law until they get me; I'm not going to be their sacrificial spectacle.

In the 5-day interim between the grand jury indictment and the suicide, a black lawyer who is a Nebraska state senator complained that in the future he would advise clients with warrants to demand "the Jake treatment," meaning tell authorities you'll surrender when you feel like it. Gardner had been living on the West Coast after receiving 1,600 death threats. Authorities gave him time to turn himself in.

The Jake treatment? Let's review the Jake treatment.

A decorated veteran confronted thugs threatening to demolish his business because of something unrelated to him or his business. He showed a weapon but did not respond with violence. (Apparently that was the terroristic threat – by the guy surrounded by terrorists attacking his business.) When attacked and knocked to the ground, he fired warning shots. When an attacker put him in a chokehold and would not let go, he fired a fatal shot deemed self-defense by a prosecutor of sterling reputation – a Democrat, for those keeping score politically and presuming that an evil conservative Republican let the racist killer off. The prosecutor has been elected and re-elected county attorney in four consecutive elections because people of all political stripes respect his judgment and professionalism.

But that was not good enough. The woke race warriors would not quit. A kangaroo court grand jury was convened to deliver a political result demanded by the angry left.

A law-abiding citizen defended himself and his business from a rampaging mob, was scrutinized by the justice system and found justified, then was railroaded into an indictment for manslaughter and driven to suicide.

That's the Jake treatment.

Scurlock had a criminal record. He had served time for violent crimes, including an armed home invasion robbery that was reduced to burglary. He had methamphetamine and cocaine in his system when he died. None of that means he deserved to die, but he was not an innocent dove. And of course he was engaged in violent criminal activity – rioting, and then attacking someone in a life-threatening way.

The left ignores the wrongdoing of the George Floyds, Michael Browns, and James Scurlocks to serve the narrative that a race war is being conducted by vicious whites against innocent blacks. Again, the wrongful death of any citizen at the hands of police is intolerable, but the left wants to tear the country apart using rare exceptions to promote the lie that America is a racist nation with racist cops.

If racism was systemic, Barack Obama would not have been elected president. He won – twice – because tens of millions of whites voted for him instead of his white opponents. That could not happen in a nation with systemic racism. The racist system would have won, not Obama.

Do black lives matter? Of course, but I'll take BLM seriously when it denounces the killing of roughly 5,000 black males every year *by black males*. That is the slaughter on which to focus if you value black lives.

I agree with those who call slavery America's original sin. Preservation of slavery was considered necessary to keep the colonies unified as they fought for independence, but it was a monumental violation of natural law. Initially the Constitution partially counted slaves as population to enhance Southern political power in Congress and in the electoral voting system for president, but did not recognize slaves as human beings. The Constitution stopped importation of slaves in 1808, but did not abolish slavery.

All true. It's equally true that the goodness and genius of America are reflected in the way Americans used the Constitution to abolish slavery and guarantee the civil rights of former slaves with a series of constitutional amendments after the Civil War.

A black man who has held leadership positions in our local Republican Party in Omaha has said numerous times that he is a Republican for three reasons: the Thirteenth Amendment in 1865 (abolition of slavery), the Fourteenth Amendment in 1868 (equal protection of law for all citizens), and the Fifteenth Amendment in 1870 (right to vote regardless of race). All were supported by Republicans and opposed by Democrats.

Blacks understandably flocked to the Republican Party in the late 1800s. Today many see things differently.

During the 2004 presidential campaign, there was a student straw poll at the predominantly black inner-city middle school where I worked. A black student was explaining to me his choice of U.S. Senator John Kerry, a Democrat from Massachusetts, over the Republican incumbent, President George W. Bush. "Bush hates black people," the student said matter-of-factly. I said I was surprised to hear that and asked how the student knew. "Because he's a Republican," the student replied, as if explaining that the sun rises in the east and sets in the west – it's simply the way things are.

I asked the student if he knew who Colin Powell was. He did. I noted that Bush's father and our 41st president, Republican George H.W. Bush, had picked General Powell to be the first black Chairman of the Joint Chiefs of Staff, the nation's highest-ranking military officer and a crucial advisor to the commander-in-chief. I noted that when Bush the son became president, he picked General Powell to be the first black Secretary of State, one of the most important positions in a presidential administration.

I asked the student if he knew who Condoleezza Rice was. He grinned and nodded yes. I noted that the younger Bush, the current president, picked Rice, a black woman, to be his National Security Advisor, and then chose her to succeed Secretary of State Powell.

I asked the student to guess my party affiliation and we both burst out laughing.

Some blacks are wary of the Republican Party because of a misconception about the Dixiecrat movement. In 1948, Southern Democrats opposed to federal racial integration policies formed a third-party movement. Nicknamed Dixiecrats, they argued for a state's right to enforce racial segregation. Their party dissolved after the 1948 election, but for the next two decades, Dixiecrat Democrats continued to fight federal civil rights legislation. Their last hurrah was in 1968 when former Alabama Governor George Wallace ran for president as a third-party pro-segregation candidate.

A few Dixiecrats became Republicans. The vast majority died as Democrats. Their movement died with them.

What has lived on is the race-baiting lie that the Dixiecrat movement relocated to the Republican Party, where it was welcomed by fellow racists. The truth is that the Republican Party has stood for racial justice from its founding in 1854 to fight slavery. Today's Republican Party must convince African-Americans invested in the Democratic Party that their future depends on the same things every American's future depends on – self-reliance, personal responsibility, and pursuit of American exceptionalism.

The same is true for Latinos. Yet some Republicans want to out-pander Democrats by offering Latinos amnesty on illegal immigration and unfettered access to the federal welfare/entitlement system. They worry that the Democratic Party's get-'em-dependent-on-us strategy will work with Latinos as it has with African-Americans.

Republicans, we will never beat Democrats at that cynical game. Even if we could, we would become accomplices in the ruination of America.

"Turn into the fire." My former boss, Treynor State Bank Chairman Mick Guttau, earned two distinguished flying crosses as a Cobra helicopter gunship pilot in Vietnam. He said "turn into the fire" was a key principle from his training. If you come under fire, don't turn or pull away; don't surrender your offensive capability and perhaps make yourself a bigger target. Attack. You're a smaller target if you turn into the fire. Go right at the threat and eliminate it.

Republicans, turn into the fire. Attack with the ideology that produces the best for the most. Invite all races and ethnicities to reject dead-end welfare/entitlement politics and instead pursue American exceptionalism.

\* \* \*

Supporting the federal welfare/entitlement system has

been a winning strategy for politicians. It appeals to two huge groups of voters: kindhearted middle- and upper-class people who care about the plight of the poor, and the growing number of people receiving government assistance. And of course citizens of all means comprise the tens of millions receiving Social Security and Medicare.

The American left is trying to replicate the fusion of Christianity and socialism accomplished in Europe, which is smothering European Christianity. Practicing the faith becomes politicized into making loud and persistent demands for more care and feeding by nanny government. Citizens seek community through common dependence on big government rather than common religious beliefs.

The scandal is that governments in Europe and America do not take from their citizens enough tax revenue to pay for what the citizenry consumes in government goods and services. Remember that a significant chunk of every dollar spent by the U.S. government is borrowed money. Our growing indebtedness to China and other potentially hostile creditors is bad enough, but where is the moral outrage from religious leaders over the crushing debt burden that deficit spending creates for our children? Why don't they demand payment for the full cost of the welfare/entitlement system they advocate? Why don't they condemn the way we steal from younger generations when we borrow and leave the tab to future taxpayers?

There was a time (July 3, 2008, in Fargo, ND) when presidential candidate Obama shared that view:

*The way Bush has done it over the last eight years is to take out a credit card from the Bank of China in the name of our*

**children, driving up our national debt from $5 trillion dollars for the first 42 presidents – number 43 added $4 trillion dollars by his lonesome, so that we now have over $9 trillion dollars of debt that we are going to have to pay back, $30,000 for every man, woman and child. That's irresponsible. It's unpatriotic.**

Bravo! That's a full-throated Tea Party proclamation.

But as president, Obama increased the debt more in his first three years than Bush did in eight, as the *San Diego Union-Tribune's* Steve Breen captured in this cartoon:

The $5 trillion debt increase reflected in the cartoon grew to $10 trillion – more than double the increase for which President Obama criticized his predecessor. The lava flow of debt expanded even faster under Obama.

Whether more dollars are collected from us as taxes to pay down the debt, or the value of our dollars is eroded by inflation because the government simply prints more money (or generates it electronically) to service the debt, it's the same result: government takes purchasing power out of our pockets and gives us nothing in return.

The left's answer: Raise taxes on the rich!

We tried that. The top federal income tax rate exceeded 90% during World War II and still hovered around 90% in the 1950s. President Kennedy brought it down to 70% in the early 1960s, a precursor of the economic policy of President Reagan – cut taxes to spur economic growth and generate *more* tax revenue. Kennedy's tax cut worked, producing a robust period of economic growth. (President Trump replicated that success with the 2017 tax cut.)

We've looked at how President Johnson followed Kennedy with the Great Society. In the 1968 presidential election, the electorate rejected liberal/progressive Democrat Hubert Humphrey in favor of seemingly conservative Republican Richard Nixon. But Nixon disengaged from gold in determining the value of the dollar, imposed wage and price controls, and in other ways moved the nation left rather than right on fiscal policy. Abandoning the gold standard as a disciplinary force was a major blow to American fiscal stability. There was nothing to restrict the government from simply printing money to fund deficit spending. It opened the way to the fiscal shenanigans of today.

By the mid-1970s, the fiscal triple whammy of the Great Society, the Vietnam War, and escalating oil prices had pummeled our country economically. America was plagued in that decade with double-digit inflation and interest rates, and nearly double-digit unemployment.

The damage was not just economic. In the late 1970s, President Jimmy Carter warned of a national "crisis of confidence." Political pundits talked about a "Carter malaise."

No wonder. The federal government took 70 cents from every dollar a citizen earned above a certain level of income (roughly $200,000 at that time), never mind state and local tax burdens. People began to question whether it was worth it to keep striving when their tax dollars went to a growing number of people who took from the system and contributed nothing. Recall D'Souza's wagon (page 46).

The succession of Johnson, Nixon (Vice President Gerald Ford became president and finished Nixon's second term after Nixon resigned over the Watergate scandal), and Carter had many Americans thinking their country was lapsing into a European socialist stupor.

Reagan succeeded Carter in 1981 and reduced the top federal income tax rate to 50% right away, and 28% by the end of his presidency. That helped lay the foundation for an unprecedented run of economic growth and prosperity for Americans in general, not just the rich (page 113). The tax cuts also produced an unexpected torrent of revenue into the federal treasury in the 1990s that pushed annual budgets into the black for a few years.

The top income tax rate has crept back up near 40% – still better than 70% when Reagan took office. The wealthy still pay most of the taxes. The last decade of federal income tax data show that the richest 1% earns up to 20% of the nation's income, but pays at least 30% of federal income taxes. The top 10% earns a little less than half of the nation's income but pays 67% of federal income taxes. The top half earns well over 80% of income and pays nearly 100% of federal income taxes. Remaining citizens pay little or nothing. Yet the myth persists that conservatives take care of the big shots and don't care about the little guys.

You know what hurts the little guy? Tax increases. The rich can maintain domiciles outside the United States to avoid taxes, or hire lawyers to maximize advantages in the tax code. The ones hurt by tax increases are those who have little or no margin in their budgets, and cannot afford multiple domiciles or a legal team to scour the tax code for specialized tax breaks.

I'd love to force those who say rising tax burdens are no big deal to field the calls I have as an elected official from people of modest means, especially senior citizens on fixed incomes, who want to know what they are supposed to do when their home valuations (and thus their property taxes) have doubled over the last 15 years, but their incomes have not. A homestead exemption helps to some degree for the elderly, but there are many people struggling to bear the tax burden necessary to fund big government at all levels. Working-class taxpayers typically pay 30% of their income to local, state, and federal taxing bodies.

That, says the left, is why we should raise taxes only on millionaires. But confiscating every dollar from the wealthy won't solve our fiscal crisis. It would be counterproductive to take more money out of the private sector by raising taxes on people who build or expand businesses and provide jobs.

I'm a middle-class guy, but I don't want my government pulling down rich people. That doesn't help me. And don't let anyone fool you, Mr. & Mrs. Middle Class, by saying the shakedown of the rich will spare you from having to pay more taxes. The tax man will be coming for you, too. He already is via Obamacare and its new taxes. It's not possible to fund our federal welfare/entitlement system without heavily taxing the middle class.

The American left rejects such concerns. It wants more spending on more "stimulus" plans. It wants the federal government to manage more of the economy. It wants to keep pushing leftward toward socialism.

The American left seems unaware that European socialism is failing. Greece, Ireland, and places in between have discovered what Lady Thatcher warned of many years ago: socialism is great until you run out of other people's money. Socialist economies squeeze the economic life out of their productive citizens. They also breed dangerous expectations in their nonproductive citizens. People who rely on (and blame) "the system" for their standard of living "rage against the system" that can no longer afford to carry them.

While studying in England during the 1986-87 academic year, I was amazed by students at England's most famous universities, Oxford and Cambridge, protesting for greater public subsidies of their elite educations. Imagine students at Harvard and Yale having the nerve to protest for greater public subsidies of their Ivy League degrees.

But look at today's news. American college students are braying about the cost of higher education and demanding "debt-free degrees." The left is clamoring for cancelation of student loans. I realize that higher education has become a lucrative racket for schools and a financial bludgeoning for students and families. Nonetheless, I can't believe students want everyone else to foot the bill for their education, including people without the ability or opportunity to attend college. I took out government-backed loans to help fund my education, but I did not expect the government – which means my fellow citizens – to pay them off for me.

The left seems to argue that the moral thing to do is jack the top income tax rate back up to 70% or more and have the government guarantee a certain standard of living for every citizen. If you question the advisability, never mind the legality or constitutionality, of having the federal government assume such a duty, you are accused of hating old people, children, and all of humanity.

For example, the left says that without Obamacare, 30 million people won't get health care. But why should the federal government raise taxes and spend money to cover uninsured citizens? Just because the government *can* do something doesn't mean it *should* do it.

But someone might suffer or die if the federal government doesn't act, the left insists.

This is where people ready to embrace limited government often lose their nerve.

This is where former Massachusetts Governor Mitt Romney ran into heavy turbulence as a 2012 Republican presidential candidate when he said "my job is not to worry about" the 47% of people dependent on the federal government. He meant worry about winning their votes, but the left spun it as Romney saying that as president he would ignore the plight of the poor.

Romney was more correct than he was willing to admit. He should have jammed it right back down the throat of the left and said: It is *not* the job of the president to promise and deliver social services.

What about people facing crises in health and other areas of life without the means to handle them? Leave them to suffer on their own?

Of course not. The Constitution limits what the *federal government* can do. State and local governments can provide social services as authorized by state constitutions and state and local statutes. There are local, regional, and national non-government social service providers, religious and secular, that are better than government at providing cost-effective social services.

And of course there is no limit to what individuals are free to do to help fellow citizens. If you believe a problem needs immediate major financial assistance, then you can engage in voluntary taxation. Donate money to a cause or form an organization to solicit donations for it. Appeal to emotion. Make a convincing case. Sell it. There's nothing wrong with a cause having to prove itself and earn support.

Years ago I served on a volunteer committee developing the fundraising pitch for my high school alma mater. We had to raise a big pile of money for a capital campaign. Our internal motto was: laugh, cry, write the check. We warmed people up with humor, then pulled on the heartstrings. The campaign succeeded because donors were convinced that the cause was worthy.

French political analyst Alexis de Tocqueville wrote a book, *Democracy in America*, based on his tour of America in 1831-32. He wrote about a dynamic society of go-getters unlike anything the world had seen before. He said America's vitality came in large part from the inclination to form grassroots associations to address all manner of political and social matters. Americans don't wait for government to act, de Tocqueville noted. They look to themselves and their neighbors first and foremost. Civic action is citizen-directed, not government-directed.

Americans practiced subsidiarity before popes identified and encouraged it. Today, though, our national policy has become: See a problem? Press the federal Expand Government button to solve it. However, we are not paying the true cost of pushing the Expand Government button. We borrow and push the bill off to younger generations.

Meanwhile, our civic muscles atrophy.

On a local radio show, an advocate for government funding of prenatal care for illegal immigrants was asked why the project couldn't be left to religious or secular social service organizations. The advocate said nongovernment funding might not be "systemic or sustainable." A funding stream is a legitimate concern, but that does not mean it's OK to use the coercive power of government to force people to fund the program.

Another economic argument is "let's use local money as leverage to get federal money." For every $1 state government spends on prenatal care, the federal government will contribute $3. We can turn a half-million dollars into $2 million: $500,000 in state tax dollars + $1.5 million in federal tax dollars. If its constitution allows it, a state can subsidize prenatal care with the help of a 3-to-1 federal contribution. But that's the mindset that is propelling out-of-control spending by local, state, and federal governments.

Regardless of the legal status of the expectant mother, the answer to the prenatal care question is yes, it would be hard to develop systemic and sustainable funding for a program outside of government, and that's exactly what should happen. It should be done outside of government and it should be hard – for donors, for agencies providing the service, and for women receiving the service. Religious, community health, pro-life, and other voices advocating the subsidy should raise the money and coordinate the service. There should be a repayment plan for the recipient, even if it takes 10 years. Maybe there should be a one-and-done rule – we'll help you for one pregnancy. Whether or not that rule is used, the recipient should be told don't have sexual relations and get pregnant again until you are married to a good husband who will be a financially and emotionally supportive father to your children.

The left would slam such an approach as "judgmental." The problem with nonjudgmental government programs is that they exacerbate problems rather than solve them. The Great Society has been a Great Failure because it rewards dysfunctional behavior instead of stopping it and eliminating the need for the service.

Skeptics claim that the call for limited government is really a way for conservatives to absolve themselves of any responsibility to help the poor. They have it backwards. Limited government doesn't get the citizen off the moral hook. It puts the citizen *on* the moral hook. Some Americans decline to give to charitable causes because they presume government is addressing the problem. Under limited government, you don't get to pass off to some government bureaucracy your duty to help fellow citizens.

In his famous 2006 study, *Who Really Cares: The*

*Surprising Truth about Compassionate Conservatism,* Arthur Brooks showed that conservatives earn less income than liberals, yet give more to charity. Conservatives are frugal, yet generous. They embrace the responsibility of the prosperous to help the struggling. Individuals and societies that ignore this responsibility endanger themselves. The stability of society erodes if pockets of suffering and frustration are allowed to fester and grow. Shirking this responsibility erodes the character of the shirkers. Willingness to contribute to the common good is necessary for a self-governing society to thrive.

If the virtue of Americans is weak and the prosperous ignore the struggling, then American society will die a deserved death, but big government is not the answer. Resorting to big government guarantees failure. We have examples all over the world, including American cities under liberal/progressive management for decades.

The best way to care for the needy is to create conditions for prosperity and generosity, as Plymouth Colony proved four centuries ago. I have worked enough in fundraising to know that Americans of all political persuasions are generous. Donors may require financial accountability and evidence of success, but they will rally to help people in need.

\* \* \*

President Obama, responding to conservative criticism of his fiscal policy in April 2012, invoked the name of Ronald Reagan to defend himself. Obama complained that Reagan wouldn't make it through a Republican presidential primary today because, having allowed some tax increases during his presidency, he wouldn't be considered fiscally conservative enough. Some Republicans make the same complaint in reaction to the fiscally conservative pressure exerted on Capitol Hill by the Tea Party.

Reagan would do just fine today. Tax hikes he approved (and tax breaks for the wealthy that he ended) would be eclipsed by his massive income tax cut that generated the greatest burst of economic prosperity in American history.

Reagan saw Obamacare coming more than four decades before Obama became president. In the run-up to the 2009 vote on Obamacare, much radio air play was given to a speech from the early 1960s in which Reagan predicted that concern about health care would be a compelling way to tug on emotions and sell socialism in America. Reagan warned that leftists would argue that millions will suffer and die unless the government guarantees universal health care.

If Reagan were running for president today, after watching spending patterns keep growing right through the 1990s and overtake the budget surpluses his tax cuts produced, and then watching Republicans continue growing government in the 2000s and run up astronomical debt, he would not advocate tax hikes to balance the budget. Reagan would say the problem is too much spending, not lack of revenue.

Big government sucks money out of the prosperity-producing machine called free-market capitalism. It entices Americans to become takers from society rather than producers and givers. Employers are afraid to expand and hire because they don't know what new taxes and mandates government might impose on them. They realize that somehow, someday, all that money we are borrowing to fund federal spending must be paid off.

# Balanced Budget Amendment

*There is no practice more dangerous than that of borrowing money; for when money can be had in this way, repayment is seldom thought of in time, the interest becomes a moth, exertions to raise it by dint of industry ceases, it comes easy and is spent freely, and many things [are] indulged in that would never be thought of if [they were] to be purchased by the sweat of the brow. . . . [I]n the mean time the debt is accumulating like a snow ball in rolling.*

*George Washington, 1797*

*I wish it were possible to obtain a single amendment to our Constitution. I would be willing to depend on that alone for the reduction of the administration of our government to the genuine principles of its Constitution; I mean an additional article taking from the federal government the power of borrowing.*

*Thomas Jefferson, 1798*

*Nobody can ever convince me that government can spend a dollar that it's not got.*

*Harry Truman, c. 1950*

The national debt was $6 trillion when President George W. Bush took office in 2001, $10 trillion when President Obama took office in 2009, $20 trillion when President Trump took office in 2017, and $28 trillion when President Biden took office in 2021. That 367% increase was partly pandemic-driven, but mostly due to unlimited government.

It's going to take boldness rather than incrementalism to reverse this course and solve our fiscal crisis. We need to fix it now with a balanced budget amendment.

The key, of course, is for annual spending to match annual revenue. Although I just rejected incrementalism, I am forced to admit that we can't snap our fingers and balance the budget in an instant. Let's have the amendment establish a 10-year graduated path to balance. In Year 1, the deficit could not exceed $900 billion. In Year 2, $800 billion. In Year 3, $700 billion, and so on by increments of $100 billion, down to zero in Year 10.

I reach back to page 62 for the limited government circle of authority drawn by the Constitution. The goal is to have the constricting pressure of smaller annual deficits force us back to limited government. No more borrowing to fund government beyond the limits of the Constitution.

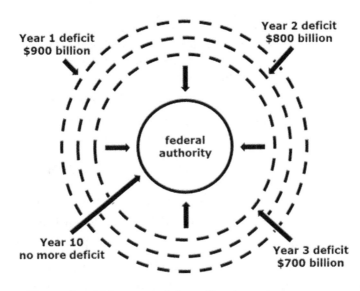

There should be a provision allowing a temporary override with a supermajority of at least 75% in both houses of Congress. That allows flexibility in case of war, pandemic, or some other demand that generates supermajority support.

One objection to a balanced budget amendment is that

it isn't necessary. Congress and the president can balance the budget right now. If they don't, the people can vote out the over-spenders and vote in budget-balancers.

In theory, that's true. In reality, the people have discovered that voting for self-proclaimed fiscal conservatives proves futile. The federal government is too big, too powerful, and too far-removed to be held accountable by ordinary citizens, and our politicians continually fail us. Without the pressure of a constitutional mandate, federal office holders won't shrink federal authority back to the limits established by the Constitution.

Politicians at all levels of government have proven themselves unable to resist the temptation of turning government into a goody dispenser. Cities and states all over the nation face bankruptcy, primarily because of accommodating politicians giving government-employee unions too much in pay, benefits, and pensions. Americans are busy working and raising families and living their lives. They don't have the time and resources to monitor government. They are at the mercy of candidates who keep betraying constituents once they are elected and disappear into the bubble of city hall or the state or federal capitol.

At the federal level, that's what the Constitution is for. It's the 24/7 written enforcer of the will of the people.

One of the best things about the Constitution is that we the people can change it whenever we want. Those who complain that we are prisoners of a document that is outdated and inflexible are wrong. We have made 27 changes to the Constitution using the amendment process. In one case (repeal of Prohibition), we undid a change made in a prior amendment. The Constitution is as up-to-date and flexible as we choose to make it.

We need another change. We need to impose our will on the federal government with a balanced budget amendment. Jefferson was right. We need to rein in the federal government with a constitutional provision that prevents the federal government from spending more than it takes in.

The beauty of a balanced budget amendment is that it should attract people on the left, the right, and everywhere in between. The lava flow of debt will engulf all of us regardless of party affiliations or positions on other issues. This should be a catalyst for bipartisan or nonpartisan cooperation. That's fun to think about. Another fun aspect is that it exposes the frauds among us who say they want to get government spending under control, but fight a balanced budget amendment because they don't want to be forced back to limited government.

Some conservatives do not support a balanced budget amendment because it does not guarantee reduced spending on smaller government. You can balance a budget by raising taxes instead of shrinking government. I would oppose that option (as I have done in office), but at least it would force fiscal truth in government. It would force Americans to pay for the amount of government they want, not push the cost off to younger generations. It would force advocates of big government to admit how much their agenda truly costs.

Another criticism is that a balanced budget amendment would plunge the nation into a recession if it caused the size of government to be reduced. If hundreds of thousands of government workers become unemployed, the argument goes, all the money the federal government pays them would be lost to the economy.

This is one of the most frustrating arguments in the fiscal debate. The government does not put new money into the economy. The government removes money from the economy by taxation and directs some of it back into the economy as wages paid to employees and other forms of spending, but it's a recycling process, not an addition of new wealth to the economy.

The money the federal government would have paid employees is not "lost" to the economy – unless you're saying the federal government will keep collecting the same amount of tax revenue and hoard the money it no longer pays to employees. The tax revenue that was needed to pay all those employees should be left in the private sector. There it can be used to hire former federal employees looking for work in the private sector – a private sector with a lighter tax burden and fewer federal regulatory costs. Let former federal employees find jobs in a private sector that has more capital to spend and is more willing to expand and hire because of less anxiety about government.

I don't mean to sugarcoat it. Fiscal reform would be painful. I know what it's like to be "between jobs." I wish I could think of a painless way to fix our crisis, but I can't. The longer we wait, the more painful it will be. The alcoholism analogy comes back to mind. If we say we can't reduce government spending because it would be too painful economically, then we are saying we must spend ourselves to death like an alcoholic drinking himself to death because it would be too painful to stop.

But if we're in a recession, the left argues, a balanced budget amendment would make it worse because the federal government would not be able to deficit-spend to soften the financial blow to the nation and put money into the economy. This flawed logic is based on the flawed legacy of the New Deal – that it saved the country with deficit spending. Again, the government does not really put money into the economy. It can put into the economy only what it takes out of the economy in taxes and other fees. Keep that money in the private sector instead of running it through government, where some of the money is lost to bureaucratic inefficiency and expense.

The federal government can pump more money into the economy by expanding the money supply, as when it showers cash on citizens in the form of stimulus payments. It can print currency or generate it electronically. None of that produces economic growth and strength. It does the opposite. It is foolhardy, banana-republic desperation that weakens the citizen economically. The inevitable inflation that results reduces the value of the money in the citizen's pocket. It is just as damaging as a tax increase.

Another argument against a balanced budget amendment is that it will not take effect until at least 38 states ratify it. The states have become just as addicted as their citizens to federal subsidies and will howl like drug addicts in withdrawal, the naysayers contend, if their federal supplier reduces or cuts off their fix because of pressure to make spending match revenue.

That's not a reason to shrink from the challenge. It's

time to force a decision on whether citizens are willing to pay the true price of the federal welfare/entitlement system. That terrifying prospect is what motivates the left (and collaborators on the right) to fight a balanced budget amendment. Remember that a significant chunk of every dollar the United States spends is borrowed money. Defenders of the status quo hide its true cost by borrowing and running annual deficits and accumulating debt. They know that if taxpayers had to pay 100% of the cost of big government, there would be a major backlash. That's why, despite President Truman's rejection of deficit spending, the federal government continues to spend dollars "that it's not got."

Hiding the true cost of the federal welfare/entitlement system allows the federal government to be the go-to provider of social services. The deception is ethical, its defenders argue, because only the federal government can marshal the resources needed to save the children or the senior citizens or anyone else who needs saving.

If so, then convince a majority of your fellow citizens to change the Constitution and make the federal government what you believe it should be – the guarantor of every American's standard of living.

You will not convince me. I am as passionate about social justice and looking out for the underdog as any liberal or progressive is. The federal government is not the answer.

It is amazing to me that people who say they care about the struggling underdog are so adamant about using the federal government to provide social services. We have decades of proof that the federal government has been a terrible vehicle for delivering social services. It's too big. It's too expensive. There are too many moving parts. It's too easy to defraud. There's no accountability to the people. There's no financial risk to spur bureaucrats to be as efficient as possible. In fact, the federal government has an advocacy program encouraging people to sign up for food stamps.

Several years ago, a successful entrepreneur who was inducted into the business hall of fame in Omaha chided the audience a bit. He said there was a lot of griping in business circles about big government and the welfare state, and a lot of bold talk about individualism and freedom and making your own way in the world without interference from government. This man who made a fortune managing capital, working at the highest levels of capitalism, spoke a word in defense of government programs. He said that when he was growing up, his family never would have made it through the crises they faced without help from the government. He said he would not be standing there accepting accolades as a successful free-market capitalist had his family not received government aid.

The question isn't whether American society should provide help for those in need. It should. The question is whether the federal government should be a provider. The answer is no. It's not authorized by the Constitution, it's a proven failure as a public policy, and we can't afford it.

# Are Republicans Ready to Lead?

The Democratic Party has led the effort to expand the American welfare/entitlement system, but plenty of Republicans have contributed to the growth of the nanny state. As mentioned on pages 115-16, in the early 2000s, big-government Republicans helped produce a 66% increase in spending featuring No Child Left Behind, a prescription drug subsidy, the Bush stimulus payout, and TARP.

Some fiscal conservatives defended the TARP vote as necessary to avert a meltdown of the nation's financial system. If that vote stood alone as a single breach of fiscal orthodoxy, that would be one thing, but it was part of a big-government Washington establishment voting pattern over a decade. It is congressional dereliction of duty when the country is sinking into fiscal failure and you pretend everything is fine with Social Security while doing nothing to address the big picture.

Republicans say they are "fighting" for a balanced budget amendment. The opportunity is there every time there is a debt ceiling showdown. There is leverage to make congressional approval of a balanced budget amendment part of an agreement to raise the debt ceiling. The Republican Party does not use that leverage.

The ultimatum should be the same regardless of when the next push to raise the debt ceiling happens: no increase in the debt ceiling until a balanced budget amendment has been added to the Constitution. Put the burden on those who want to raise the debt ceiling. Make them get moving, in Washington and at the state level, to accomplish approval of a balanced budget amendment if they want to raise the debt ceiling again.

Exactly what is the debt ceiling? It's a limit on federal borrowing created by Congress. It's not in the Constitution. It's done by federal statute through an act of Congress.

There almost always has been a national debt, with upward spikes at times of crisis such as the Civil War or World War I. It was during the year the United States entered World War I, 1917, that Congress established a debt ceiling.

Sustained and ominous growth of the debt occurred during the New Deal in 1930s. In 1939, Congress strengthened debt ceiling restrictions to limit borrowing by the federal government.

Enhanced restrictions are meaningless if not enforced. Because the debt ceiling was created by legislative action, it can be changed by legislative action. Congress has raised the debt ceiling *more than 90 times*. By routinely raising the debt ceiling, Congress has rendered it virtually meaningless – except that periodic debates about whether to raise the debt ceiling send nervous tremors through financial markets because of feverish speculation that America will default on its debt-financing obligation.

When Congress raised the debt ceiling in October 2013, a supersize headline on the front page of my local newspaper blared: BACKING AWAY FROM THE BRINK.

That was misleading. Our country is in terrible fiscal shape, but there need not be any threat of default on our debt. The Fourteenth Amendment says: "The validity of the public debt of the United States . . . shall not be questioned." That means the Constitution requires America to service its debt, meaning we make the periodic debt payments on what we have borrowed to finance deficit spending. There is no default on American credit if we follow the Constitution and pay that obligation first.

Then there is the problem of insufficient money in the treasury to pay for the remaining spending that has been approved. The federal government should cut spending to match revenue or raise revenue to match spending. It should not keep borrowing more money to cover the difference.

An Oct. 17, 2013, news item at www.nbcbayarea.com ridiculed Senator Rand Paul for saying there's enough revenue to cover the debt-financing obligation; pay it, then prioritize remaining spending according to what's left in the treasury. The story relied on a Berkeley Law School professor who served in the U.S. Treasury's Office of Tax Policy from 2010-12. This former Obama administration bureaucrat is an example of what we're up against. He said federal government computers are programmed to pay bills in the order they are received; they aren't set up for prioritized spending. He said there was "absolutely no authority" for prioritizing spending and it would be "illegal" to do so.

He's wrong. There is legal authority to prioritize spending. *It's called the Constitution.* If the computers aren't programmed to make the debt-financing payment first, then reprogram the computers. The Constitution mandates that America service its debt. The Treasury Department's computer system is not exempt.

After the debt is serviced, Congress and the president can get back into the budget to prioritize and reduce spending. It might be a healthy exercise to go through each line item and say pay this first, pay this second, and so on.

While serving as president, Obama said raising the debt ceiling does not increase the debt. He said when we raise the debt ceiling, we're not spending any more than has been approved in the budget.

True, but there was not enough money in the federal treasury to cover the level of spending that was approved. We were maxed out on borrowing authority, so how did President Obama propose that we pay for the amount of spending not covered by existing revenue? By raising the debt ceiling and borrowing more money – thereby increasing the debt! I suppose you can say raising the ceiling by itself does not increase the debt, but the purpose of doing it is to utilize the new borrowing authority to take on more debt to finance continued deficit spending.

President Obama has daughters the same ages as two of mine. Why did he try to hide the way he was setting up our daughters for a fiscal thrashing? Has he achieved that super-rich status that will allow him to insulate his family from whatever economic disaster ravages the rest of us? Or is he so steeped in leftist ideology that he is blind to basic principles of government finance?

I have experience with this kind of situation. My first two years in the Nebraska Legislature (2001-02), there were special sessions in addition to the regular annual legislative sessions. The national economy already was sliding into recession in 2001 when 9/11 happened. The special sessions were necessary because the struggling economy meant state revenue kept falling short of projections. Like most states, Nebraska requires that the state budget balance every year.

There wasn't enough money in the state treasury to cover the amount of spending approved, so we went back into the budget to reduce spending.

Why is that option *never* considered on Capitol Hill? It's never considered because cutting spending to match revenue would require leadership and tough decisions. Instead, all we hear is that if we don't raise the debt ceiling, the government will default on its debt and America will become a disgraceful deadbeat nation. Politicians and their media allies whip up a panic that blots out the option of reducing spending.

If the federal government is running out of funds to pay for spending it has approved, it has three options: 1) cut spending to match revenue, 2) raise revenue to match spending, or 3) borrow more money to cover the difference. Option 3, raising the debt ceiling to borrow more money, is for fiscal cowards.

President Obama did not cut spending because he believed in big government and his left-wing base would have erupted. He did not raise taxes to the degree necessary because the taxpaying public would have erupted. So he tried to take the sting out of increasing the debt, ease our consciences, and drain the issue of its moral urgency by promoting the fiction that no new debt is incurred when the debt ceiling is raised. But it *is* new debt. The spending is on the books, but not the debt to pay for it. That's why the debt ceiling is raised – to borrow more money.

I have been chastised for saying that on the debt ceiling, President Obama was hiding the truth or was blinded by left-wing ideology. I'm told it's the kind of personal attack that demeans the public debate. If you believe someone is misrepresenting the truth, or is so misguided that he does not see the truth, are you not allowed to say it? Politicians, whatever their ideology, will not be held accountable if justified criticism is declared out-of-bounds because it might be considered a personal attack. I had no personal beef with President Obama, but any way you spin it, raising the debt ceiling to borrow more money is the present stealing from the future by loading more debt burden onto the future.

I don't mind a president saying we should raise the debt ceiling and take on more debt because reducing spending would damage the nation. I disagree, but that's a policy issue over which reasonable people can differ. I do mind him saying that borrowing more money to cover unfunded spending doesn't increase the debt. Back on page 2 is the 2006 Senator Obama statement against raising the debt ceiling because it would mean "shifting the burden of bad choices today onto the backs of our children and grandchildren." He was convicted in 2011 by his own words in 2006.

When confronted in 2011 with his 2006 statement against raising the debt ceiling, President Obama offered the lame excuse that his 2006 position was political posturing by a new senator who didn't grasp the situation. What about his 2008 campaign statement (page 177) about President Bush running up the debt? How many times can you say "I didn't mean what I said" before your integrity is shot?

I'm adamant on this because it's one of the main reasons I wrote this book. Advocates of big government will say whatever is necessary to mind-massage the public, including pivoting 180 degrees on raising the debt ceiling. They try to play Jedi mind tricks and tell us we do not see the debt increase that we plainly see. Don't let them hypnotize you into nodding along with their "bad choices" that are piling a massive debt burden "onto to the backs of our children and grandchildren." Think of your children and grandchildren being crushed financially by the national debt. If you're young, think of *yourself* being crushed by the debt burden being created now. Reject the liberal/progressive spell the left is trying to cast on you.

I don't mean to place all blame on the left for the debt ceiling charade and the rest of our fiscal crisis. During the Obama presidency, House Republicans whined about being unable to fix our fiscal crisis because the House is only one-half of one-third of the federal government. The Constitution gives fiscal primacy to the House. The House is supposed to be a power-House on fiscal policy. The House was given the power of the purse because it's the part of the federal government closest to the people, with members facing election every other year. The House is supposed to drive policy on taxing and spending. Part of the reason for the Senate and the presidency seizing policy-making power on fiscal issues has been the passivity of the House.

I disagree with those who say raise the debt ceiling with no strings attached, then reform the budget. It will never happen. The same "we'll fix it before the next crisis" refrain surfaces every time the debt ceiling is breached. Those who utter that refrain never deliver on that promise. Why expect that to change?

The House should tell any president to forget about raising the debt ceiling until a balanced budget amendment has been added to the Constitution. Congress immediately should crank out to the states a balanced budget amendment creating a 10-year path to balance (page 190), and states should approve it as soon as possible. Otherwise the debt ceiling should not be raised and the federal government should buckle down to the brutal task of cutting the budget to make spending match revenue.

Either we dramatically chop spending now to match available revenue, or we do it in a more measured manner over 10 years under the pressure of a constitutional provision requiring a balanced budget. Fiscal reformers can no longer do business-as-usual and raise the debt ceiling without getting anything meaningful in return. If the House doesn't have a majority willing to do that, then voters need to press candidates on this and send to Congress those who will form the needed majority.

I can't resist sharing this again:

> *I wish it were possible to obtain a single amendment to our Constitution. I would be willing to depend on that alone for the reduction of the administration of our government to the genuine principles of its Constitution; I mean an additional article taking from the federal government the power of borrowing.*
>
> *Thomas Jefferson, 1798*

Jefferson saw the danger that expanded government would be funded by borrowing. Some apologists for deficit spending note that Jefferson, as president, resorted to borrowing to fund the Louisiana Purchase. True, but at 4 cents per acre, the deal to finance the $15 million purchase price over 20 years was fiscally sound. Meanwhile, Jefferson had annual budget surpluses in all eight years of his presidency. The Louisiana Purchase was paid off as planned and in the 1830s America enjoyed its only debt-free period.

That kind of fiscal responsibility is in our national DNA. We need to rediscover it.

If a president won't agree to a balanced budget amendment, then the House should leave him no option but to make the debt-financing payment without taking on more debt. If he refuses and lets the federal government default on its debt-financing payment, that would unleash unnecessary financial chaos for the nation and world. It would be a violation of the oath to "preserve, protect, and defend the Constitution," which requires financing of the debt.

Congressional Democrats were willing to let the budget process stall – resulting in a partial shutdown of the federal government – in order to block border wall funding in 2018 (page 76). Status quo Republicans run scared from the term "shutdown," which describes the closing of some federal offices when funding runs out because of a failure by the two houses of Congress, or Congress and the president, to reach a budget agreement. Republicans get nervous about being branded unreasonable extremists by hostile media.

Republicans should turn into the fire and attack. They should go on offense and say: "Of course we must shut down huge chunks of the federal government, permanently. The question is whether we do it immediately in a haphazard fashion, or more gradually over 10 years in compliance with a balanced budget provision in the Constitution."

If a president pushes back against a balanced budget

amendment, the House position should be:

> *This budget services the debt and funds defense and other functions of government. We are not shutting down anything. We are funding government. Sign this budget or veto it and shut down the government. It's your choice. But you are a president, not a dictator. The Constitution gives us the power of the purse and any budget you get WILL NOT EXCEED AVAILABLE REVENUE. Will you risk debt default and jeopardize national security, Social Security payments, and other functions of government because you want to keep stealing from the future by running up more debt?*

If a president refuses to cooperate, then he owns resulting shutdowns, debt default, and whatever else follows.

The left regularly threatens to shut down the federal government if the budget does not subsidize Planned Parenthood. Congress should produce a budget that says to the left and any president:

> *This budget services the debt and funds defense and other functions of government, but not an organization that cannibalizes aborted babies for money. That $500 million has been redirected to women's health providers that do not engage in such activities.*
>
> *We are not shutting down anything. We are funding government. Taxpayer funding for Planned Parenthood is 1/10,000 of the budget. Only an over-the-top zealot for abortion would shut down 99.99% of government to protest .01% that still is going to women's health.*
>
> *Sign this budget or veto it and shut down the government. It's your choice. But you*

*are a president, not a dictator. The Consti-*
*tution gives us the power of the purse and*
*any budget you get WILL NOT FUND*
*PLANNED PARENTHOOD. Will you risk*
*debt default and jeopardize national secu-*
*rity, Social Security payments, and other*
*functions of government because you*
*want to give taxpayer dollars to an organ-*
*ization that brags about aborting babies in*
*ways that maximize the commercial value*
*of the victims' body parts for sale?*

If we prioritize and reduce spending immediately, what does that look like? On a monthly basis in round numbers, absent something extreme such as a pandemic, the U.S. collects $290 billion in revenue and spends $370 billion, with $30 billion spent on servicing the debt. The Constitution requires that the debt payment be made, so we start there. Social Security and Medicare recipients paid into those programs and planned their retirements on them, so those benefits must be paid. Contractors must be paid for goods and services delivered, though contracts for future projects might be casualties.

The debt-financing payment, Social Security, and Medicare total about $170 billion per month, leaving about $120 billion in unspent revenue. But there's still $200 billion per month in spending that must be covered.

To eliminate that deficit of $80 billion per month, other budget items would be subject to significant cuts. Most of the reduction would come from nonmilitary payroll. I am sorry for the pain this would cause people who would lose their jobs, but it has to happen. We can't keep going on the way we have been. The question is whether it happens immediately or gradually over a decade.

I prefer the gradual approach so those affected have time to plan their next move, but only if the Constitution is amended to require the budget to balance within a decade. Absent that guarantee, the budget cutting starts now and goes deep enough to avoid additional borrowing.

If I could get an audience with leading defenders of the status quo, Republicans as well as Democrats, my question would be: What is your end game? We can't keep borrowing or generating extra money forever to cover our deficit spending. Eventually creditors will pull the plug. Even if they don't, the value of our currency will be destroyed. We don't want to live in a society where the top tax rate is back up to 90% and it costs $100 to buy a loaf of bread. That's not what we want for our children and grandchildren.

I suppose defenders of the status quo already have given their answer: raise taxes and have the federal government take over more of society. But that still won't pay for all the spending. Plus it kills jobs and economic growth as business owners – the non-cronies not getting special favors from the government – go into a protective shell.

We who want better are up against people who think our capitalist system will keep producing enough revenue to serve government no matter how hard and often government bashes the capitalist system. The bashers of capitalism are going to produce a living hell for us, and an enduring hell for our children and grandchildren.

Several friends have asked why I advocate such a high-pressure course of action. My experience serving in local and state elected office and working in local, state, and federal government tells me that there is ***no way*** defenders of the status quo will change anything unless they are subjected to enormous pressure. That means denying the option of borrowing and forcing an immediate and severe budget-cutting showdown if they won't accept a balanced budget amendment.

Even that kind of pressure might not be enough. Recall the alcoholism analogy. You can't negotiate with people who don't want to change. I don't see defenders of the status quo ever weaning themselves and the nation from the unsustainable system they have created. They must be defeated in elections. We need a new majority serious about fixing our fiscal crisis by restoring limited government.

\* \* \*

Defeatist Republicans say: What can we really do to challenge the Washington status quo?

Don't curse the darkness and give in. Light a candle and fight for your convictions. Light a candle in every district and state across the country. It's a numbers game. District by district and state by state, win seats and build a majority that *can* change the system, as the Tea Party is doing.

I was hard on Speaker Gingrich earlier in this book, but he was brilliant in seeing the need for, and executing, the Contract with America national strategy in 1994. We must embrace that kind of national approach and break out of the typical congressional "fiefdom" mentality. Too many representatives have decided that the country is going down the drain, but they're happy as long as they can get some pork from the federal barrel for their districts.

It isn't just members of Congress. The argument is the same in districts across the country: we have to stick with our incumbent; he's the chairman of a committee that can help our local businesses; we can't save the country, so we want someone in Congress who will get whatever he can for us while there's still something to get.

The minimal value of an incumbent's position for most of us drops to zero for everyone when the value of our currency collapses and our economy collapses because of the failure of dozens of status quo committee and subcommittee chairmen to do anything meaningful to fix our fiscal crisis.

The Tea Party understands that we are facing the third major crisis of our national history. I know I'm right about this because Dr. Larry Arnn, president of Hillsdale College, sees it similarly. A few years ago, one of my brothers signed me up for the free online class on the Constitution offered by Hillsdale. One of the first things I came across was a similar argument about America facing a moment of truth that ranks with the American Revolution and the Civil War. We did not have to break out of our colonial relationship with England. We could have split into separate nations in the 1860s. We made choices about what we wanted to be and where we wanted to go as a nation.

We have another choice to make. The issue of limited government versus unlimited government is as fundamental to the future of America as the issue of independence versus colonialism was in the 1770s, and abolition/union versus slavery/secession was in the 1850s. There were strong and passionate arguments for rejecting independence, and for allowing slavery and secession, just as there are strong and passionate arguments today for unlimited government. I'll say it again: reasonable people are not going to agree on everything, so it comes down to majority rule. I and others of like mind must convince a majority of fellow citizens to join the crusade to restore limited government.

Speaking of the 1850s, the Republican Party had better wake up before it goes the way of the Whig Party, which the Republican Party displaced. For two decades starting in the early 1830s, the Whigs (a party name taken from British politics) were the other major political party along with the Democrats. On slavery, Whigs tried to remain neutral and preserve the status quo, much like modern Republicans try to remain neutral and preserve the status quo on the federal welfare/entitlement system.

A major party remains a major party by taking a strong position on the defining issue of the era. Democrats were willing to die for slavery and secession. Republicans ran Whigs off the stage of American politics because Republicans were willing to charge into territory where Whigs feared to tread – a bold position in favor of abolition. The Whig Party became irrelevant because nobody on either side of the abolition/union versus slavery/secession debate was interested in a party afraid to take a decisive position on the issue that would determine the nation's future.

The Democratic Party is a force today because it has taken an emphatic "yes" position on the defining issue of our time – whether to embrace unlimited government and the federal welfare/entitlement system as the way to provide the best for the most. Bursts of Republican strength at the federal level, starting with Reagan in 1980, have happened when voters thought the Republican Party stood for limited-government conservatism.

The Tea Party is trying to save the Republican Party, not ruin it. The Republican Party won the presidency in 2016 because the Tea Party rallied to Donald Trump. I'm not calling for the Tea Party to displace the Republican Party as the Republicans displaced the Whigs. I'm calling on Republicans to embrace and incorporate the Tea Party movement as a catalyst for another Gingrich-style national effort. This time the goal is to remove the looters from Congress and build a majority of crusaders for limited government. There is an opportunity to rekindle a Reagan coalition that includes Democrats who don't want to be fiscally incinerated by the lava flow of debt.

Political consultants say that's crazy talk. They say when voters are addicted to big government, you don't win elections by promising small government. Regardless of what people say, they love Social Security and Medicare and the rest of the welfare/entitlement system, and they will smash anyone who messes with the status quo and tries to do something foolish like balance the budget and restore limited government.

If that's true, then we're done as the nation that produces the best for the most. America will decline into an expanding group of whiners demanding that a shrinking group of providers pay more taxes to subsidize the whiners.

This is where leadership comes into play. Leadership sometimes requires you to stake out a new position and start waving your arms and shouting: "Hey, we're going the wrong way! Our future is this way, not that way!"

I know from experience that challenging the status quo and trying to lead in a new direction can be risky. As a state senator, I tried to overhaul Nebraska's K-12 education funding system. As a county commissioner, I tried to pursue city-county merger. I was squashed in both cases by defenders of the status quo. Some were office-holding colleagues. Some were bureaucrats. Some were unions and other special interests.

You don't lose if you don't give up.

The Tea Party is proof that a growing number of voters are snapping out of the welfare/entitlement trance that has numbed the electorate for most of the last century. It's OK now for candidates and politicians to talk to voters as rational adults capable of handling reality.

In 2009, Republican candidate Chris Christie told New Jersey voters that as governor he would challenge the public-sector unions. He did so with such conviction that people all over the country wanted him to run for president in 2012, and he did in 2016.

In 2010, Tea Party congressional candidates all over the country told voters they were going to challenge the status quo. Voters liked what they heard and produced a Republican majority in the House because of the jolt of enthusiasm generated by Tea Party candidates.

Republican candidate Scott Walker told Wisconsin voters in 2010 that if elected governor he would challenge the status quo dominated by public-sector unions. He was elected and did so. Defenders of the status quo tried to throw Walker out, but in a 2012 recall election he won a higher percentage of votes than he did in 2010. Walker's 2014 re-election victory made three wins in four years. Like Governor Christie, he developed a national following that generated a presidential campaign in 2016. Relentless attacks by the left eroded Walker's support enough that he lost by a percentage point in his 2018 re-election bid, but it was quite a run for a conservative in a traditionally blue state.

Critics started chiseling a tombstone for the Tea Party after the 2012 election, but that cycle yielded Senator Cruz from Texas, a Tea Party favorite who probably would have won the 2016 Republican presidential primary if not for Trump.

In Nebraska's May 2014 Republican Senate primary, political newcomer Ben Sasse ran as a Tea Party candidate and won a dominating victory in a field including three other very strong candidates. A month later came the stunning primary election upset of House Majority Leader Eric Cantor by Tea Party candidate Dave Brat in Virginia. Sasse and Brat won in November 2014 as part of a wave of Republican victories across the country. The force that generated the wave was the Tea Party.

President Trump beat the establishment of both major parties in 2016 because the Tea Party saw him as the populist champion who would "drain the swamp" in D.C.

Establishment Republicans say they steer clear of Tea Party "extremism" so they can live to fight another day. But fight for what? What are they fighting for other than their paychecks and pensions? They talk Tea Party to constituents at home in their districts, but vote establishment when they're back in Washington.

It reminds me of socialist George Orwell's *Animal Farm*, an allegory slamming the Stalinist Soviet Union as a betrayal of socialism. Farm animals were the exploited workers of the story. They counted on their leaders to fight for change and improve their lot. As the animals watched a meeting between their leaders and human leaders, they couldn't tell the difference between the two groups. Leaders of the two groups had become indistinguishable. The agendas of the animal leaders and the human leaders were basically the same – make deals to preserve their positions and maintain the status quo.

Status quo Republicans remind me of the Scottish nobles in the movie *Braveheart*. The nobles despised populist William Wallace and his grassroots movement fighting for Scotland's independence from England. They joined Wallace for a few battles and feigned loyalty to the cause, but in the big showdown with the English king, the Battle of Falkirk, with Wallace and his foot soldiers engaged in battle and counting on the nobles to serve as cavalry, the nobles rode away from the field. The Scots were routed.

The betrayal by the nobles is historical fact, but history does not tell us why they did it. Was it cowardice? Were they jealous of Wallace? The movie portrayed it as a deal with the English king to expand the nobles' land holdings.

Whatever their motives, the nobles acted to preserve their positions and maintain the status quo.

Establishment Republicans treat the Tea Party the same way the Scottish nobles treated the Wallace movement. They play along with the populist Tea Party when it suits them, but ultimately they want the Tea Party to fail and go away. Sometimes they help make it happen.

Voters can cross party lines in a Mississippi primary

election. In a 2014 Republican primary run-off election in Mississippi, establishment Republicans pulled a "Falkirk" and collaborated with the other side. They inflamed black Democrats against Tea Party challenger Chris McDaniel with racially provocative messages, and recruited them to vote for incumbent U.S. Senator Thad Cochran in the Republican primary. It worked. Cochran won 51% of the vote.

Some Republican candidates and office holders were spooked and stampeded into abandoning presidential candidate Trump when the Access Hollywood groping clip became public a month before the November 2016 election. Trump was not my choice among the primary election candidates, but I did everything I could to help him win the general election because with Trump there was a chance of getting the kind of course correction our country so desperately needs. Don't tell me that the way to strengthen the Republican Party and best serve the nation was to squander a winnable race, let a thoroughly corrupt Hillary Clinton become president, and let the left gain a more commanding position.

The Falkirk Republicans who abandoned Trump at the moment of truth tried to cover their betrayal by proposing a crazy, desperate, pathetic, bush-league plan – swapping in Trump's running mate, Mike Pence, as a magic candidate right before the election. Pence is a fine man, but he had not run for president and was not well-known by the general public. This is like having your football team's offense down near the opponent's goal line in the final minute of the game with a chance to score a touchdown and win the championship; suddenly you pull your starting quarterback, the one who got you in position to win the championship, and replace him with someone who has been solid in practice as a backup, but has not played in a game all season. What are your fans going to think of that? What are Republican voters supposed to think when record numbers of them picked Trump, but Republican Party leaders still wanted to deny them their choice?

After Trump won, Never Trumpers and those who said Trump should step down as the nominee called for a healing balm of Lincolnesque good will – malice toward none, charity for all. They said let's not get sidetracked by revenge and payback; let's move forward and focus on policy. It reminded me of a scene in *Monty Python and the Holy Grail*. An overzealous Sir Lancelot goes charging into a crowd gathered for a wedding, swinging his sword, slashing and killing several people, including the best man. The father of the groom, who wants the wedding to proceed no matter what so he can expand his land holdings, intervenes and says: "This is supposed to be a happy occasion; let's not bicker and argue about who killed who[m]."

There were gaping holes in Trump's back where some people on the right stuck knives. Trump was properly gracious in his victory speech, but there should have been some degree of accountability for the terrible wrongs done by Falkirk Republicans to someone who won the Republican presidential nomination fair and square.

Never Trumpers were back at it in 2020. They undermined the Trump candidacy and helped the candidate backed by socialist Green New Dealers, advocates of males in women's bathrooms, kneelers for the national anthem, and practitioners of the society-wrecking violence typical of "antifa" and Black Lives Matter.

Maybe we should call Never Trumpers "Black Lives Matter" Republicans. Most BLM protesters are hypocrites. They want to have it both ways. They love to bash police, but they want that thin blue line to continue to exist. They behave as if they want a world without police, but they would not want to live in and be responsible for the societal damage that would result if they got their way. They want police to rescue and protect them when they need it. It boils down to: I want police protection, but I won't demean myself by supporting the police.

It's the same with BLM Republicans. They would have lived in, and been responsible for, the economic and societal damage that would have resulted if they had gotten their way and prevented Trump from winning in 2016. It boils down to: I want the benefits of a Trump victory, but I won't demean myself by supporting him.

We'll see how it works out for them now that they got in 2020 the Trump defeat they said they wanted.

Conservatives must make these connivers own the 2020 Trump defeat and then shove them out of the way and take control of the Republican Party. A major mistake by conservatism was not fully capitalizing on the Reagan phenomenon. The Republican establishment despised Reagan, just as it despises Trump. The establishment put up with Reagan because it had no choice. Like Trump, Reagan broke through to the people and won.

After Reagan, the establishment pushed forward for president one of its own – Reagan's vice president, George H.W. Bush. He road Reagan's coattails to victory in 1988.

In 1992, President Bush lost his bid for re-election because he could not help his establishment nature. As a candidate in 1988 he had promised no increase in the federal tax burden – "read my lips, no new taxes" – but as president he signed a tax increase into law. That sealed his 1992 defeat.

The Republican Party continued nominating establishment candidates for president. In 2000, I thought I was voting for a Reagan conservative in George W. Bush, but he increased government spending at more than twice the rate President Clinton did in the 1990s (page 115).

The establishment doesn't care about the Constitution or limited government or founding values. The establishment doesn't want to change the game of big government. The establishment wants to be in charge of the game.

We must make conservatism the guiding ideology of the Republican Party, but there is debate about what "conservative" means. Dr. Arnn at Hillsdale says conservatives believe that "things that have had a good reputation for a long time are more trustworthy than new things." A new thing or idea should not be adopted simply because it is new; it must prove it is superior to what it seeks to replace.

The flipside of that premise is that nothing is immune from scrutiny. Just because something has been around for a long time does not mean it deserves continued support. A conservative will embrace change if the facts justify it.

That brings us back to the argument that will decide the future of America.

The left argues for a new way based on the New Deal (featuring Social Security), the Great Society (featuring welfare payments, Medicaid, and Medicare), Obamacare, and Green New Deal Build Back Better socialism. The left says the new way is proving itself superior to, and thus should replace, the old way based on capitalism and limited government under the Constitution.

I argue that 80 years of facts and evidence prove that the new way is inferior to the old way. And it is not the "old" way. Limited-government capitalism is the timeless, ageless, eternal way to provide the best for the most. The first three years of the Trump presidency, featuring reduction of tax and regulatory burdens, reminded us what America can do and be when it moves *toward* limited-government capitalism instead of away from it.

American conservatism at its core means belief in limited government under the Constitution. You can't claim to be conservative if you support unconstitutional welfare/entitlement programs. Yet many conservatives support Social Security and Medicare as things with a good reputation for a long time that should be preserved.

Buckle up; it's time to examine the "good reputation" of two leftist poison pills that are killing the American way of life.

# Social Security & Medicare: The Problem

By permission of Jeff Koterba.

The cartoon above was published in April 2012 in the *Omaha World-Herald* to mark the centennial of the Titanic. It shows what's in store for the fiscal and ideological mistakes called Social Security and Medicare.

\* \* \*

Social Security was sold to the public as a retirement system, but it is pure socialism. The clue is in its very name.

The left engineered enactment of the federal income tax in 1913 to grow the federal government according to the progressive agenda. Twenty years later the left wanted more revenue for bigger government. Answer: Social Security, a flat tax on income stacked on top of the progressive income tax. Some of it goes to retirement benefits to keep everyone happy, but Social Security was ruled constitutional by the

Supreme Court as a way of raising "social insurance" revenue for unrestricted redistribution of wealth. Read the 1935 statute creating Social Security. Or just look at your paycheck. FICA stands for Federal *Insurance* Contributions Act, not Federal *Retirement* Contributions Act.

The constitutionality of Social Security was based on a flawed interpretation of Article I, Section 8, Clause 1 (page 125) as a grant of unlimited taxing authority to Congress. The Supreme Court said the federal government can levy a tax for the "general welfare" and spend it any way it wants. Social Security has been treated as an all-purpose slush fund for all manner of federal spending. That was fun until the demand for payments to Social Security recipients surpassed the supply of FICA payroll tax revenue coming in.

Some people are furious to learn that there is no buildup of Social Security savings because any surplus revenue has been scooped off and spent on other government programs. But at the time the constitutionality of Social Security was challenged, the fact that FICA payroll tax revenue could be spent on anything was cited as proof that the tax served the general welfare and, therefore, was constitutional.

Citizens also are infuriated to learn that they have no right to Social Security benefits as retirees. The Supreme Court has ruled that contributors to Social Security do *not* have a contractual right to receive retirement benefits. That sounds crazy, but go to the Social Security Administration website and type in *Flemming v. Nestor*. It's a 1960 Supreme Court ruling confirming that the federal government can do anything it wants with FICA payroll tax revenue and change the deal for the taxpayer at any time.

Ephram Nestor sued the federal government for Social Security benefits. He had paid into Social Security for 19 years and became eligible for benefits in 1955. The next year he was cut off because he was deported for having been a communist in the 1930s. Nestor argued that because he had paid into Social Security all those years, he had contractual and property rights to receive benefits regardless of his political beliefs and status. The Supreme Court said no, Social Security is an unconditional redistribution-of-wealth tax, not an annuity or pension plan or retirement fund.

Think about that: making payments to Social Security during your working life does *not* create a right to receive retirement benefits when your turn comes. Admit it: you side with the former communist on this one. I certainly do.

*　*　*

Do an Internet search for "Social Security checks to dead people" and you'll find that Social Security spends hundreds of millions of dollars annually paying benefits to dead people, overpaying benefits to live people, and paying benefits to the wrong people.

Even if the bureaucracy worked flawlessly, Social Security is fiscally unsustainable. According to Social Security's website, when Social Security was created in 1935, Congress was told that the payroll tax for a citizen would never exceed 3%, and no more than $3,000 of annual income would be subject to the tax. That would be a maximum annual tax of $90. Today the rate is 6.2% and the amount of annual income subject to the Social Security payroll tax is nearly $140,000. If you make $100,000 a year, that's an annual tax of $6,200.

Add another $1,450 (1.45%) per year for Medicare, enacted in 1965.

The Social Security website says Congress also was told in 1935 that by 1980 Social Security would pay out $3.5 billion per year and have a reserve of $47 billion.

Reality: By 1980, Social Security was paying out more than $120 billion per year and was approaching bankruptcy. Emergency amendments to Social Security were adopted in 1983. That's when Social Security became known as the "third rail" of American politics, as in the live electric rail running parallel to the tracks of a subway train – touch it and you die. Such was the addiction of the American people to this entitlement. Despite the fiscal calamity Social Security had become, the prime directive of politicians was to do whatever was necessary to preserve Social Security.

Social Security now exceeds $1 *trillion* annually.

The numbers are similarly calamitous for Medicare. When it was created in 1965, it cost $3 billion per year and was projected to cost $12 billion per year in 1990.

Reality: Medicare cost $107 billion in 1990. It exceeded $500 billion in 2010. It's nearly $700 billion today.

What accounts for the massively mistaken numbers? The main reason is that average American life expectancy in 1935 was just shy of 62 years. Today it approaches 80. Creators of Social Security did not expect many Americans to actually collect the benefit. Remember, these were leftists looking for additional revenue to fund their dream of a national liberal/progressive/socialist mega-state. Social Security revenue was intended for that, not retirees.

The left figured out how to get some of it back. Social Security benefits initially were not taxed. They are now.

During the Obama administration, Republicans accused Democrats of trying to cut $700 billion from Medicare over 10 years to help fund Obamacare. News agencies quoted President Obama saying the same thing in 2009. Then he and Democrats said there was no cutting of Medicare, just an elimination of waste, fraud, and abuse. Even if that's true, that means there is on average $70 billion a year of waste, fraud, and abuse in Medicare!

I dare you to peer into the future at the unfunded liability for Social Security and Medicare. Estimates vary, but the consensus is that unfunded liability is from $50 trillion to $100 trillion for Social Security and Medicare, with about two-thirds of it Medicare. That's right; as bad as the numbers are for Social Security, in the long run Medicare is an even worse fiscal nightmare. Add obligations for federal pensions and the subsidized prescription drug entitlement of 2003 and, any way you figure it, we're well north of $100 trillion in unfunded entitlement liability.

This means taxpayers are on the hook for more than $100 *trillion* to fund these entitlement payments. It's further proof that limited government is not extremism; America is in an extreme fiscal crisis because it has abandoned limited government. If all of us live out our lives according to statistical probabilities, we will collect more than $100 trillion in entitlement benefits. There are about 100 million taxpayers, so if you break down this liability by taxpayer, that's a tax burden of $1 million apiece. Let's say the payout will happen over the next 50 years. That's an annual average of $2 trillion, or $20,000 per taxpayer – in addition to the tax burden for the rest of government. Younger generations are destined for a lifelong fiscal mauling.

\* \* \*

I get it. Americans have developed a warm, fuzzy feeling for Social Security and Medicare. We all pitch in together and take care of each other. That was the approach Plymouth Colony took in the early 1620s before the switch to capitalism (pages 97-98). The creators of Social Security and Medicare produced a disaster because they did the same thing Plymouth Colony did initially; they strayed from natural law and the founding values of self-reliance and personal responsibility.

Politicians talk tough on fiscal reform and say "everything is on the table." Then you find out that the two biggest things on the table, Social Security and Medicare, together more than 40% of the federal budget, are taken off the table.

"Any serious plan to tackle our deficit will require us to put everything on the table," said President Obama in an April 2011 speech supporting an increase of the debt ceiling. Then in the same speech he took Social Security and Medicare off the table. Why? Because of "a conviction that each one of us deserves some basic measure of security and dignity . . . so we contribute to programs like Medicare and Social Security, which guarantee us health care and a measure of basic income after a lifetime of hard work."

Obama also said in that speech that "we saved millions of seniors from poverty with Social Security and Medicare" and that America "would not be a great country without those commitments."

Republicans are equally culpable for the failure to reform Social Security and Medicare. In 2012, then-Indiana Governor Mitch Daniels delivered the Republican response to President Obama's State of the Union Address. The middle part was a love letter to Social Security and Medicare: "We must unite to save the safety net [comprised of Social Security and Medicare] so future Americans are protected" by these "proud programs." He wanted to pretend the numbers can work if we means-test for benefits. He ignored the reality that there can be no such thing as limited government while Social Security and Medicare exist.

If that's the ideology we now embrace – that the "proud" mission of our "great country" is to have the federal government guarantee citizens a certain standard of living and save us all from old age – then I say again that we're done as the nation that produces the best for the most. The proud mission of our great country is to provide the best for the most, but not through a federal welfare/entitlement system.

In 2010, President Obama led a celebration of the 75th birthday of Social Security. If Social Security is as American as baseball and apple pie, why were President Obama and congressional Republicans using the *defunding* of Social Security as a way to score political points on each other? I'm talking about the temporary reduction of the payroll tax that funds Social Security, the 2% cut that expired at the end of 2012. It was celebrated as a middle-class tax cut, which it was, but what about funding Social Security benefits while the revenue stream that funds Social Security was reduced? Democrats wanted to pile an extra tax on top of "the rich." Republicans initially made bold statements about budget cuts to make up for the reduced revenue for Social Security. They abandoned that charade and agreed to let the deficit increase by $100 billion.

Until 2011, Social Security collected enough revenue to pay benefits to retirees. Then demographics finally caught up. Payments to recipients began to exceed revenue. The disparity will grow as baby boomers retire.

In the face of this reality, the director of the Office of Management and Budget said Social Security is not part of the fiscal problem. How do people in such positions get away with saying such things?

The OMB director was referring to the fact that pre-2011 Social Security revenue surpluses were used to buy U.S. Treasury bonds. He said Social Security is not a fiscal problem because those bond purchases will be paid back to Social Security with interest by the U.S. Treasury.

But what does that mean? It means that surplus Social Security revenue was not put in a "trust fund" or "lock box" for safe keeping until retirees need it. Surplus funds were sent to the federal treasury to purchase bonds. Social Security got paper IOUs called bonds while the federal treasury got dollars from Social Security that were spent on other government programs. There is no Social Security surplus. The "asset" on which Social Security relies is a stack of paper, a stack of Treasury IOUs to pay off bonds held by Social Security. But the federal government is running annual deficits as its debt soars. Where will the federal treasury get the funds needed to pay back those IOUs? And that's not counting a tsunami of retiree claims about to break over the nation as baby boomers become eligible for Social Security.

Then-Texas Governor Rick Perry, while still a Republican candidate for president in 2012, was right to call Social Security a Ponzi scheme. It's a multi-level system with a lot of money flowing through it, but no real assets. One level of "investors" has to shake down the next level below them. Or in this case, one generation of Americans shakes down the next generation. If the younger generation complains about the increasing tax burden, the older generation says: "When it's your turn, you can demand whatever you need from the next generation. Meanwhile, shut up and pay up because it's our turn to cash in."

Defenders of Social Security say they have paid into the program and are entitled to collect from it. But there is no correlation between contributions and benefits. Like any Ponzi scheme, the system is great for those who get in early. The first regular Social Security recipient, Ida May Fuller, paid $24.75 into the program and lived long enough to receive nearly $23,000 from it. The return is not as good for those who get in later and pay into Social Security for 40 years. If you live long enough it can still be a net gain financially, but you'd better be healthy and have long-life genes. A 2011 Urban Institute study concluded that a couple retiring after paying $598,000 into Social Security would receive only $556,000 in benefits if the husband lived to 82 and the wife to 85.

In 1940, there were 160 workers contributing to Social Security for every 1 recipient of benefits. That ratio is now 3-to-1. As workers contribute more to fund retirees who live longer, and as taxes increase while benefits decrease to keep the system solvent, the likelihood grows that people will collect from Social Security less than they put in.

Some people die before collecting anything from Social Security, never mind the value of what they contributed. And because surpluses over the years have been spent on other areas of government, the well-meaning citizen who has contributed to Social Security his whole working life has to become a shakedown thug and squeeze younger taxpayers for higher payroll taxes to fund his retirement as the ratio of workers to retirees goes down.

It's not as if Social Security provides a king's ransom. The average annual payout is $15,000 and the maximum is $30,000. Because previous annual Social Security revenue surpluses have been squandered, confiscatory taxes will be required to maintain even those meager benefit levels.

The Treasury Department owes Social Security a lot of money, roughly $2.5 trillion. But there's no money in federal coffers to pay back Social Security. Additional revenue will be required of taxpayers to repay Social Security and keep up with those 15-figure unfunded liabilities. Taxpayers will have to be gouged for higher payroll taxes or higher income taxes, or both. Some analysts predict that the federal government will go after citizens' private retirement accounts and any other piles of money the federal government thinks it can raid. We're on the road to Cyprus, the European nation raiding its citizens' bank accounts to pay for failed liberal/progressive/socialist fiscal policies.

* * *

I was working for Senator Hagel from Nebraska in 1999 and we were riding to a speech he was to give. We got to talking about entitlements and I said Social Security was a terrible policy and we had to find a way out of it. The man who had won election to the Senate in 1996 on the slogan "less government, more personal responsibility" slowly shook his head no. He said the people had become too accustomed to Social Security and would not give it up. I don't dispute Senator Hagel's analysis at that time. I hope the Tea Party is changing that reality.

It is a challenge. In the debt ceiling showdown in the summer of 2011, President Obama used Social Security to scare recipients into demanding that Republicans raise the debt ceiling. He wondered aloud whether Social Security payments for the next month would go out absent an agreement to raise the debt ceiling.

That brings to mind what former Vice President Al Gore screamed about the way he claimed President George W. Bush marshaled political support for the decision to invade Iraq: "He played on our fears!"

Nanny government's warning that Social Security checks might be delayed was a lesson in what is really at stake: power. Again, no one can look at Social Security and say it's fine, leave it on autopilot. Yet many Democratic and Republican office holders do just that. Why? Because a powerful voting bloc of Social Security recipients now exists, and it's about to grow dramatically. That power flows to you if you can convince that bloc that you are its savior and protector. Make that bloc dependent on you, and you can wield significant power by telling benefit recipients that they'll be cut off if they can't help you get those other bums to agree to whatever the savior/protector says is necessary to keep the Social Security checks coming.

When Governor Perry, running in the 2012 Republican

presidential primary, denounced Social Security as a Ponzi scheme, rival Mitt Romney said the Republican Party would be "obliterated" if it nominated for the presidency someone critical of Social Security. If that's true, it's because Republicans as well as Democrats have failed to lead on reform of Social Security. Instead of being honest about the failure Social Security has proven to be, establishment Republicans intone the same stale rhetoric about protecting Social Security and cherishing senior citizens.

There is no debate or division among Democrats, at least not among party leaders. The Democratic Party is the pro-welfare/entitlement party. Democrats will fight to the political death to preserve welfare/entitlement programs, and Social Security is the granddaddy of them all.

The consensus of the social engineers who want to preserve Social Security is: OK, the initial plan and projections were flawed, but now we know all the variables and have some experience on which to base future plans and projections; it's the greatest government program of all time and now we know how to perfect it.

Conservative economist Friedrich Hayek called this the fatal conceit of leftist planners. Hayek drew from Adam Smith, who said:

> *The man of system . . . is apt to be very wise in his own conceit; and is often so enamoured with the supposed beauty of his own ideal plan of government, that he cannot suffer the smallest deviation from any part of it. . . . He seems to imagine that he can arrange the different members of a great society with as much ease as the hand arranges the different pieces upon a chess-board.*

The left does not know everything about the present, never mind the future. No person, think tank, or government agency, no matter how smart and well-intentioned, can comprehend and plan for every contingency of the human condition, especially the farther into the future you try to exercise control. No one knows for sure what demographic changes will occur, or what triumphs and calamities will affect America and the world. Why do we allow the left to impose on America untenable social engineering schemes such as Social Security and Medicare? Let American society evolve and adapt with personal and communal initiative at the state and local level instead of expanding, and growing more dependent on, the federal government to handle every challenge.

That can be a hard sell because there is political gain to be achieved by scaring the hell out of people and then promising to save them with the federal government. Democrats run the same basic ad on Social Security against Republicans everywhere, claiming that Republicans are enemies of senior citizens if they challenge the status quo on Social Security.

I understand the reluctance to deal with Social Security and Medicare, but if Republicans won't take the lead on Social Security and Medicare reform, then they do not deserve the support of fiscal conservatives. Why support a party that won't do anything meaningful to stop entitlement spending from spinning out of control? Why support a party trying to out-promise Democrats on Medicare, which in the long run is more of a budget-buster than Social Security? Why support a party that ignores a future featuring unfunded federal entitlement liability of $50 trillion to $100 trillion, nothing in the federal treasury to cover the IOUs to Social Security, and one generation shaking down the next for ever-increasing payroll taxes?

This is the fiscal reality that has driven me to the Tea Party. I'm done with politicians who play at the fringes of the problem while these giant fiscal asteroids of unfunded entitlement liability are coming at us. Maybe Jeff Koterba can help drive the point home with a cartoon showing asteroids labeled "Social Security" and "Medicare" on a collision course toward America. Fix it now and destroy the asteroids before they clobber us.

# Social Security & Medicare: The Solution

The solution is that we phase out Social Security and Medicare and take responsibility for our own retirement and health care.

I envision a buyout of Social Security and Medicare for Americans under age 55. The federal government would pay back with interest every dollar citizens under 55 have contributed to Social Security and Medicare. The buyout would be financed by selling federal government bonds. Using a ballpark figure of $10 trillion at 5% interest to cover the buyout, the federal government would pay bondholders $500 billion per year for 80 years, then an additional $10 trillion when the bonds reach maturity. That additional $10 trillion would be funded by putting $100 billion in an interest-bearing account and leaving it alone for 80 years.

That sounds like a long time, but remember that it took 80 years to get into this predicament. It also sounds like a lot of money, spending $50 trillion to pay off $10 trillion. But it pales in comparison to the many trillions more we'll have to spend if we continue the status quo. And this expenditure is stable from year to year with an end in sight.

Citizens 55-or-over would be allowed to participate in Social Security and Medicare if they don't want to participate in the buyout. Social Security and Medicare would be phased out over 40 years or so as participants die.

The FICA payroll tax would be eliminated, so the return to limited government becomes all the more imperative. We'll need a trillion dollars per year to fund recipients in the phase-out period. That funding must come from money freed up by the dismantling of departments of government outside the authorization of the Constitution.

Economists whose judgment I trust warn that a buyout of this magnitude could attract a huge portion of investment capital that otherwise would go to the private sector. I do not want to starve the private sector of capital. If there is a better way to accomplish a phase-out, I will support it. But we must do it. We must find a way to reimburse Americans for their FICA payroll tax contributions and work our way out of Social Security and Medicare.

The left will fight this. It doesn't want the federal government to lose the power that comes from making Social Security and Medicare recipients dependent on the federal government as the guardian of recipients' retirement and health care benefits.

The left will argue that people aren't competent to provide for their own retirement and health care. Conservatives have faith in the common man. Americans don't need to have their interests managed by a government that "knows better." Of course there are some people who need to have their affairs managed by others, but most people can manage their own retirement and health care. If citizens want guidance, they can get it from the private sector, the public sector, or volunteer organizations.

A common criticism is that it's too risky to expose people's retirement investments to the ups and downs of the stock market. Those totally invested in one company or stock are vulnerable, but those who hold on to an array of stocks generally recover over the long-term what they lose in short-term crises. Mutual funds or exchange-traded funds, which rely on holdings in dozens of companies or stocks, are relatively crisis-proof. If you want more certainty, invest in bonds, annuities, trusts, or some other form of virtually risk-free investment.

That's what most people believe Social Security is, a risk-free guaranteed retirement payment. You make regular contributions during your working life in return for guaranteed regular payments in retirement. But remember that the law does *not* recognize Social Security as a contract for retirement benefits. Politically, there would be an uproar if the federal government stopped paying Social Security retirement benefits to recipients who have paid into the system expecting such benefits. Yet the fact remains that the federal government can do anything it wants with your payroll tax revenue and change the deal on you at any time. A private sector financial program locking in payments for the recipient would be backed by law as a binding contract.

There is a way for the government to fund Social Security that is not available to the private sector. The government can raise taxes and collect more revenue. Some triumphantly cite this as proof that Social Security is the best option for funding retirement. I see it as proof that Social Security is an economy-wrecking financial sledgehammer.

If the government is afraid to raise taxes high enough to pay off the Treasury IOUs held by Social Security, it could sell bonds. However, paying off existing debt by generating new debt still sticks future taxpayers with the tab for today's overspending. (My solution creates new debt, but it would be capped, controlled, and eventually retired.)

Advocates of Social Security present various "what ifs." What if the value of the dollar plummets, so I am paid in retirement with dollars worth less than the ones I paid in to my private sector retirement program? What if the company paying my annuity goes out of business? What if I get caught up in an Enron type of scandal in which a corrupt company destroys my next egg?

The only way to eliminate all economic risk is to adopt a totalitarian system with the government controlling all aspects of economic life. Yet even that is not a permanent guarantee of economic safety because eventually such a system will dry up and fail for lack of productivity and prosperity. See: Venezuela, one of the richest and most successful countries in South America 15 years ago, reduced by a decade of socialist tyranny to an economic disaster area collapsing in spasms of poverty, corruption, and violence.

There is no such thing as a guarantee of total economic security. If you want a government that will make such a promise and destroy an economy trying to deliver on it, move to a socialist or communist country. In America, we're getting off the road that leads to the defunct Soviet bloc, Cyprus and much of Europe, Cuba, Venezuela, North Korea, and other leftist failures.

Critics have said: you propose a phase-out of Social Security and Medicare without offering a solution to replace them. I do offer a solution – but it doesn't involve the federal government. The solution is you. The solution is me. The solution is Americans taking responsibility for our own retirement and health care. The idea is to wean ourselves from Social Security and Medicare and put the federal welfare/entitlement system in America's rearview mirror.

What if people mismanage their retirement funds? What if they misjudge taxes and other expenses in retirement and run out of money? What if they make no provision at all for retirement?

The answer is that they will have to keep working, or go back to work. Or rely on state and local government social services. Or religious and secular non-government social services. Or relatives and friends.

The federal government is not authorized by the Constitution to set up a social insurance system. Aside from that, the federal government is not supposed to protect citizens from bad decisions. There's too much of that happening now and it encourages more bad decisions. The prospect of hardship if you arrive at retirement age without anything to retire on is a healthy incentive. It brings back into play the fundamental American values of self-reliance and personal responsibility, which are being snuffed by the federal welfare/entitlement system.

A caller berated me when I made this argument while hosting a talk radio show. He said I made him "sick" because I was a "phony Christian" who had a "heart of stone." That kind of reaction is what I had in mind when I said it has become extremist hate speech to say that Americans ought to be responsible for themselves.

Some say a buyout of Social Security and Medicare is feasible only if Americans are forced by law to put buyout money into retirement and health care plans of the citizen's choosing. I don't like that kind of mandate, but if the deal won't happen without that kind of condition, then so be it.

On Medicare, defenders of the status quo argue that health care is too expensive to expect senior citizens to be able to afford it without government subsidies. That raises a different set of issues that requires a book of its own on competition, tort reform, health savings accounts, and other elements of an affordable health care system based on choices in free and transparent markets rather than government domination. The path we are on is wrong; Medicare was one of the biggest mistakes; let's quit compounding it.

Some voices on the right say the answer to solvency for Social Security and Medicare is to move the eligibility age to 70 or 75, something more in line with the longevity of Americans, and keep adjusting it as necessary. That would relieve fiscal pressure, but would not solve the long-term fiscal and psychological problems that come from violating the Constitution and embracing socialism.

The left says the answer is to subject all income to the payroll tax. The rationale for capping the Social Security payroll tax at a certain level of income is that benefits also are capped. If you subject all income to the payroll tax, do you remove the cap on benefits? A lefty would say tax all of the income of the wealthy and still cap or means-test benefits. That would fit the original vision of Social Security as a no-strings-attached social insurance tax. It would fit the Obama vision of using government to "spread the wealth around" and redistribute it however government wants.

I would rather get the federal government out of the unconstitutional, socialist, budget-busting business of providing a guaranteed minimum standard of living in retirement.

# Move Faster on Rest of Budget

Even under the best scenarios, phasing out Social Security and Medicare will take several decades. We have to move faster on the rest of the budget.

For limited government to be restored, entire departments of the federal government must be abolished, starting with those outside Article I, Section 8 except for final-phase Social Security and Medicare. Everything else outside the parameters of Article I, Section 8 must be eliminated or pushed down to the state level. Even programs within constitutional parameters must be scrutinized.

Fix it now – adopt as soon as possible a balanced budget amendment that stair-steps the annual deficit down to zero in 10 years (page 190) and start the process of restoring limited government – but it might take a decade to dismantle the federal welfare/entitlement system (except for final-phase Social Security and Medicare) and the rest of the unconstitutional federal bureaucracy, and build up the revenue needed to achieve an annual budget surplus.

There will be wailing and gnashing of teeth at the prospect of returning to limited government and dismantling the federal welfare/entitlement system.

For example, some will object that state taxes would skyrocket if Medicaid and other services subsidized by the federal government became the sole obligation of states. That could be true. The shrinking of the federal government should leave more money in the pockets of taxpayers. States will have to decide if they want to preserve the status quo and collect from their citizens the share of taxes the citizens used to pay to the federal government, or change existing welfare/entitlement systems. I would not want my state to raise the state tax burden enough to soak up my federal tax savings and preserve the status quo, but there should be greater efficiency, or at least greater accountability to me as a state taxpayer, in a welfare/entitlement system run by my state rather than the federal government.

Maybe a state wants to replicate Romneycare in Massachusetts (named for then-Governor Mitt Romney), a government-managed health care system considered a model for Obamacare. Maybe a state wants to pursue a Ben Carson model. Carson is a renowned doctor who was a 2016 Republican presidential candidate and Secretary of Housing and Urban Development in the Trump administration. He advocates health care for all, including the poor, using health savings accounts in a system that can accommodate government and charitable subsidies, but also requires responsibility by the health care consumer. Maybe a state wants to utilize elements of both approaches and come up with its own model. Let's practice true federalism. Stop pretending that one size fits all. Let states experiment and innovate. Remember subsidiarity – get as small and local as possible. I know from serving in state and local governments that the closer you get to the people and the smaller the unit of government, the better bang for the buck you get for health care and other government services.

The left rejects this approach. Well-meaning people have told me they want a uniform standard of health insurance coverage throughout the country managed by the federal government. They worry that someone in one state might have better coverage than someone in another state.

For the sake of leveling uniformity, they would sacrifice the dynamic progress generated by the free market. Remember the lesson of Lady Thatcher (pages 86-87): even those in the lower rungs of decentralized free-market systems are better off than the mass of citizens trapped in the uniform misery of systems dominated by national governments.

Some on the right as well as the left point to slavery and civil rights as examples that some issues must not be left to the states. I agree that liberty and other basic civil rights should not vary from state to state. That's why the Constitution was amended to guarantee such rights nationally and authorize the federal government to protect them.

We could amend the Constitution to allow the federal government to intervene in the health insurance industry, but I think it would be a mistake. We have ample evidence from our experience with social services and health care that increased federal government involvement makes such systems more expensive and less effective, and raises the exasperation level for practitioners as well as patients.

What's really at issue is the character of Americans. The left believes that the federal government is the only way to take care of people because individuals, nongovernment organizations, and lower levels of government can't be trusted to do the job. I have a hard time convincing some conservatives to restore limited government because they are worried about people who are struggling.

As a conservative, I see the flaws in human nature, but I also see the good. When I look at American history, I see warts, but I see many more manifestations of goodness – most of it emanating from individuals and nongovernment organizations, not government. Americans embrace the principle of helping the underdog. Skeptics need to be reminded, or maybe shown for the first time if they've been educated in a system dominated by the left, that the best way to help the struggling is through local efforts with government in a supporting role, not acting as the main provider of aid.

A disabled veteran told me he was in his 40s and his benefits were tied in with Social Security. He asked, "Am I screwed if you succeed in shutting down Social Security and Medicare for people under 55?"

Absolutely not. People disabled because of their service to our country have a claim to federal support. Having a standing military and protecting the nation are firmly within Article I, Section 8 of the Constitution. That includes taking care of wounded warriors.

In the case of non-veterans drawing federal disability benefits, perhaps we create a transition period to allow states to decide how they want to handle such cases. We're not going to cut people off without notice and leave them hungry and homeless, but the goal is to shut down the federal government as a provider of social services.

The long-term answer to the problem of poverty is a growing economy and a cultural/attitudinal move back to self-reliance and personal responsibility. That will reduce the number of people needing assistance and maximize the number doing well. It's the only permanent solution.

*     *     *

The phase-out of Social Security and Medicare might take several decades, but I would allow no more than 10 years to bring the federal budget into balance. I have no faith in plans for a balanced budget that take longer than a decade, especially plans that push the pain off to the outlying years. There's no guarantee that future Congresses would stick with the plan. Future office holders might say, "Why should we do the heavy lifting and carry out the painful reforms to accommodate slackers who wanted to cruise through their careers and leave the hard work to their successors?" Former Congressman Ryan deserved credit for being one of the few people on Capitol Hill to propose actual budgets, but his plans took too long to achieve balance.

The Simpson-Bowles Commission's proposal for fiscal reform, a mixture of spending cuts and tax increases plus the preservation of Social Security and Medicare, has not gotten much traction on Capitol Hill. It would be an improvement on the status quo, but I was counting on former U.S. Senator Alan Simpson (R-WY), a co-leader of the commission, to lead the way out of Social Security. As a senator he was a critic of Social Security. Either he changed his mind or he could not garner support for a phase-out.

When the commission was convened in 2010, some economic analysts said America was in fine fiscal shape compared to other Western nations. The other co-leader of the commission, former Clinton White House chief of staff and nationally prominent Democrat Erskine Bowles, responded to that rosy assertion by calling America "the best-looking horse in the glue factory." There are Democrats willing to acknowledge the fiscal truth.

Some defenders of the status quo cite the bullish performance of the stock market during certain intervals in recent years as evidence that all is well economically. It's misleading. For much of the Obama administration, the Federal Reserve bought $85 billion a month in government bonds and mortgage-backed securities to prop up financial markets and provide money to fund government spending. This trillion-dollar per year fiscal shell game is called "quantitative easing" or "monetizing the debt," political jargon meant to confuse citizens so they don't understand what kind of financial burden this places on them.

I must not be smart enough to understand the transaction. Defenders of this policy say it does *not* add to the debt. I see an annual trillion-dollar purchase of bonds and securities that will have to be paid off by taxpayers.

There's another consideration. The stock market is a psychological profile of investors that does not necessarily reflect the true economic condition of the nation. The stock market was surging upward in the summer of 1929 before the crash that produced the Great Depression. We may look better fiscally than other Western nations right now, but we're headed in the same direction toward fiscal failure.

From 2008 through early 2010, the American economy lost more than 8 million jobs. There was rejoicing on the left in May 2014 when it was announced that 48 consecutive months of job growth had produced more than 8 million new jobs. It was cited by the left as proof that Obamacare, "monetizing the debt," and the overall Obama agenda were good for the economy. Yet economic experts, including the self-described liberal Economic Policy Institute, said a truly healthy and recovering economy would have produced at least 15 million new jobs during those 48 months.

What we have been doing is not working. Fiscal reform requires more than tweaking the status quo. The goal is to wean ourselves from the federal welfare/entitlement system and close it down, not find ways to keep it going. Every year we wait worsens the fiscal damage, especially as baby boomers begin receiving Social Security and Medicare benefits.

Some Republicans join Democrats in saying there can be no debt reduction without tax increases. I disagree. Don't take more money out of the economy. A growing economy is just as important to debt reduction as spending cuts. More money in the economy – plus employer confidence that government is not going to expand and impose more mandates and taxes – will produce more jobs, more economic growth, and more tax revenue.

What about tax cuts? I would support a federal income tax cut if it is in addition to, not instead of, spending cuts. President Reagan cut tax rates, but spending increased during his presidency, especially on defense. This produced huge deficits until the economic benefits of the tax cuts manifested themselves in unprecedented prosperity and tax revenue in the 1990s. Annual budget surpluses that materialized in 1998-2000 did not continue because there was no meaningful change in spending patterns. The continued increases in spending overtook revenue and put annual budgets back in the red.

President Trump pushed Congress to enact cuts in taxes and regulatory burdens that spurred economic growth not seen in 50 years. That's good, but it's not enough. There must be an equally zealous effort to reduce the size and scope of the federal government. Otherwise, in the never-ending race to balance the budget, revenue will not be able to overtake and permanently stay ahead of spending.

I could support a flat tax on income, a national sales or consumption tax often called a fair tax, or the Herman Cain 9-9-9 plan. My focus is on spending. Changing the way we raise revenue won't matter if we don't bring spending under control.

# Fiscal Conservatism Needs Social Conservatism

The focus of this book is fiscal policy, but I want to make a point about social conservatism: If the left is allowed to drive a wedge between fiscal and social conservatives, there is no chance for a conservative majority and no chance for fiscal conservatism to prevail. Fiscal conservatives, remember the lesson of Reagan and at least tolerate social conservatives. It's the only way to advance fiscal conservatism.

All you righties who despise the social issues, don't be duped when lefties whisper in your ear: "We can do business with you. It's those social conservative fanatics who must be kept out of the political arena." Forget it. They're lying. They hate fiscal conservatives as much as they hate social conservatives. They know they can defeat you by separating you from social conservatives. They're afraid your fiscal conservatism will rise to power if buoyed by an alliance with social conservatism.

The alliance is natural. Former U.S. Representative Michele Bachmann (R-MN) put it well: "Social conservatism *is* fiscal conservatism."

Why is there relentless pressure for expanded social services? Because liberal/progressive Great Society orthodoxy holds that fathers and two-parent families are relics of the judgmental and politically incorrect past.

With TV character Murphy Brown leading the propaganda campaign a generation ago, young women were told that they can have children out of wedlock and it's fine, just a lifestyle choice. On screen and in stars' actual lives, Hollywood glorifies single parenthood.

In a 2014 Thanksgiving radio commentary, television news icon Tom Brokaw spoke approvingly about his daughter utilizing a sperm bank to become a single mother.

Out-of-wedlock birth usually is a disaster for the child, for the single parent, and for the society that has to deal with the consequences. For individuals and for society, the best "program" for personal, emotional, and financial development is a sequential progression of education, job, marriage, and then production of children in a family that has a father as well as a mother.

Some who misunderstand natural law say nature encourages reproduction without regard for nuclear families. Perhaps that's true in the animal world, but the natural law formula for humans is one man, one woman, one family. As discussed earlier (page 138), decades of social science evidence and thousands of years of human experience show that the best chance for healthy individual and communal development is in a society based on the nuclear family.

Life doesn't always follow the ideal script. My family came together in an unusual way. When I met the woman who would become my wife, she was the mother of two children she had adopted as a single woman. When I worked at an inner-city middle school, I met single parents doing a heroic job of raising children. They were heroic because the odds are stacked against success in that situation. We still need to strive for the norm of the nuclear family with a father as well as a mother.

\* \* \*

There's a growing chorus on the right saying: social issues cost us votes, especially among young people; it's too hard to fight popular culture with deeper concepts; let's adopt an "anything goes" position on social issues.

That won't work. Adopting an "anything goes" approach to social issues undermines the ideological discipline needed to fix the nation's fiscal crisis.

The founders believed limited government depended on civic virtue, bolstered by religion, because limited government requires commitment to absolute principles that require self-discipline. Limited government means saying "no" and telling people they are wrong to expect certain things of government. It is not realistic to think you can achieve limited government while also saying there are no absolute rules in life, no boundaries, no limits, no such thing as natural law, no timeless values from which it is dangerous to deviate.

This relates to the earlier discussion of natural law and relativism (pages 91-94). Natural law says truth exists outside ourselves and is the same for everybody; we must find it and, if necessary, adjust to it. A relativist believes truth exists within himself and is not necessarily the same for everybody; there is no need to search for, or adjust to, anything outside himself. To succeed, advocates of limited government must break through that shell of self-centered relativist pride with natural law.

The left peddles the notion that happiness is indulging in whatever you want without anyone judging you. A 2012 campaign ad compared voting for Obama to having sex with him. It featured lefty icon Lena Dunham: cute, clever, sassy, willing to trivialize sexuality. She found Obama attractive and cool, simultaneously smooth and edgy. She said he cared about her and accommodated her every inclination without being judgmental. Voting becomes an exercise of emotion, even something flirtatious and romantic, rather than an exercise of intellect.

Fiscal conservatives, do you really think it's possible to find in an "anything goes" cultural morass the ideological discipline necessary for fiscal conservatism? I don't. If we concede on one front – the social issues – we will be flanked and routed by the left on the fiscal front. The left is beating our brains out with the social issues. We'll never get to the fiscal issues, especially with young people. They've already been conditioned to believe that we have nothing of value to offer in the political conversation because we are on the "wrong" side of the social issues.

Even if we can get to the fiscal issues, the left has trained young relativists to scoff at economic principles. Who cares about the debt? There are no absolute fiscal principles, just as there are no absolute social or moral principles. Raise taxes on the rich. Raise the debt ceiling. Borrow more money. Print more money. Do whatever is necessary to keep the party going.

The fiscal hangover will be awful, with the young holding the tab for the party. We who see what is coming must convince the young that there are absolute principles in life, including financial realities that will body-slam the young if we don't find our way back to limited government.

I said earlier (page 65) that we must show the young that the left is selling them out fiscally. We also must show them that the left is selling them out on social issues. Then they will be more likely to listen to us on fiscal issues.

It's a fine line to draw, a careful threading of the needle. We on the right don't want to manage you socially or morally; we are presenting reality and explaining why it is self-destructive for you to reject us and our ideas, and instead embrace people and ideas that are ruining your world.

The right must convince people of all ages to care about natural law, the belief that there are basic ground rules humans must follow to thrive as individuals and communities. But even if everyone agrees that natural law must be followed, who gets to decide what conforms to natural law? Some believe same-sex marriage is a deviation from natural law. Some believe with equal certainty that it's not. If there are differences of opinion on what conforms to natural law, then majority will prevails.

If we make the wrong choices, if we pursue policies that deviate from natural law, we will know because of the negative results for individuals and society. Look at the damage done to our country because a majority supported, or at least condoned, slavery and then Jim Crow segregation. Look across the country today at millions of individuals and huge sections of society ruined by the federal welfare/entitlement system. Look at the harm done to marriage and the family as sexual union has been turned into a recreational sport instead of an experience shared only by people totally committed to each other.

Natural law does not lie. It reveals inescapable truth. As the members of Plymouth Colony learned in the 1620s (pages 97-98), natural law cannot be ignored or defied. As

253

the founders knew, natural law is as binding in the political/social/cultural world as the law of gravity is in the physical world. Natural law will tell you if you are getting it right or wrong.

We on the conservative right cannot surrender on natural law. Without natural law to reinforce the argument for limited government, we will be speaking a strange language that makes no sense to people formed by a popular culture that bounces from issue to issue in relativistic bliss, with no one allowed to judge anyone else's words or actions by objective standards. The Declaration of Independence, the Constitution, and the idea of limited government make sense only if there are timeless, absolute standards by which human society ought to be governed.

*   *   *

The quest to restore limited government in harmony with natural law is made more difficult when conservatives commit social issues gaffes that reinforce the stereotype of thoughtless, heartless curmudgeons with no mercy for suffering people. If somebody concludes that I say Americans have no obligation to help each other, then I have failed as an author. Natural law includes the moral imperative to help people in need. My point is that such help should not be provided through the federal government.

# Conclusion

*The revenue creates pensioners, and the pensioners urge for more revenue. The people grow less steady, spirited, and virtuous, the seekers more numerous and more corrupt, and every day increases the circles of their dependents and expectants, until virtue, integrity, public spirit, simplicity, and frugality become the objects of ridicule and scorn, and vanity, luxury, foppery, selfishness, meanness, and downright venality swallow up the whole society.*

*John Adams, 1775*

Adams' warning of how government subsidies can sap civic vitality reads like a critique of the modern welfare/entitlement system.

The original 1960s *Star Trek* television series broke new cultural ground with a black female in a leading role and relationships that transcended races and even species. Yet for all its futuristic focus, the show had a recurring theme of old-fashioned conservatism bordering on libertarianism. There must be a dozen episodes in which the crew of the starship *Enterprise* encounters what seems to be a utopia, or a plan for a utopia to be established. But it usually turns out that the intended beneficiaries of the utopia are required to sacrifice their freedom.

In one episode, benevolent-but-determined humanoid robots had the technology and ability to supply all human needs. They wanted to use this power to rule humans. The robot leader said of humanity, "We cannot allow any race as greedy and corruptible as yours to have free run of the galaxy." But they didn't plan to take over by force:

*We shall serve them. Their kind will be eager to accept our service. Soon they will become completely dependent upon us. Their aggressive and acquisitive instincts will be under our control. We shall take care of them. We shall serve them and [they] will be happy – and controlled.*

It was a leftist's dream society. No capitalist "acquisitive instincts." No competition. No striving to meet needs. Everyone dependent on government. Everything under control – as long as humans allowed themselves to be chloroformed into status quo stagnation.

Captain James T. Kirk and his crew overcame the robots and freedom prevailed.

In another episode, Kirk and crew encountered a world similar to Earth, but where the Roman Empire never fell – in part because slaves had become content under government-provided health care and old-age pensions.

Before you dismiss these as over-the-top examples that could never happen in real life, recall how President Obama jerked the chains of Social Security recipients during the debt ceiling standoff in the summer of 2011.

I contend that voters are looking for candidates who will restore limited government. But I also say we have a nanny state because people like what big government provides and reward politicians who make it happen.

The dichotomy is explained in part by the fact that in a nation of more than 300 million people, you will find folks at all points on the political spectrum. The balance of power can shift back and forth.

Yet it is true that some of the same people who call for

limited government also support big-government politicians and policies. How many people at Tea Party rallies also belong to AARP, the American Association of Retired Persons, a left-wing advocacy group strongly supportive of Social Security and unlimited government? Human beings and human communities are capable of thinking, saying, and doing contradictory things.

The Nebraska state budget was in crisis when I was a state senator from 2001-04. At a legislative hearing one year, the committee chairman – a senior senator who was a gentle soul – got purple in the face, the veins bulging from his neck, as he fumed about two letters from the same constituent. In one hand he held a letter from earlier in the year in which the constituent asked why the idiots in the legislature couldn't do what everyone else in the state had to do – cut the budget to make spending fit income. In his other hand, the committee chairman held a more recent letter from the same constituent. In the second letter, the constituent asked how the idiots in the legislature could consider reducing funding to subsidize dental care for the poor. The committee chairman demanded to know which it was going to be: cut the budget, or raise taxes to provide subsidized dental care and other things people want from government even as they decry fiscal irresponsibility.

Part of the problem is the illusion of freedom that takes root in a welfare/entitlement system.

The truth is that bigger government means reduced freedom. But how can that be? When government takes control of health care and subsidizes more of it, doesn't that enlarge my freedom by taking that financial pressure off me? When government provides me more subsidized services, it's not oppressing me; it's providing me benefits that raise my standard of living and free me up to enjoy life more.

Acceptance of more government services also means acceptance of more government regulations. But it's the psychological surrender that truly traps citizens who become dependent on government. The Great Society has created dysfunctional second- and third-generation cycles of squalor and despair because recipients become accustomed to living on government handouts, and the system encourages them to remain in this condition.

Even with Social Security and Medicare, citizens become trapped in dependence on government and lose their American spirit. At a presentation about this book, someone spoke up in praise of the federal welfare/entitlement system. He said that without Social Security, he'd be dead. He wanted to see the federal government take over more of society and have America embrace socialism.

That is worrisome. A typical American man's survival depends on the federal government supporting him at a subsistence level, and he's comfortable with that arrangement. I'm more worried about the internal spread of that kind of American-spirit-is-dead resignation than I am external threats from ISIS or the Chicoms.

Don't forget that someone's freedom has to be encroached upon to provide government-funded benefits. The subsidies and services of the federal welfare/entitlement system are not free. To pay for them, government taxes its citizens. When government takes your property – in this case, money you have earned – and gives it to someone else in the form of a subsidy or service, that is an encroachment on your freedom. Productive citizens start questioning why they are in effect in servitude to nonproductive citizens. Remember Plymouth Colony in the 1620s (pages 97-98).

People have paid into Social Security so it feels like a return on investment. But now we are consuming more in benefits than we are producing in revenue for Social Security. The federal government used to count on Social Security surpluses to fund other areas of government. Now Social Security puts more pressure on current and future taxpayers by adding to annual deficits and the debt.

*　*　*

The unlimited government of today violates the Constitution, but some Americans say so what? We want a federal government that does more than the founders intended. We skipped the step of amending the Constitution and we vote for politicians who preserve and expand the federal welfare/entitlement system.

Reject such thinking. Even if there were no Constitution to limit the federal government, using the federal government to fix societal problems is a colossal mistake.

GOP stands for Grand Old Party, a nickname for the Republican Party. In a column entitled *GOP to move past 1980s?* that ran in our local newspaper Jan. 25, 2015, *Washington Post* liberal/progressive E.J. Dionne Jr. wrote:

> *Admitting that it is neither the '80s nor the '90s anymore is the first step toward backing away from the Reagan-Thatcher view of economics that has been surprisingly durable for 35 years: that markets need little regulation, that social programs are overrated or even harmful, and*

**that taxes should always be kept as low
as possible.**

I laughed out loud at the words "surprisingly durable." Only a lefty could be surprised that the economic philosophy that animated the Reagan and Thatcher administrations is still popular. That economic philosophy remains popular, and always will be, because it is the objective, eternal truth. Following that formula, and in the process restoring limited government, is not going backwards or back in time. It is applying values that are timeless; they apply equally in the past, present, and future. The last part of Dionne's statement – promote free markets, de-emphasize social programs, and reduce taxes – is the formula for a society that produces the best for the most. We should be perfecting it, not moving away from it to the next leftist deviation from natural law.

A 2010 editorial in the local newspaper endorsing the local congressman for re-election criticized "unrealistic calls for a return to 1920s-style government." That was a shot at the Tea Party challenger. In other words, quit barking about limited government. The genie of big government was let out of the bottle by the New Deal in the 1930s and no serious person wants to put the genie back in the bottle.

Stuffing the genie back in the bottle is exactly what needs to happen. The Tea Party often is dismissed as nutty extremism. What's nutty is the smug superiority of those who look at government gone wild and act like it has been a self-evident success despite the socio-economic devastation and fiscal debacle it has produced.

The burden of proof is not on those of us who want the kind of government that produced the greatest nation on

Earth. The burden of proof is on those who want to continue deviating from that model, a deviation that is ruining the nation psychologically as well as financially.

For anyone willing to look at the situation honestly, the fiscal bender the nation has been on, especially over the last two decades, should destroy the illusion that the federal welfare/entitlement system produces freedom and progress.

Even some defenders of the welfare/entitlement system were alarmed at where the Obama administration took the nation. Millions of people get their health insurance through unions, and unions were big supporters of Obamacare. Yet unions scrambled just like employers did to get out from under the mandates of Obamacare. Unions obtained most of the waivers and exemptions from Obamacare.

\* \* \*

Asch experiments, named for the scientist who in the 1950s researched the inclination of people to conform to the majority, often are cited as confirmation for the adage that people would rather be wrong together than be right alone.

On YouTube are videos of experiments in which an unsuspecting subject ends up conforming to the rest of the group's absurd thoughts or actions because of the pressure people feel when they are out of sync with what seems to be the norm. There's one in which a group of people compared a line about 8 inches long to a set of three lines in which one was 4 inches, one was 8 inches, and one was 12 inches. The participants were asked which line in the set was the same length as the 8-inch line. (The length of the lines was not given. I'm guessing at the actual lengths.) All but one of the participants were instructed in advance to pick the wrong line from the set. They said with certainty that the 12-inch line from the set was the match to the 8-inch line. The unsuspecting subject who was not part of the pre-arranged scam looked around in puzzlement at the others and hesitantly picked the correct match, the 8-inch line, rather than join the consensus and choose the 12-inch line. On the next go-round, though, he fell in step with the rest of group and picked the wrong line as the match. The expression on the guy's face showed that his mind was grinding on it: "I must be missing something. Apparently it looks right to everybody else. They seem absolutely certain. I don't want to look like an idiot or a troublemaker."

Something similar happens in politics. People are bamboozled and bullied into conforming to group-think by those who make the most noise. For example, Obamacare advocate Jonathan Gruber was caught on video yucking it up with fellow economists, bragging about how he sold Obamacare to the public by exploiting what he called the stupidity of Americans. Gruber celebrated the fact that Obamacare was so confusing that people were stunned into not objecting, even if they weren't convinced.

Liberal/progressive Democrat Howard Dean, a physician who ran for president in 2004 and later served as chairman of the Democratic National Committee, broke rank and denounced Obamacare as something produced by elitists who don't understand the American people. But the left understood the American people well enough to know that it needed to hide the truth to get Obamacare enacted.

Obamacare is part of the overall campaign to convince us that a bigger government means a better society. We who know that's wrong must dig in and argue two points:

1. **Harmonious communal life begins with people being responsible for themselves and their families.** Then society can be strong, stable, and prosperous enough to produce extra resources to help those who are not able to take care of themselves or their families.

2. **Where there is need for extra help, the federal government is not the answer, and not just because it is unconstitutional.** The federal government generally does not solve the problem and often makes it worse.

\* \* \*

I finally pushed all the way through Ayn Rand's *Atlas Shrugged*. Conservative friends had been urging me for years to read Rand's view of an America in which left-wing collectivism has prevailed. The productive people go on strike, which hastens the collapse of the national economy that already was under way because of the relentless attacks on capitalism, individual excellence, and personal responsibility. I find Rand's "objectivist" philosophy troubling, but I love her evisceration of the elitist liberal/progressive political and economic agenda.

I encounter a growing number of conservatives who think America has reached the *Atlas Shrugged* stage. They shake their heads in weary pessimism at my scenario for fiscal reform and restoration of limited government. They have given up on the American people. They say too many are addicted to nanny government. Too many believe the answer to every problem is to push the Expand Government button. Too many believe government is made of money, or that it can requisition whatever money it needs from "the rich." Too many are brainwashed into believing they are not responsible for themselves. That's what they've been taught by 80 years of liberal/progressive indoctrination.

I have not reached that stage of pessimism, but the longer we wait to dismantle the federal welfare/entitlement system, the harder it will be to make the required course correction.

I've been told to talk about the problem, but not offer a solution and thereby make myself a target. That's the establishment way: admire the problem. Establishment Democrats and Republicans do the same thing: admire the fiscal crisis, but don't be foolish enough to propose a solution and become a target.

Look what happens to people such as Paul Ryan when they propose solutions. It really is right out of the pages of *Atlas Shrugged*. The few people willing to lead are gang-tackled by those who criticize whatever deviates from the status quo, especially if it threatens the gig they have going.

The problem with "let it all go to pieces and let the left own the wreckage" is that we don't want that mess for our families and our country. And it won't play out that way. *Animal Farm* and *Atlas Shrugged* provide instructive examples of how the left spins blame for its failed policies away from itself and onto the right. The left controls enough of the media to dominate the national conversation. It has conditioned much of the public to accept as unquestioned truth whatever it hears from the same leftist voices that dismiss American exceptionalism and related ideas.

Here's an example of what I mean. Who was the villain

in the Monica Lewinsky scandal? Hint: It wasn't Bill Clinton, married and father of a daughter, who used the power of his office as president of the United States to sexually exploit a 23-year-old female intern, and then was kicked out of the legal profession by a judge in his home state (whom he had appointed while governor) for lying under oath about what happened. No, the second president to be impeached was not the villain. The villain was Judge Kenneth Starr, the investigator trying to find the truth being hidden by the perjuror-in-chief. The co-villains were the members of what the first lady called a "vast right-wing conspiracy" hellbent on harassing her innocent husband.

President Clinton should have been banished from the stage of national politics in disgrace as a liar and a brute to women. (Millennials, look up Juanita Broaddrick, Kathleen Willey, and Paula Jones.) The one-man war on women should never have been heard from again. But the left decided the narrative was that Judge Starr and fellow sexophobic Republican fanatics waged a shameful personal attack on a president over a private matter. President Clinton was the victim, not the villain. He has been lionized as a political rock star whose *credibility* President Obama tapped to help sell Obamacare and other policies.

Why revisit that unpleasant episode? Because it shows why the right can't expect the failure of Obamacare and the left-wing agenda to be a self-evident truth. Media magicians will turn failure into an alternate reality that serves the left. The lesson will be that the federal government has to take *more* control over society. The left now calls for outright socialism. A dispirited and desperate American populace might go along if it is successfully disconnected from its ideological heritage by the left.

For example, the longer Obamacare remains the law and people grow accustomed to the idea of relying on the federal government for health care, the harder it will be to disengage. Notice how Democrats now use "he wants to repeal Obamacare" as an attack on Republican candidates, and fearful Republicans deny it or insist that they just want to fix it.

In *Atlas Shrugged*, with the collectivist ideology taking over society, a man expounds on the virtues of capitalism and self-interest and striving for excellence, and how they maximize human progress. A woman disagrees with him. The man invites her to explain where his analysis is wrong. The woman has no interest in examining his view intellectually. She says she "feels" rather than "thinks." She can't identify flaws in his logic and sees no need to do so. She simply feels he's wrong and that's what matters to her. The man says when society is in ruins because the feelers have prevailed over the thinkers, and the feelers say they are sorry and didn't realize what would happen, they will not be forgiven.

Conservatives could wait for our economy to collapse and then have the satisfaction of telling lefties, "We told you so and we don't forgive you." I'd rather jump in now and turn things around so the collapse doesn't happen. Instead of passively waiting for negative scenarios to put our country into even worse condition, the right must go on offense and administer ideological shock therapy to wake the public out of its compliant trance.

*Atlas Shrugged* was published in 1957. Since then,

we've seen what happens when the feelers get what they advocate. Europe has been pulverized economically and psychologically by socialism. In America, poverty has metastasized instead of disappeared. We'll save for another time a review of the damage the feelers have done to American education.

Feelers are prevailing over thinkers. Thinkers are afraid to go after Social Security and the rest of the leftist megastate because they know feelers will explode.

When I say thinkers, I don't mean elites. Some thinkers are elites, but there are people holding prestigious places in the world, leaders of business and government and academia, who are clueless feelers. There are people with little education or social status who hold non-prestigious places in the world, but they are clear-headed, rock-solid thinkers.

This nation was founded and made great by thinkers as well as doers. Public policy was based on thought rather than emotion. The challenge is to get today's thinkers to engage and reclaim control of the political process. Passion is welcome – in fact, it's necessary to inspire the electorate – but not thought-eclipsing hysteria.

I believe that on fiscal issues there is a majority of clear-headed, rock-solid thinkers to the right of center on the political spectrum, Democrats and Independents as well as Republicans. All understand that the kind of consensus needed today has nothing to do with establishment Republicans and Democrats alternately playing tug-of-war and reach-across-the-aisle-compromise, whatever it takes to preserve the status quo. The goal is to build a majority far enough to the right on the political spectrum to accomplish the reactionary act of going back to limited federal government and undoing nearly a century of unlimited federal government.

What I advocate is a modest adjustment of the center of gravity in American politics. It's doable if a majority of the American people realizes that the federal government has moved too far to the left and needs to return to the path charted by the founders – not out of blind reverence for the founders, but because it's the best way to govern a capitalist democratic republic. The media and political establishment will call it right-wing reactionary extremism, but it's close to where most Americans already are.

Let's go back to the diagram of the political spectrum:

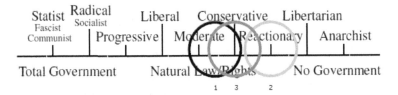

James Q. Wilson's *American Government* is the gold standard in college textbooks on American civics. On page 166 of the 12th edition, Wilson says that 40% of Americans identify themselves as moderate, 30% as conservative, and 20% as liberal. In the diagram above, the black circle (1) is an approximation of where the majority is. The light gray circle (2) is where the majority must relocate to accomplish a return to limited government. That would be reactionary, going back to a previous standard. Once that change is accomplished, my hope is that the center of gravity in America settles at the dark gray circle (3), a conservative position preserving limited government as the status quo.

Impossible? Not if Americans accept the facts and decide they don't want the federal government to ruin the country financially. The choice of government is between limited and unlimited; there is no other alternative.

\* \* \*

Small business owners are a no-nonsense breed. One of my advocacy jobs was for an organization composed primarily of small business owners fighting taxes and regulatory mandates at city hall. Big businesses may have political and social issues that cloud their agendas. Some of them benefit from bailouts, Obamacare, and other big government programs. At the grassroots entrepreneurial level where small businesses operate, there's virtually no margin for error. Things tend to be more black-and-white.

Boxer the horse in *Animal Farm* was a loyal laborer who endured the exploitative demands of his socialist/communist rulers. His mantra was, "I will work harder." When Boxer broke down from overwork, the rulers (fellow animals) rewarded his devotion and sacrifice by selling him to a slaughterhouse.

Steel magnate Hank Rearden in *Atlas Shrugged* tried to overcome the blood-sucking effect of increasingly onerous government mandates by improving productivity at his steel mill. He finally realized that the left-wing collectivist government was punishing his success and squeezing everything it could out of him until his business was destroyed. He abandoned his business and joined an underground movement to remake society based on liberty and initiative.

Small business owners tend to react the same way as Boxer and Rearden. They prefer to work harder and be more productive rather than waste time and energy fighting city hall or the state or federal capitol. But they are learning what Boxer learned too late and Rearden learned just in time. Elected officials and bureaucrats steeped in leftist ideology will keep exploiting you. You have no choice but to push back. You must defeat them – or surrender and become "woke" as so much of the business world has done. Even then, they still will keep exploiting you. There are people at all levels of government who impose nonsensical regulations that generate outrageous fines. They either don't understand what harm their policies do, or don't care.

Employers fired employees, did not hire new ones, and reduced employees' hours because the utopians imposing government-run health care on us didn't check with employers about the impact of such a plan. Or they didn't care. Despite President Obama's promise to the contrary, people were thrown off their insurance plans because the utopians misjudged, or didn't care about, their scheme's impact on consumers of health care.

Some argue that Obamacare's true purpose is to wipe out insurance in the private sector. I'm not sure about that, but I am sure that the left rejects the idea that the public sector exists to serve the private sector. Part of American exceptionalism is that the private sector is the main stage of American life, the engine of growth and progress and prosperity. The left sees the public sector as the main event, with the private sector in a supporting role subject to taxes and mandates deemed necessary to serve the public sector.

Do not underestimate the power and arrogance of the "deep state" bureaucracy at all levels of government. Some bureaucrats are professionals genuinely dedicated to good government who leave personal politics out of their jobs. More typical, though, is the liberal/progressive staffer with contempt for conservative elected officials and the voters who put them in office. These bureaucrats aren't subject to term limits or worried about being turned out by dissatisfied voters, so they ignore, stall, or defy elected officials and preserve the status quo.

Then along come elected officials such as President Obama who want to give more policy-making power to the federal bureaucracy – and use it to harass political opponents. That got President Nixon hounded out of office.

The solution is to rein in government at all levels and purge the bureaucracy. It begins with putting the federal government back in the circle of authority (page 62) called Article I, Section 8 of the Constitution.

Establishment voices complain that returning to limited government is childish. What strikes me as childish is status quo Democrats and Republicans fighting for control of a raft that is going over the fiscal falls because neither of the contending sides will change course. Unbridled spending is producing record deficits and driving the nation toward a fiscal Niagara Falls. At times the rivals play nicely with each other – as they allow the raft to careen toward the edge. Americans must elect leaders who will paddle in reverse or make for the shore – whatever it takes to get off the course we've been on, and do it before we get so close to the edge that it's too late to avoid going over the falls.

If someone criticizes you for advocating limited government and says we need "adult" leadership to solve our fiscal crisis, press him for specifics. If we don't use the Constitution to limit the parameters of government, then where are the lines drawn on what is acceptable and what is too much? Was Jefferson wrong when he warned that once you break out of constitutional parameters, there are no limits?

Keep pressing. What is your fiscal policy? Where does it leave us and our descendants? How does it pay for current spending and future unfunded liabilities?

Your critic might dismiss you as unreasonable and abandon the topic. Status quo defenders are not serious about solutions. They just want to escape such uncomfortable conversations.

Maybe your critic will say the summer 2011 debt ceiling deal's combination of spending cuts and tax increases is an example of sensible compromise. Really? Congress passing the buck to a super committee that failed was good public policy? Relying on proposed spending cuts and tax increases that may not happen, and even if they happen will *add* $7 trillion to the debt over 10 years, is good public policy? Remind your critic that American credit was downgraded *after* passage of that debt ceiling deal because the financial markets saw what a non-solution it was.

\* \* \*

Those of us who voted for President Trump in 2020 were dealt a staggering blow by his defeat.

The number one goal of the left is to crush your soul, crush your spirit, leave you thinking all is lost, there is no hope, you and your views are finished. Don't you sometimes feel like you're in one of those scenes from *Lord of the Rings* in which the good guys are surrounded by waves of monsters, fiends, ghouls, dragons, and all manner of demonic forces, closing in? There's no way the good guys can survive, never mind prevail.

And yet they do. They find the will to fight, and ultimately win, because they know the truth, they refuse to be separated from the truth, and they will not give up on the truth. That unbreakable bond with the truth drives them on to give without counting the cost or heeding the wounds, as St. Ignatius said.

J.R.R. Tolkien, author of *Lord of the Rings*, was a Christian writing fiction about the real-world battle between good and evil that he witnessed in Europe when the Nazis were on the march. We have real-world examples from American history. They remind us not to let fatalist cynicism sap our strength.

"Can't be done." That's the biggest obstacle I face in selling my proposal. Conventional wisdom says we can't undo Social Security and Medicare and the rest of the federal welfare/entitlement system. People are conditioned to rely on the federal government to take care of them. The status quo is here to stay. Forget about challenging it.

Ah, conventional wisdom. It told President Reagan in the 1980s that he couldn't say "tear down this wall" in Berlin, call the Soviet Union an "evil empire," and act like he intended to defeat communism and actually win the Cold War. Conventional wisdom said the Soviet Union is here to stay; we must accept that reality and stop pretending that our political values and form of government are superior.

Reagan stayed the course. The Soviet Union declined and finally perished, a victim of American resolve and the inherent flaws in a leftist system that rejected natural law and natural rights.

Did you see the movie *Lincoln*? It shows how President Lincoln was told in early 1865, even by abolitionists, that it would be impossible to find enough votes in the House of Representatives to pass a proposed constitutional amendment to abolish slavery. Conventional wisdom said the North is about to win the Civil War and preserve the Union; be satisfied with that and forget about abolishing slavery.

Lincoln, of course, defied conventional wisdom and pursued the effort to abolish slavery.

Conventional wisdom said it was a suicide mission for General George Washington to attack the 1,500 Hessian troops garrisoned in Trenton, New Jersey, on Dec. 26, 1776. The Hessians, German mercenaries hired by the British, were considered the best soldiers in the world. They had superior weapons and supplies. They held a defensible position. They were part of the British force that had routed the Americans in New York in late August.

Washington's army was cold, hungry, exhausted, and humiliated from being driven out of New York and pursued for the previous four months across New Jersey into Pennsylvania. Reduced by casualties and desertions from 20,000 to 2,000 (several hundred of whom were sick or wounded or both), the ranks likely would be further depleted in another week as many commissions would expire at the end of the year.

Conventional wisdom said the revolution was demolished. Some of Washington's fellow officers recommended accepting the terms of surrender offered by the British.

They considered Washington a lunatic for believing it was possible to defeat the Hessians, fight on, and win independence from that era's rising global superpower.

Washington agreed with his critics that the situation was dire, but he disagreed with their response. He turned into the fire and attacked. He believed his army, and the revolution, could survive if the Americans struck an immediate, dramatic, and victorious blow. The revolutionaries needed to prove to *themselves*, as well as England and the rest of the world, that their cause was not lost. The stunning triumph over the Hessians at the Battle of Trenton put America back on the path to independence.

The common thread running through these three examples is the power of truth.

Reagan knew the truth: socialism/communism was economically wrong, politically wrong, and morally wrong. America's values are superior because they are based on natural law and 4,000 years of Judeo-Christian teaching. That is the truth, and Reagan would not be separated from, or give up on, the truth.

Lincoln knew the truth: slavery was a cancer that would kill America unless it was removed from the body politic. He would not be separated from, or give up on, the truth.

Washington and the founders knew the truth: they were being denied their God-given rights, and efforts to negotiate a peaceful solution were rejected. They pledged their lives, their fortunes, and their sacred honor to the cause of independence. It was not rhetorical flourish or posturing. Some lost their fortunes. Some lost their lives. You don't take that kind of risk unless you know the truth, refuse to be separated from it, and refuse to give up on it. You resolve to make the truth happen, or die trying.

Now *you* know the truth: the movement toward bigger government is ruining America. Will you refuse to be separated from the truth, never give up on it, and use it as motivation to fight for a return to limited government under the Constitution?

Look at the challenges America has overcome. I'm simply saying that we take responsibility for ourselves and fellow citizens as individuals, organizations, and communities at the local or state level, not hand it off to the federal government and bankrupt ourselves in the process. If we can't do that, then we are not worthy of the legacy established by our forebears.

I am optimistic about America's future. The American Dream is alive and well. Earlier (page 44) I mentioned two of my adult sons. They began life scavenging for food and struggling to survive in a Third World orphanage. They have graduated from American universities and have good jobs at good businesses. They are taxpaying citizens living the American Dream.

I want an America that rewards my children with freedom and prosperity for working hard and playing by the rules, not an America that treats them as worker bees who exist to serve the national mega-state and the political ruling class in Washington.

Conventional wisdom says it's too late for that. Conventional wisdom says we've lost too much ground to the belief in big government. Conventional wisdom says that to be good, moral, and do its job, the federal government must be unlimited in its authority.

This is another case in which conventional wisdom will be proven wrong. But we've run out of time. Like General Washington in December 1776, we have no choice but to turn into the fire and attack if we want to succeed. As baby boomers retire, there is not enough Social Security and Medicare revenue to pay their benefits, and there is not enough money in the federal treasury to repay all the Social Security and Medicare funds already spent on other programs. The debt looms as an immoral fiscal assault on younger generations. We are losing our "can do" American spirit built on self-reliance and personal responsibility. We need to prove to *ourselves*, as well as critics and cynics, that we still can live the American Dream and hand it on intact.

We need to fix it now.

# French Dessert

If you don't have the time or patience to work your way through *Atlas Shrugged*, then enjoy a few slices of a French delicacy called Bastiat. (BAHS-tee-yah is my best American phonetic attempt.) That's Frederic Bastiat, probably the cleverest guy you've never heard of. He was a 19th century French political philosopher who was on the scene when European socialism developed. He fought it with arguments that resonate today.

Bastiat is part of the reading list for a college American civics course I have taught as an adjunct professor. His name also has come up when I have hosted radio shows. Despite stereotypes of talk radio being a forum for bomb-throwing barbarians, callers to my talk radio show brought up Bastiat on their own. It's as if he had a crystal ball and foresaw the negative economic, social, and political consequences that would befall socialist Europe – and America to the degree that it has adopted socialist policies.

Below are observations from Bastiat with occasional comments in brackets from me. *Bon appetit.*

- *We cannot doubt that self-interest is the mainspring of human nature. It must be clearly understood that this word is used here to designate a universal, incontestable fact, resulting from the nature of man, and not an adverse judgment, as would be the word selfishness.* [Echoing Adam Smith's concept of mutually beneficial self-interest.]
- *By virtue of exchange, one man's prosperity is beneficial to all others.*
- *The profit of the one is the profit of the other.* [Capitalism is based on mutually beneficial transactions.]

- *If socialists mean that under extraordinary circumstances, for urgent cases, the State should set aside some resources to assist certain unfortunate people, to help them adjust to changing conditions, we will, of course, agree. This is done now; we desire that it be done better. There is, however, a point on this road that must not be passed; it is the point where governmental foresight would step in to replace individual foresight and thus destroy it.* [Citizens should be responsible for their own health care and retirement.]

- *When under the pretext of fraternity, the legal code imposes mutual sacrifices on the citizens, human nature is not thereby abrogated. Everyone will then direct his efforts toward contributing little to, and taking much from, the common fund of sacrifices. Now, is it the most unfortunate who gains from this struggle? Certainly not, but rather the most influential and calculating.* [He's describing TARP!]

- *The socialists declare that the State owes subsistence, well-being, and education to all its citizens; that it should be generous, charitable, involved in everything, devoted to everybody; . . . that it should intervene directly to relieve all suffering, satisfy and anticipate all wants, furnish capital to all enterprises, enlightenment to all minds, balm for all wounds, asylums for all the unfortunate, and even aid to the point of shedding French blood, for all oppressed people on the face of the earth. Who would not like to see all these benefits flow forth upon the world from the law, as from an inexhaustible source? . . . But is it possible? . . . Whence does [the State] draw those resources that it is urged to dispense by way of benefits to individuals? Is it not from the individuals themselves? How, then, can these resources be increased by passing through the hands of a parasitic and voracious intermediary? . . . Finally . . . we shall see the entire people transformed into petitioners. Landed property, agriculture, industry, commerce, shipping, industrial companies, all will bestir themselves to claim favors from the State. The public treasury will be literally pillaged. Everyone will have good reasons to prove that legal fraternity should be interpreted in this sense: "Let me have the benefits, and let others pay the costs." Everyone's effort will be directed toward snatching a scrap of fraternal privilege from the legislature. The suffering classes, although having the greatest claim, will not always have the greatest success.* [Unless they have good lobbyists.]

- *Life, faculties, production – in other words, individuality, liberty, property – this is man. And in spite of the cunning of artful political leaders, these three gifts from God precede all human legislation, and are superior to it. Life, liberty, and property do not exist because men have made laws. On the contrary, it was the fact that life, liberty, and property existed beforehand that caused men to make laws in the first place.* [Summary of natural law and natural rights.]

- *It is impossible to introduce into society a greater change and a greater evil than this: the conversion of the law into an instrument of plunder.*

- *When plunder becomes a way of life for a group of men in a society, over the course of time they create for themselves a legal system that authorizes it and a moral code that glorifies it.* [It's now hate speech to question welfare/entitlement programs.]

- *But how is this legal plunder to be identified? Quite simply. See if the law takes from*

*some persons what belongs to them, and
gives it to other persons to whom it does
not belong. See if the law benefits one citizen at the expense of another by doing
what the citizen himself cannot do without
committing a crime.*

- *No legal plunder: This is the principle of justice, peace, order, stability, harmony, and
  logic. Until the day of my death, I shall pro-
  claim this principle with all the force of my
  lungs (which alas! is all too inadequate).*

- *Socialism, like the ancient ideas from which
  it springs, confuses the distinction between
  government and society. As a result of this,
  every time we object to a thing being done
  by government, the socialists conclude that
  we object to its being done at all. We disap-
  prove of state education. Then the socialists
  say that we are opposed to any education.
  We object to a state religion. Then the socialists say that we want no religion at all.
  We object to a state-enforced equality.
  Then they say that we are against equality.
  And so on, and so on. It is as if the socialists were to accuse us of not wanting persons to eat because we do not want the
  state to raise grain.* [Not everything important must be, or ought to be, done by
  government.]

- *If the natural tendencies of mankind are so
  bad that it is not safe to permit people to be
  free, how is it that the tendencies of these
  organizers are always good? Do not the legislators and their appointed agents also belong to the human race? Or do they believe
  that they themselves are made of a finer
  clay than the rest of mankind?* [The left believes the masses need to be saved from
  themselves by an enlightened and morally
  superior elite. But as Bastiat notes, the
  elites are subject to the same flaws of human nature that afflict the rest of us. How

did you like having one of "these organizers" as president from 2009-16?]

- *Whatever the question under discussion – whether religious, philosophical, political, or economic; whether it concerns prosperity, morality, equality, right, justice, progress, responsibility, cooperation, property, labor, trade, capital, wages, taxes, population, finance, or government – at whatever point on the scientific horizon I begin my researches, I invariably reach this one conclusion: The solution to the problems of human relationships is to be found in liberty.*

# Merry Capitalist Christmas

O good tidings of great joy. The saga (pages 49-52) of the uncle teaching his nephews about capitalism has another chapter:

*My nephews' arrival at the family Christmas gathering [December 2013] was slightly delayed as they were busy finishing up snow removal for their customers. Yes, not only have they learned what's involved in managing a family's finances and the importance of saving for the future, but now they are learning first-hand about business. They do lawn mowing during that season, leaf removal in the fall, and now snow removal for quite a list of folks in their small Iowa town. They also provide these services for free for some elderly neighbors and their church, so they know about the importance of helping others who truly need it.*

*What's interesting is to see how they approach figuring out how much to charge – what the competition is charging, their equipment maintenance and fuel costs, etc. One nephew is becoming an expert with spreadsheets. The other is keenly aware of watching the expenses and bottom line since the majority of their profits goes straight into their college savings funds.*

*I can assure you that nothing any current/future progressive teacher/professor tries to pass off as gospel will have any impact on these two young men now. I am so proud of how much they've learned and how well they put that knowledge into productive action.*

# Famous Quotations on Debt

The list below (with a few bracketed comments by me) is heavy on founders, whose hostility to debt was rooted in natural law. To them, the downward pull of debt on a man's character was as certain and relentless as the downward pull of gravity on a man's body. The same principle applied to the nation. The founders also rejected the modern practice of one generation pushing its spending burden off to future generations.

**John Adams** (2nd president):

*There are two ways to enslave a nation. One is by the sword. The other is by debt.*

*The consequences arising from the continual accumulation of public debts in other countries ought to admonish us to be careful to prevent their growth in our own.*

**Ambrose Bierce** (caustic 19th century political commentator nicknamed "Bitter Bierce"):

*Forgetfulness. A gift of God bestowed upon debtors in compensation for their destitution of conscience.*

**Rev. William Boetcker** (Presbyterian minister famous for his Ten Cannots published in 1916):

- *You cannot bring about prosperity by discouraging thrift.*
- *You cannot strengthen the weak by weakening the strong.*
- *You cannot help little men by tearing down big men.*
- *You cannot lift the wage earner by pulling down the wage payer.*
- *You cannot help the poor by destroying the rich.*

- *You cannot establish sound security on borrowed money.*
- *You cannot further the brotherhood of man by inciting class hatred.*
- *You cannot keep out of trouble by spending more than you earn.*
- *You cannot build character and courage by destroying men's initiative and independence.*
- *You cannot help men permanently by doing for them what they can and should do for themselves.*

**Calvin Coolidge** (30th president):

*There is no dignity quite so impressive, and no independence quite so important, as living within your means.*

**Benjamin Franklin** (leader among founders):

*Rather go to bed supperless than rise in debt.*

*Think what you do when you run in debt: you give to another power over your liberty.*

**Alexander Hamilton** (1st Treasury secretary):

*Allow a government to decline paying its debts and you overthrow all public morality – you unhinge all the principles that preserve the limits of free constitutions. Nothing can more affect national prosperity than a constant and systematic attention to extinguish the present debt and to avoid as much as possible the incurring of any new debt.*

*When the credit of a country is in any degree questionable, it never fails to give an extravagant premium, in one shape or another, upon all the loans it has occasion to make. Nor does the evil end here; the same disadvantage must be sustained upon whatever is to be bought on terms of future payment. From this constant necessity of borrowing and buying dear, it is easy to conceive how immensely the expenses of a nation, in a course of time, will be augmented by an unsound state of the public credit.*

**Daniel Hannan** (modern British politician):

*You cannot spend your way out of recession or borrow your way out of debt.*

**Herbert Hoover** (31st president):

*Blessed are the young, for they shall inherit the national debt.*

**Thomas Jefferson** (3rd president):

*I place economy among the first and most important of virtues, and public debt as the greatest of dangers to be feared.*

*The same prudence which in private life would forbid our paying our own money for unexplained projects, forbids it in the dispensation of the public moneys.*

*But with respect to future debt; would it not be wise and just for that nation to declare in the constitution they are forming that neither the legislature nor the nation itself can validly contract more debt than they may pay within their own age, or within the term of 19 years.*

*We must not let our rulers load us with perpetual debt. We must make our election between economy and liberty or profusion and servitude. . . . A departure from principle in one instance becomes a precedent for [another] . . . till the bulk of society is reduced to be mere automatons of misery. . . . And the fore-horse of this frightful team is public debt. Taxation follows that, and in its train wretchedness and oppression.*

*It is a wise rule and should be fundamental in a government disposed to cherish its credit, and at the same time to restrain the use of it within the limits of its faculties, never to borrow a dollar without laying a tax in the same instant for paying the interest annually, and the principal within a given term; and to consider that tax as pledged to the creditors on the public faith.*

*The multiplication of public offices, increase of expense beyond income, growth and entailment of a public debt, are indications soliciting the employment of the pruning knife.*

*The principle of spending money to be paid by posterity, under the name of funding, is but swindling futurity on a large scale.*

*We shall all consider ourselves unauthorized to saddle posterity with our debts, and morally bound to pay them ourselves.*

*It is incumbent on every generation to pay its own debts as it goes, a principle which if acted on would save one-half the wars of the world.*

**James Madison** (4th president):

*To say that the United States should be answerable for twenty-five millions of dollars without knowing whether the ways and means can be provided, and without knowing whether those who are to succeed us will think with us on the subject, would be rash and unjustifiable. [I]n my opinion, it would be hazarding the public faith in a manner contrary to every idea of prudence.*

*I go on the principle that a public debt is a public curse and in a republican government a greater than in any other.*

*I regret, as much as any member, the unavoidable weight and duration of the burdens to be imposed, having never been a proselyte to the doctrine that public debts are public benefits. I consider them, on the contrary, as evils which ought to be removed as fast as honor and justice will permit.*

**Lyn Nofziger** (conservative advisor in the Nixon and Reagan administrations):

*The reason this country continues its drift toward socialism and big nanny government is because too many people vote in the expectation of getting something for nothing, not because they have a concern for what is good for the country. A better educated electorate might change the reason many persons vote. If children were forced to learn about the Constitution, about how government works, about how this nation came into being, about taxes, and about how government forever threatens the cause of liberty, perhaps we wouldn't see so many foolish ideas coming out of the mouths of silly men.* [That's why I wrote this book.]

**Thomas Paine** (revolutionary pamphleteer, author of *Common Sense* and *The American Crisis*):

*As parents, we can have no joy, knowing that this government is not sufficiently lasting to ensure any thing which we may bequeath to posterity: and by a plain method of argument, as we are running the next generation into debt, we ought to do the work of it, otherwise we use them meanly and pitifully. In order to discover the line of our duty rightly, we should take our children in our hand, and fix our station a few years farther into life; that eminence will present a prospect, which a few present fears and prejudices conceal from our sight.* [See page 43: America Is Robbing Its Children.]

**Wendell Phillips** (New England abolitionist):

*Debt is the fatal disease of republics, the first thing and the mightiest to undermine governments and corrupt the people.*

**Ezra Pound** (American expatriate leftist poet):

*Wars in old times were made to get slaves. The modern implement of imposing slavery is debt.* [In 2013, a lefty critic in the media crudely attacked former Alaska Governor Sarah Palin for making the same point.]

**Ayn Rand** (author of *Atlas Shrugged*):

*Inflation is not caused by the actions of private citizens, but by the government: by an artificial expansion of the money supply required to support deficit spending. No private embezzlers or bank robbers in history have ever plundered people's savings on a scale comparable to the plunder perpetrated by the fiscal policies of statist governments.* [America has shown that non-statist governments also perpetrate such plunder.]

**Ronald Reagan** (40th president):

*These United States are confronted with an economic affliction of great proportions. We suffer from the longest and one of the worst sustained inflations in our national history. It distorts our economic decisions, penalizes thrift, and crushes the struggling young and the fixed-income elderly alike. It threatens to shatter the lives of millions of our people. But great as our tax burden is, it has not kept pace with public spending. For decades, we have piled deficit upon deficit, mortgaging our future and our children's future for the temporary convenience of the present. To continue this long trend is to guarantee tremendous social, cultural, political, and economic upheavals. You and I, as individuals, can, by borrowing, live beyond our means, but for only a limited period of time. Why, then, should we think that collectively, as a nation, we are not bound by that same limitation? We must act today in order to preserve tomorrow.* [In other words, fix it now.]

*People are tired of wasteful government programs and welfare chiselers, and they're angry about the constant spiral of taxes and government regulations, arrogant bureaucrats, and public officials who think all of mankind's problems can be solved by throwing the taxpayers' dollars at them.*

*We could say they [governments] spend like drunken sailors, but that would be unfair to drunken sailors, because the sailors are spending their own money.*

**George Washington** (1st president):

*To contract new debts is not the way to pay old ones.*

*As a very important source of strength and security, cherish public credit. One method of preserving it is to use it as sparingly as possible, avoiding occasions of expense by cultivating peace, but remembering, also, that timely disbursements to prepare for danger frequently prevent much greater disbursements to repel it; avoiding likewise the accumulation of debt, not only by shunning occasions of expense, but by vigorous exertions in time of peace to discharge the debts which unavoidable wars have occasioned, not ungenerously throwing upon posterity the burden which we ourselves ought to bear.*

*No pecuniary consideration is more urgent, than the regular redemption and discharge of the public debt: on none can delay be more injurious, or an economy of time more valuable.* [That's the father of our country's 18th century gentlemanly way of saying, "Fix it now."]

# Maxwell Bio

**Education**    **University of Nebraska – Lincoln**
J.D. (law degree)

**Oxford University**
M.Stud. (master of studies degree in
American history)

**Boston College**
B.A. (bachelor of arts degree in
political science)

**Work**    **Retire SMART**
Media and public relations for financial advisory firm.

**St. Barnabas Classical Academy**
High school history teacher.

**Salem Media Group – Omaha**
Talk radio host and account executive at KOTK. Also
host on local stations KFAB, KKAR, KOIL, and KCRO.

**TS Bank**
Trust Officer: managed trust accounts and develop
new clients.

**Omaha Alliance for the Private Sector**
Executive Director: advocated from the private sector perspective primarily on issues at city hall.

**Fatherhood-Family Initiative**
Executive Director: promoted the role of fathers in
families and emphasized the importance of the
father-son relationship.

**Grace University**
Adjunct Professor: taught course called Introduction
to American Politics.

**Bellevue University**
Adjunct Professor: taught course in the American
Vision & Values political science curriculum as part
of the Kirkpatrick Signature Series.

**Nebraska Coalition for Ethical Research**
Executive Director: advocated stem cell research
that does not involve destruction of human embryos.

**Douglas County Board**
Commissioner: served a 4-year term.

**Nebraska Legislature**
State Senator: served a 4-year term.

**Jesuit Academy**
Development Director: responsible for fundraising and public relations at an Omaha inner-city Catholic middle school for boys.

**U.S. Senator Chuck Hagel**
Special Assistant: drafted floor speeches, columns for newspapers and magazines, and other items.

**Omaha World-Herald**
Editorial Writer: helped prepare daily opinion statements; edited letters to editor and op-ed columns.

**Kennedy, Holland, DeLacy & Svoboda**
Associate: worked in the litigation department on defense of medical malpractice cases. That firm later dissolved into two new firms with new names.

**Nebraska Court of Appeals**
Law Clerk: helped Judge William Connolly research legal issues and draft opinions.

**Other Items**    Married with seven children ages 17-31.

Author of three self-published books.

Omaha Citizen Patrol neighborhood watch.

YMCA youth baseball coach.

Full-time worker at Pine Street Inn homeless shelter in Boston.

Teacher and coach in Kingston, Jamaica, as member of the Jesuit Volunteer Corps, a service program similar to the Peace Corps for graduates of Jesuit universities.

Graduate of Creighton Preparatory School, Omaha's Jesuit high school.

Batboy and then player for the Westside Chapel men's fastpitch softball team, a perennial contender for Omaha city championships and regional competition.

Won a free piece of cheesecake at a Georgetown pizzeria for playing a spirited, if somewhat choppy, rendition of *Has Anybody Seen My Gal?* on an old-fashioned piano. This has nothing to do with anything, but it's something that people seem to remember.

And they remember this: beloved humorist **Mary Maxwell** (21 million hits on YouTube for "Mary Maxwell Home Instead") is my mother.

Made in the USA
Middletown, DE
28 April 2022

64890993R00166